FREE BOOKS

www.*forgottenbooks*.org

You can read literally <u>thousands</u> of books
for free at www.forgottenbooks.org

(please support us by visiting our web site)

Forgotten Books takes the uppermost care to preserve the entire content of the original book. However, this book has been generated from a scan of the original, and as such we cannot guarantee that it is free from errors or contains the full content of the original. But we try our best!

Truth may seem, but cannot be:
Beauty brag, but 'tis not she;
Truth and beauty buried be.

To this urn let those repair
That are either true or fair;
For these dead birds sigh a prayer.

Bacon

GREEK AND ROMAN MYTHOLOGY

BY

JESSIE M. TATLOCK

ILLUSTRATED

NEW YORK
THE CENTURY CO.

Copyright, 1917, by
THE CENTURY CO.

297

Printed in U. S. A.

PREFACE

WHILE familiarity with classical mythology is generally recognized as essential to the understanding of literature and art and to the preservation of a great and valuable part of our artistic and spiritual heritage, the method of assuring such a familiarity to the rising generation differs in different schools. In many the stories of the gods and heroes are read in the lower grades from one or another of the children's books based on the myths, and any further knowledge of the subject depends upon the study of Vergil and other Latin or Greek writers and on the use of reference books in connection with reading in English literature. In many schools, however, experience has proved that as even the most elementary knowledge of mythology gained in childhood cannot be presupposed, and as the knowledge gained from the occasional use of reference books is unsubstantial and unsatisfactory, a systematic course in mythology for students of high-school age is necessary. It might seem that to such students this subject would be so simple as to present no difficulties, but the fact is that to those who come to its study, as surprisingly many do, with such entire unfamiliarity that the name of Apollo or Venus conveys nothing to them, the mass of new and strange names and the divergence of the conceptions from those to which they are accustomed make the study not a little difficult. After many years' experience with such students the writer has been led to believe that there is need for a text book in a style to appeal to those who have outgrown children's books, but of content so limited and treatment so simple as to make it possible for the average boy or girl to assimilate it in a course of about thirty lessons. To secure brevity and simplicity only the most famous and interesting of the stories have been incorporated in this book; certain others are briefly mentioned in the index. In reading a narrative it is difficult for an inexperienced student to distinguish between the important names and those that merely form part of the setting of the story. The mention of any names beyond those that should be remembered has therefore been avoided, and the effort has been made by reiteration and cross-reference to impress these names upon the student.

In preparing an elementary book on mythology there are naturally two purposes to be kept in mind: (1) By a sympathetic and accurate treatment to give understanding and appreciation of the character and ideals of the people among whom the mythology developed. Any study that gives this understanding and appreciation of one of the peoples through whom our own spiritual life and civilization has come to be what it is is believed by the writer to be important to an intelligent valuation of our present life and ideals and to a sane building for the future. (2) By placing the familiar stories in their proper relation to enable the student better to understand references in literature and representations in art, ancient and modern. Because of the subjective element in the treatment of mythology in later ages the conceptions have become confused. It is the writer's belief that to avoid confusion and misunderstanding on the student's part the subject should not be treated through the medium of modern writers and artists, whose interpretation of Greek thought and religion has been affected by the thought and religion of their own times, but that by the use of ancient sources, careful study of the people's own understanding of their mythology, direct quotation and free reproduction of the works of Greek and Latin poets, illustrations drawn from Greek sculpture and painting, the effort should be made to leave an honest picture of the mind of the Greeks. Therefore reference has not been made in the text to English poems based upon the myths, but it has been left to the individual teacher carefully to introduce such illustrations and parallels; an appendix suggests a few of the more notable. Another

misunderstanding that it is sought to avoid is the
popular association of these anthropomorphic conceptions and imaginative tales with the Romans.
The writer has wished to make it clear that what
is known as classical mythology is a product of
Greece, and that in general the Latin writers have
merely retold stories that were not original with
their people. The Greek names have therefore
been employed primarily, even though they are
less familiar than the Latin. It may seem in-
consistent that this has been done even when the
version of a tale as it appears in the work of some
Latin poet, e.g., Ovid, has been followed, but it
is not the nomenclature, which is Latin, but the
subject matter and the conception of the tale,
which is Greek, that has been followed. Where
the story is mainly of Latin development Latin
names have been used. Perhaps it may seem
that too scant attention has been paid to Roman
gods, but when one deals with Roman deities
one quickly gets out of the realm of mythology
into that of ritual and history, subjects which
seem out of place in such a book as this.

In spelling Greek names the most familiar and
the simplest English spellings have been used.
In most cases ει has been transliterated by English _i_. (Poseidon is a common exception, and
_e_ takes the place of ει before the terminations
_a, as, us._ as Me de′a, Au ge′as.) _K_ has been ren-
dered _c_, αι by _æ_, οι by Latin _us_. In these incon-

sistencies the usual and permissible custom is followed. In the index and upon their first mention the accent on names of more than two syllables is indicated, and in an appendix a few simple rules of pronunciation are given.

While in many instances in a foot-note the version of a story followed has been indicated, and in case of direct quotation the reference has been given, in an elementary book such as this the use of many notes has been avoided as undesirable. In many stories one author has not been followed exclusively, but various features have been borrowed from various sources. Those chiefly followed are: Homer, the *Homeric Hymns,* Hesiod, Pindar, Æschylus, Sophocles, Euripides, Apollodorus, Apollonius Rhodius, Hyginus, Pausanius, Vergil, and Ovid. In quoting from the *Iliad* the translation of Lang, Leaf, and Myers has been used; from the *Odyssey,* that of Butcher and Lang; and from the *Homeric Hymns,* that of Lang. Of modern authorities consulted the most important are: Preller's *Griechische Mythologie* revised by Robert (unfortunately incomplete); Wissowa's *Religion und Kultus der Römer;* separate articles in Roscher's *Lexikon der griechischen und römischen Mythologie;* the *Pauly-Wissowa Real-Encyclopädie der classischen Altertumswissenschaft.* Frazer's *Golden Bough,* Jane Harrison's *Prolegomena to the Study of Greek Religion,* Lawson's *Modern*

Greek Folklore and Ancient Greek Religion,
Warde Fowler's *Roman Festivals,* and many
other books and articles have been helpful and
suggestive. The comprehensive works of Collignon, Baumeister, Overbeck, Furtwängler, and
others have, of course, been taken as authorities
in dealing with representations in art.

J. M. Tatlock.

December, 1916.

CONTENTS

PAGE

INTRODUCTION xix

PART I. THE GODS

CHAPTER

I THE WORLD OF THE MYTHS 3

II THE GODS OF OLYMPUS: ZEUS . . 16

III HERA, ATHENA, HEPHÆSTUS . . . 36
    I Hera 36
    II Athena 40
    III Hephæstus 49

IV APOLLO AND ARTEMIS 55
    I Apollo 55
    II Artemis 80

V HERMES AND HESTIA 91
    I Hermes 91
    II Hestia 98

VI ARES AND APHRODITE 105
    I Ares 105
    II Aphrodite 109

VII THE LESSER DEITIES OF OLYMPUS . 122
    I Eros 122
    II Other Deities of Olympus . . 139

VIII THE GODS OF THE SEA 143

IX THE GODS OF THE EARTH 153

X THE WORLD OF THE DEAD . . . 186

Contents

PART II. THE HEROES

CHAPTER		PAGE
XI	STORIES OF ARGOS	199
XII	HERACLES	210
XIII	STORIES OF CRETE, SPARTA, CORINTH, ÆTOLIA	228
	I Stories of Crete	228
	II Stories of Sparta	234
	III Stories of Corinth	236
	IV Stories of Ætolia	241
XIV	STORIES OF ATTICA	244
XV	STORIES OF THEBES	256
XVI	THE ARGONAUTIC EXPEDITION	266
XVII	THE TROJAN WAR	280
XVIII	THE WANDERINGS OF ODYSSEUS	305
XIX	THE TRAGEDY OF AGAMEMNON	326
XX	THE LEGENDARY ORIGIN OF ROME	331
	APPENDIX A	355
	APPENDIX B	356
	INDEX	363

LIST OF ILLUSTRATIONS

FIG.   PAGE

1. Omphalus, copy of a stone bound with fillets that was set up at Delphi to mark the center of the earth (Museum at Delphi) 4

2. Rhea offering Cronus the stone in place of Zeus (Vase in Metropolitan Museum) . 6

3. Zeus (Metropolitan Museum) . . . 17

4. Dirce tied to the bull (National Museum, Naples) 27

5. Head of Zeus found at Otricoli (Vatican) 31

6. View of ruins at Olympia 33

7. Hera, "Borghese Juno" (Glyptothek Ny Carlsberg, Copenhagen) 37

8. Ganymede and the eagle (Vatican) . . 39

9. Head of Hera (Museo delle Terme, Rome) 40

10. Lemnian Athena (Albertinum, Dresden) 41

11. Birth of Athena (Gerhard — *Auserlesene Vasenbilder*) 43

12. Athena "Minerva of Velletri" (Louvre) 45

13. Hephæstus and the Cyclopes preparing the shield of Achilles (Palazzo dei Conservatori, Rome) 50

14. Apollo from the pediment of the temple at Olympia 54

FIG.   PAGE

15. The sun-god in his chariot (Vase in British Museum) 56

16. Foundations of Apollo's temple at Delphi 57

17. Apollo as leader of the Muses (Vatican) . 60

18. Niobe and her daughter (Uffizi, Florence) 69

19. Asclepius (Capitoline Museum, Rome) . 75

20. Artemis of Versailles (Louvre) . . . 81

21. Artemis of Gabii (Louvre) 83

22. Actæon killed by his dogs (Vase in Boston Art Museum) 86

23. Sleeping Endymion (Capitoline Museum, Rome) 87

24. Hermes in repose (National Museum, Naples) 93

25. Hermes (Olympia) 97

26. Hestia, so-called (Rome) 99

27. Genius and Lares (Wall-painting from Pompeii) 101

28. Ares with Eros (Museo delle Terme, Rome) 104

29. Bearded Mars (Museo delle Terme, Rome) 106

30. Aphrodite of Cnidos (Museo delle Terme, Rome) 107

31. Birth of Aphrodite from the sea (Museo delle Terme, Rome) 110

32. Judgment of Paris (Tomb of the Anicii, Rome) 111

33. Venus of Arles (Louvre) 114

34. Eros, or Cupid (Capitoline Museum, Rome) 123

FIG.   PAGE

35. Cupid and Psyche (Capitoline Museum,
    Rome) 127

36. Clio (Vatican) 140

37. Thalia (Vatican) 141

38. Terpsichore (Vatican) 142

39. Poseidon (Athens) 145

40. Marriage of Poseidon and Amphitrite
    (Vase in Glyptothek Ny-Carlsberg) . 148

41. Head of a sea-god 149

42. Cybele in her car (Metropolitan Museum) 153

43. Demeter (Glyptothek Ny-Carlsberg) . . 155

44. Demeter, Triptolemus, and Persephone
    (Athens) 159

45. Triptolemus in the dragon-drawn chariot
    (Eleusis) 162

46. Dionysus (Museo delle Terme, Rome) . 163

47. Silenus with Dionysus (Vatican) . . . 167

48. Bacchic procession (National Museum,
    Naples) 168

49. Youthful Dionysus (National Museum,
    Naples) 172

50. Bacchic procession (Vase in Metropolitan
    Museum) 173

51. Pan and a nymph (Terra Cotta from Asia
    Minor) 175

52. Votive offering to Pan and the nymphs
    (National Museum, Athens) . . . 179

53. Dancing Satyr (National Museum, Na-
    ples) 180

54. Faun of Praxiteles (Capitoline Museum,
    Rome) 181

FIG.   PAGE

55. Athena and Marsyas (Reconstruction made in Munich) 182

56. Apollo and Marsyas (National Museum, Athens) 183

57. Charon in his skiff (Vase in Metropolitan Museum) 188

58. Heracles carrying off Cerberus (Gerhard. *Auserlesene Vasenbilder*) 191

59. Parting of Orpheus and Eurydice (National Museum, Naples) 193

60. Carpenter making the chest for Danaë and Perseus (Vase in Boston Art Museum) 201

61. Head of Medusa Rondanini (Glyptothek, Munich) 203

62. Perseus killing Medusa (Metope for Selinunte) 205

63. Atlas supporting the heavens (National Museum, Naples) 207

64. Heracles (Vatican) 211

65. Heracles strangling the serpents (Wall-painting from Pompeii) 214

66. Five of Heracles' labors (Borghese Gallery, Rome) 215

67. Heracles killing the Hydra (Gerhard. *Auserlesene Vasenbilder*) 217

68. Heracles carrying the boar (Metropolitan Museum) 218

69. Amazon (Capitoline Museum, Rome) . 219

70. Heracles in the bowl of the sun (Gerhard. *Auserlesene Vasenbilder*) 221

FIG. PAGE

71. Nessus running off with Dejanira (Vase in Boston Art Museum) 226

72. Europa on the bull (Wall-painting from Pompeii) 228

73. Dædalus and Icarus (Villa Albani, Rome) 231

74. The Dioscuri (Ancient statues now set up before the king's palace in Rome) . . 234

75. Chimæra (Archæological Museum, Florence) 237

76. Bellerophon and Pegasus (Palazzo Spada, Rome) 239

77. Meleager (Vatican) 242

78. Cephalus and the dawn-goddess (Vase in Boston Art Museum) 246

79. Theseus killing the Minotaur (Vase in Boston Art Museum) 251

80. Theseus and the rescued Athenians (Wall-painting from Pompeii) . . . 252

81. Centaur and Lapith (Metope from the Parthenon) 253

82. Cadmus and the dragon (Vase in Metropolitan Museum) 257

83. Œdipus and the Sphinx (Vase in Boston Art Museum) 261

84. Phrixus and the ram (Metropolitan Museum) 266

85. Centaur (Capitoline Museum, Rome) . 268

86. Medea preparing the magic brew (Gerhard. *Auserlesene Vasenbilder*) . . 276

87. Medea preparing to kill her children (Wall-painting from Pompeii) . . . 278

FIG.   PAGE
88. The persuasion of Helen (National Museum, Naples) 285

89. Sacrifice of Iphigenia (National Museum, Naples) 289

90. Priam ransoming Hector's body (Vase in Vienna) 299

91. Laocoon and his sons (Vatican) . . . 302

92. Priam slain on the altar (Vase in the Louvre) 304

93. Odysseus and the Sirens (Vase in British Museum) 313

94. Odysseus appearing before Nausicaa (Vase in Munich) 318

95. Odysseus makes himself known to Telemachus (Vase in Metropolitan Museum) 322

96. Odysseus avenging himself upon the suitors (Vase in Munich Museum) . . 325

97. Æneas wounded (Wall-painting from Pompeii) 332

98. Æneas fleeing from Troy (Gerhard. *Auserlesene Vasenbilder*) 337

99. The wolf with Romulus and Remus (Capitoline Museum, Rome) . . . 349

INTRODUCTION

PRIMITIVE people, as they have looked out on
the world about them, on the sea and the trees,
on the sky and the clouds, and as they have felt the
power of natural forces, the heat of the sun, the
violence of the wind, have recognized in these
things the expression and action of some being
more powerful than themselves. Able to understand only those motives and sensations that are
like their own, they have conceived these beings
more or less after their own nature. The Hebrews, indeed, at an early time recognized one
supreme God, who had created and who directed
all the world according to his will, but most other
early people have seen living, willing beings in
the forms and powers of nature, and have worshiped these beings as gods or feared them as
devils. Physical events, such as the rising and
setting of the sun, or the springing and ripening
of the grain, are to them actions of the beings
identified with sun or grain. In accounting for
these acts, whether regularly recurring, as the
rising of the sun, or occasionally disturbing the or-
dinary course of nature, as earthquakes, eclipses,
or violent storms, stories more or less complete

grow, are repeated, and believed. These stories told of superhuman beings and believed by a whole people are myths, and all these myths together form a mythology.

The mythology of any people is interesting because it reflects their individual nature and developing life; that of the Greeks is more interesting to us than any other, first, because it expresses the nature of a people gifted with a peculiarly fine and artistic soul; secondly, because our own thought and art are, in great part, a heritage from the civilization of Greece. Much of this heritage comes to us quite directly from the Greek writers and artists whose works have been preserved. The dramas of Sophocles and Euripides hold an audience in America as they held those in Athens, because their art is true and great; the noble youth of the Hermes of Praxiteles, or the gallant action of the horsemen in the frieze of the Parthenon satisfy us in the twentieth century as they did the Greeks in the fifth and fourth centuries B.C. But more of this heritage comes down to us through the Romans, whose genius taught them to conquer and govern without destroying, and who learned from the nations that they conquered, Egypt, Asia, and Greece, all that centuries of rich civilization had to give. The civilization of the modern world, America as well as Europe, is rooted deeply in the civilization of Rome, and through Rome in that

of Greece. Greek thought and Greek principles
run through our law, our government, our stand-
ards of taste, our art, and our literature. The
very personages of Greek mythology are familiarly known to-day in the United States, divorced
from religious meaning but set up before our
eyes as symbols of truths that are in the very
nature of things. The winged Mercury (the
god of travelers, whose Greek name was Hermes)
waves his magic wand above the main entrance
to the Grand Central Station in New York; the
noble head of Minerva (the Greek Athena, the
goddess of wisdom) is set above the doors of our
libraries and colleges, and the adventures of
Ulysses (or Odysseus) and of many other Greek
heroes are painted on the walls of our Congres-
sional Library. Even in our daily language there
is still a hint of mythology: our troops still march
to martial music, the music of the war-god Mars,
and we eat at breakfast cereals, the gift of the
corn-goddess Ceres; the Muses of Pieria are not
too far away to inspire the music of our western
world.

These beliefs and stories have been handed
down through so many ages and modified in so
many ways that confusion as to their real origin
has naturally arisen. It is Greek, not Roman.
The Romans did not develop an original mythology but took over stories from the Greeks and
others and told them of their own gods. It was

the Greek Zeus, not the Roman Jupiter, who had
so many love adventures; it was the Greek Aphrodite, not the Roman Venus, who received the
golden apple from Trojan Paris. Classical
mythology is the expression of the nature and
thought of the Greeks, not that of the Romans.
For the Greeks were by nature artistic; they in-
stinctively expressed their ideals, the truth as they
saw it, in poetry, story, and sculpture, and because imagination, insight, and love of beauty
were united in them, their stories and their art
have an appeal that is universal.

The religion and mythology of the Greeks was
not a fixed and unchanging thing; it varied with
different localities and changed with changing
conditions. For when we speak of Greece we
do not speak of a nation in the strict sense —
that is, a people under one central government —
but of the Greek race: "Wherever the Greeks
are, there is Greece." So the mythological stories
grew and changed as they passed from Asia
Minor to Greece, or from Greece to the islands
of the Ægean Sea, to Italy and Sicily. Moreover, the independence of the individual in the
Greek states, where men thought for themselves,
and no autocratic government or powerful priesthood exerted undue restraint, fostered variety and
permitted artists and poets so to modify tradition
as to express something of their individual ideas.
This added infinitely to the richness of mythology

and art. Local conditions, too, and local pride, in a country broken both geographically and politically into small divisions, added variety to religious customs. In mountain districts the god of the sky and storms was most feared and worshiped, in the fertile plains, the gods of earth and harvest, while on the coast men needed the favor of the gods who were powerful over the sea and protected commerce. Local heroes gathered stories about themselves, and local pride led people to place important events, such as the birth of a god or some important manifestation of his power, in their own localities. Many different places claimed to be the birthplace of Apollo, and the fires of Hephæstus burned within many a volcano (called after his Latin name, Vulcan). Furthermore, as they came in contact with other peoples and became familiar with their religious stories and ceremonial, they incorporated much that was of foreign origin into their own religion. The stories connected with Dionysus, or Bacchus, and the extravagant rites celebrated in his honor were imported from the East, and the Aphrodite of Asia Minor was far more Asiatic and sensual in character than the Aphrodite of Greece. Finally, since mythology is not based on authority but grows from the soul of the people, it necessarily follows that as Greek life and thought grew and developed, as social conditions changed, as art was perfected and poetry and philosophy grew less simple, the telling of the myths and their interpretation changed and developed. Mythology was a living, growing thing, impossible to seize and fix in a consistent system. It must be regarded as a mass of legend, handed down through the people and poets of generation after generation, continually reflecting the developing life and soul of a great and vital race. When different versions of a story are found, one is not necessarily more authentic than another; in the present book that version is given which has become most famous in art and literature.

Before proceeding to the mythological stories that spring from the Greek religion, it is well to notice some of the more marked characteristics of that religion.

(1) It was polytheistic, it was the worship of many gods. The supremacy of Zeus, "father of gods and king of men," over the other gods did not make the religion a monotheism any more than the hegemony or leadership of one Greek state over others made Greece one united nation.

(2) The religion was, in origin, a worship of the powers of nature. This is natural to primitive men everywhere, because these are the first powers outside of themselves of which men are conscious. The intensity of the Greek sun, the nearness of the sea and its importance in the daily life of the people, the mountain barriers

about them, all tended to emphasize men's dependence upon nature. But as the Greeks developed in intelligence and civilization, as their thoughts and their lives became less simple, and abstract ideas entered into the government of their actions, these nature gods assumed ethical or moral meanings. So the thunder of Zeus, originally his weapon as sky-god, became the symbol of his world power as god of law and order. The clear, illuminating brightness of the sun made of the god of light, Apollo, the all-seeing prophet, who in his worshipers required purity. Athena, who, owing to the story of her birth from her father Zeus's head when Hephæstus had cleft it, is generally supposed to have represented the descent of the storm when the thunderbolt has opened the heavens, almost lost this original meaning, and became the goddess of practical wisdom and of skill in war.

(3) It was an anthropomorphic religion — that is, the gods were conceived in the forms of men, greater and more beautiful and of a finer substance, yet such as men could understand and represent. While a more spiritual conception leads to a loftier ideal, this Greek conception of the gods as of like nature with men exalts and ennobles human life and the human body and offers subjects for poets and sculptors. A purely spiritual god can never be so represented as even in part to satisfy his worshipers, but the noble

dignity of Zeus, the king of gods, was so realized by the sculptor Phidias that his great gold and ivory statue quite worthily expressed to the people their ideal. What gulf there was between gods and men was bridged by the existence of heroes or demigods, sons of gods by mortals, and of nature and powers half human, half divine.

(4) To worship and propitiate these gods, in nature so close to men, so easily understood, men needed the help of no powerful priesthood gifted with peculiar sanctity and mysterious knowledge and powers. At the great shrines, it is true, there were priests and priestesses devoted to the gods' service, and there were men and women peculiarly inspired by the god to interpret his will and give warning and promise for the future; but these prophets only occasionally or indirectly controlled people's actions and had little authority in determining religious belief and practice. Each father was his family's priest; each man could offer his own prayers and his own sacrifice and be understood and accepted by the god he addressed. When the family ate and drank, part of the meat and drink was offered to the gods. When they danced and sang, the gods, called on to be present, enjoyed a pleasure like their own. Even games and athletics were shared by the gods. Apollo threw the discus with his friends, and Hermes was famous for his swiftness of foot. So athletic contests became a form

of worship. Business as well as pleasure was a repetition of divine actions and therefore joined with religion. Hermes was a shepherd and understood the needs of other shepherds; Hephæstus was a smith, and no human smith needed an interpreter to call upon him for aid in his craft. The gods experienced and understood, too, the different relations of life. The maiden Artemis readily lent an ear to girls who were in trouble, and the offering of their childish playthings was acceptable to her. Hera, as wife and mother, was always ready to champion mortals in those relations, while the rights of kings were very dear to Zeus, the king of gods. So all the acts of daily life, all the simple things that men used, finding their counterpart among the Olympians were ennobled and filled with religious meaning.

The gods of the Romans were just as closely connected with daily life as were those of the Greeks, but the number of deities to be recognized was vastly multiplied, and they did not appear to their worshipers as distinct personalities. No act of life, from the cooking of the family meal to the declaration of war, but was under the special care of some divinity. No material thing, from the oven in which the bread was baked to the city of Rome, but had its own indwelling deity. Even to know the names of all these innumerable divinities, much more to give them all distinct characters and to determine the

best way to approach each one, was quite impossible for the busy practical citizen. Hence,
a purely conventional system of religious ceremonial and invocation ran through Roman life,
just as unquestioningly observed as the other
conventions and regulations to which the citizens
were subject. Each family under its father as
head worshiped its own gods of the home and
family about its own hearth, and no one could
hold his place in the family without performing
his duty to the family gods. So the state, as
the greater family, had its own deities, its own
hearth in the shrine of Vesta in the Forum, its
own religious head, first the king, later under
the Republic the Pontifex Maximus. State and
religion were one and indivisible; failure in religious duty was failure in national duty, and a
wrong committed against the civil law was a
sin against the gods. This was a strong civiliz-
ing side of religion that made for good morals
and good citizenship, but it lacked the inspira-
tion of a more personal faith. Nor had the
Roman gods sufficient individuality to bring into
existence any body of mythology, such as that of
the Greeks. The stories we are accustomed to
associate with the Roman gods are either borrowed from the Greeks or were late creations
of imagination inspired by and modeled on the
traditions of Greek mythology.

PART I
THE GODS

GREEK AND ROMAN MYTHOLOGY

CHAPTER I

THE WORLD OF THE MYTHS

THE knowledge that the world we live in is a sphere and but one of an endless number that are whirling through space with incredible speed, is not a knowledge that we have by nature or by experience; we must be persuaded of this scientific fact. For as we look around us and above us, we seem to stand at the very center of a circular plane, vaulted by the sky, across whose spacious arch the sun travels by day and the moon by night. This was the view held by the Greeks of early times. To them the world was flat and round, a disk whose central point was in their own native land, in Central Greece, at Delphi, the holy place of all their race. Near and far were counted from Delphi; it was with the sacred permission of the oracle established there that those daring colonists set out who brought Greece to the shores of Asia Minor, to Africa, and Italy.

Beyond those lands to which Greek enterprise and civilization penetrated lay distant lands inhabited by strange people and monsters, the tiny race of Pygmies, one-eyed giants, and serpents. Far in the North lived a good and happy people, the Hy per bo're ans, and to the South "the

Fig. 1.　Omphalus, copy of a stone bound with fillets that was set up at Delphi to mark the center of the earth.

blameless Ethiopians." These had no dealings with other men, but were specially loved by the gods, who paid them frequent visits and ate at their tables. Beyond all lands, and circling the disk of earth, ran the Stream of Ocean, a great and mysterious river without a farther shore.

The account of the beginning of this world, as the Greek poets tell it, is in one respect quite unlike the account that is found in the first chapter of Genesis. For while the Hebrews were taught that God, who existed from the beginning, created our universe of heaven, earth, and sea, and all the forms of life, ending in man, the Greeks believed that the natural world came into being by birth or generation, and that even the gods whom they worshiped were the children and successors of an earlier and more elemental race of beings.

Thus, in the beginning was Chaos, a formless misty void; next came Gæa (Earth), and Eros (Love), most beautiful of immortals. From Chaos sprang Er'e bus (the darkness under the earth) and Night. From these two were born Æther (the light of heaven) and Day. But Gæa, touched by Eros, bore U'ra nus (Heaven), the sea and all the hills. Then Uranus and Gæa were united by Eros and became the parents of the Titans, who represent the great ungoverned forces of nature, and the three Cy clo'pes, who are the rumbling thunder, the lightning, and the thunderbolt; lastly, they gave birth to the hundred-handed giants, who represent the violence of the sea. When Uranus, fearing his children, the Cyclopes and the hundred-handed giants, drove them back into the earth, Gæa in her distress called upon the Titans for deliverance.

The greatest of them, Cronus, obedient to his mother's call, attacked his father, and having maimed him with a sickle, seized his power.

Birth of the gods. After this, Cronus married his sister Rhea and became the father of six children; but since he had been told that a son should overthrow his

Fig. 2.   Rhea offering Cronus the stone in place of Zeus.

rule, as he had overthrown that of his own father, he adopted the extraordinary precaution of swallowing his children as soon as they were born. Thus Hes'ti a (Vesta), De me'ter (Ceres), and Hera (Juno) Po sei'don (Neptune), and Hades (Pluto), came to the light only to be devoured.

When Rhea bore her last son, Zeus (Jupiter), she saved him from the fate of his brothers and sisters by giving to Cronus a stone wrapped in baby's clothes in his place. The infant was kept for safety in a cave in Crete, where he was nourished on honey and the milk of the goat Am al the'a, while the Cu re'tes, mountain spirits of Crete or priests of Rhea, drowned his cries by clashing their spears on their shields.

When Zeus was grown, by giving Cronus a strong potion he forced him to disgorge the five children he had swallowed. He then declared war upon him. The gods, as Zeus and his brothers and sisters should now be called, fortified themselves on Mt. Olympus, in Thessaly, and for ten years the war raged without ceasing. The rugged mountains and jumbled rocks of Thessaly bear witness to the fury of the battles. Finally Gæa advised Zeus to loose from their prison under the earth the Cyclopes and the hundred-handed giants. After this, armed with the thunderbolts given him by the Cyclopes, and assisted by the convulsions of sea and land caused by the hundred-handed giants, Zeus gained the victory. Those Titans who had taken Cronus' part were buried deep in Tartarus, as far below the earth as earth is below heaven.

The three brothers now divided the world between them. Zeus, chosen as king, was supreme over heaven and earth, as truly a sky-god as his grandfather Uranus had been. Poseidon was lord over all the waters, and to Hades was given the realm that bears his name below the earth, and dominion over the dead.

Although Gæa had aided and abetted the gods in their war against Cronus, she resented the complete subjugation of her sons. Therefore she brought forth Typhon, a fearful monster, from whose shoulders grew a hundred serpent heads, with darting tongues and fiery eyes, and from whose throats came fearful sounds, like the bellowing of bulls, the howling of dogs, the roaring of lions, and the hissing of serpents. Under him all the earth was shaken, the waters seethed; even Hades below trembled at the convulsion of the world. But Zeus seized the thunderbolts, his gift from the Cyclopes, and overthrew Typhon, scorching all his hundred heads. This monster, too, was buried beneath the earth, but still from his uneasy writhing at times the earth trembles, and the flames from his nostrils shoot up through the craters of volcanoes.

To Zeus were born many sons and daughters, and when other enemies threatened his power, he had their assistance in overcoming them. This new war was brought on by a race of giants who had sprung from the blood of Uranus, when he was wounded by his son Cronus. Not all are agreed as to just what the form of the giants was, but artists sometimes depicted them with the tails of serpents, and armed, as a tribe of savage men might be, with tree-trunks and rocks. These, too, Zeus with the help of his brothers and children overthrew and buried. After this his rule was undisputed.

Much of this story of the world is allegory. Day springs from night; heaven and earth are the parents of the powers of nature. It is all a development from the lower to the higher, from unordered forces of nature, to nature ordered by thought, justice, and beauty. And this development comes through love and birth, and through struggle, in which the higher gains the rule by crushing the lower. It is the story of science, history, and the spiritual life, told as an allegory.

Meaning of the myths.

Of the origin of man in the world the Greeks had three explanations: he was born of the earth, as in the story of the earliest king of Athens, who rose from the ground, half man, half serpent; or he was descended from the gods, Zeus is called " Father of gods and men "; or — and this came to be the accepted account — he was molded out of clay by the Titan's son, Pro me'theus, and given life by A the'na, the wise daughter of Zeus. A Greek gentleman of the second century A.D., traveling in his own country, was shown a small brick hut in which, he was told by the natives of the place, Prometheus had fashioned the first man. Large masses of clay-colored stone lay

The creation of man.

about, and the credulous tourist says that it had the odor of human flesh.[1]

The gift of fire.

When he had created man, Prometheus gave him the gift of fire, which raised him above all other animals and enabled him to make use of the world about him by forging weapons and tools for agriculture. Fire was the means and the symbol of civilization. But Prometheus fell under the displeasure of Zeus for his favor toward man; for when a joint meeting was held to determine what part of beasts offered in sacrifice was due to the gods and what to men, he prepared a cunning device. He cut up an ox and divided it in two portions; in one was the flesh covered by the hide, and in the other the bones temptingly covered by fat. Then he told Zeus once for all to choose what should be his portion. And Zeus, although he saw the deceit, chose the bones and fat, because he wanted to bring trouble on Prometheus and his creation, man. So the gods deprived men of fire and denied them their means of livelihood, until Prometheus stole it once more from heaven, bringing it secretly in a hollow reed. For this defiance of his power the god punished Prometheus by having him bound to a rock in the Caucasus Mountains, where an eagle ever tore at his liver, which ever grew again. Although at any time he might have won his

[1] Pausanias, X. 4. 3.

freedom by telling Zeus a secret which he alone knew, the much-enduring Titan bore this torture for ages. The two were at last reconciled and Prometheus set free, by Her'a cles (Hercules), the son of Zeus, who, as part divine, part human, was suited to act as mediator between the gods and man's self-sacrificing friend and benefactor.

Because of the theft of fire, against men, too, **Pandora.** Zeus devised evil.

For fire will I give them an evil thing wherein they shall rejoice, embracing their own doom. So spake the father of men and gods, and laughed aloud. And he bade glorious Hephæstus speedily to mingle earth with water, and put therein human speech and strength, and make, as the deathless goddesses to look upon, the fair form of a lovely maiden. And Athena he bade teach her handiwork, to weave the embroidered web. And he bade golden Aphrodite shed grace about her head and grievous desire and wasting passion. And Hermes, the messenger, the slayer of Argus, he bade give her a shameless soul. (Hesiod, *Works and Days*, 56 ff. Translation by A. W. Mair.)

Now when he had fashioned the beautiful bane in the place of a blessing, he led her forth where were the other gods and men. . . . And amazement held immortal gods and mortal men, when they beheld the sheer delusion unescapable for men. For from her cometh the race of woman-kind. Yea, of her is the deadly race and the tribes of women. A great bane are they to dwell among mortal men, no help-meet for ruinous poverty, but for abundance. (Hesiod, *Theogony*, 585 ff. Translation by A. W. Mair.)

Although Prometheus (Forethought) had warned his brother Epimetheus (Afterthought) never to accept anything from Zeus, Epimetheus foolishly received this woman, Pan do'ra, at the hands of the gods' messenger, Hermes. She had with her a jar which she was commanded on no account to open. But curiosity was too strong. The instant the lid was raised out flew ten thousand little winged plagues, diseases, pains, and sins; no one on earth could escape them. Only Hope stayed within the mouth of the jar and never flew out. So in this Greek story the hitherto peaceful, innocent world received its burden of trouble through the curiosity of the first woman, just as in the Bible story the innocence of the Garden of Eden was lost through Eve.

The Four Ages. The Greeks were not quite consistent in their explanations of the coming of sin and trouble into the world, for while in the one account it all came when Pandora opened her jar, the account of the Four Ages shows a gradual deterioration. For, first of all, in the Age of Gold mortal men lived like gods, knowing neither sorrow nor toil. The generous earth bore fruit of herself, and there was neither numbing frost nor burning heat to make shelter necessary. This was during the reign of Cronus, known among the Romans as Saturn. The men of this age never grew old and feeble, but when death came, it came like a peaceful sleep. And when this race was hidden in the earth Zeus made of them good spirits who watch over mortals. The second race, that of the Silver Age, the gods made inferior to the first in mind and body. The time of helpless infancy was long, and the time of manhood short and troubled, for they could not refrain from injuring one another, and they failed to give worship and sacrifice to the gods. Yet the men of this age, too, had some honor, and lived on as spirits under the earth. Next came the Age of Bronze, when men insolently delighted in war. Of bronze were their homes, of bronze their armor, and their hearts were as hard as their weapons. Last of all was the Age of Iron. By day there was no end to their weariness and woe, nor by night to their anxieties. Family love was lost, parents neglected, and friendship and the rights of hospitality forgotten. Might became right, and respect for truth and plighted faith was made of no account. Reverence and Justice, veiling their heads, forsook men and withdrew to Olympus.

When Zeus, then, saw how utterly wicked men had become, he resolved to clear the earth of them all. To the council summoned in heaven destruction by fire seemed a method too dangerous to the homes of the gods; a flood over the earth was a safer plan. To this end, Zeus shut up the north wind and all the others that drive

The Flood of Deucalion.

away the clouds, and sent out the rainy south wind, and he called upon his brother Poseidon to let out the waters under his control. The flood spread over the fields and broke down the standing grain; it carried away the flocks with their shepherds, the houses and the holy shrines. Sea and land, all was one now, a limitless ocean. Fishes swam in and out among the branches of the trees, and awkward seals stretched themselves where lately the nimble goats had played. The water-nymphs swam wonderingly among the houses. The birds, flying long in search of a resting-place, fell exhausted in the watery waste. The human race perished, all but the son of Prometheus, Deu ca'li on, and his wife Pyrrha. These good people, taught beforehand by the wise Titan, had constructed a great chest in which they had gathered all that was necessary for life, and when the flood came they took refuge in it themselves, and floated for nine days until the chest touched ground once more on Mt. Parnassus. When Zeus looked down and saw all the violent race of men swept off the earth, and only this one man, a lover of justice and a devout worshiper of the gods, left alive with his wife, he called upon the north wind to disperse the clouds and upon Poseidon to recall his waters. Then Deucalion and Pyrrha stepped out of the chest and saw a waste and unpeopled earth about them, and in their loneliness they called upon the gods for help.   The oracle made answer that they should cast behind them the bones of their mother.   Knowing that the god could never order them to be guilty of the impiety of disturbing the tomb of their mortal parent, Deucalion divined the true meaning of the mysterious command.   The earth is the mother of all and the stones are her bones.   With heads reverently veiled they descended the mountain, casting stones behind them.   Those that Deucalion threw assumed the forms of men, those that Pyrrha threw, the forms of women.   So the earth was repeopled.[2]

[2] Apollodorus, I. 7; Ovid, *Metamorphoses*, I. 260 ff.

CHAPTER II

THE GODS OF OLYMPUS: ZEUS

Mt. Olympus. WHILE the gods of the Greek religion were personifications of natural powers, yet they were conceived after the fashion of human beings, both in bodily form and in their needs and passions. They were born, grew, married, and suffered, though death never came to them. These beings, like men, only greater and more beautiful, must have cities and homes like those of men, only greater and more beautiful. So the Greeks of the mainland looked up to the cloud-capped peak of Mt. Olympus, majestic, mysterious, eternally enduring, and saw there, under the arch of heaven, the golden halls of the divine city.

There, as they say, is the seat of the gods that standeth fast forever. Not by winds is it shaken, nor ever wet with rain, nor doth the snow come nigh thereto, but most clear air is spread about it cloudless, and the white light floats over it. Therein the blessed gods are glad for all their days. (*Odyssey*, VI. 42 ff.)

It was a true celestial city, conceived after the model of the Greek city-states. At the gates of cloud the Hours stood as guardians, within the walls rose the palaces of the gods, and on the

16

Fig. 3. Zeus.

topmost peak, the acropolis, was the great hall where the members of the Olympic Council gathered for deliberation or for feasting. Ambrosia was the food served at these banquets, and nectar, poured into the cups by Hebe, the goddess of youth, nourished the ichor flowing in the gods' veins instead of blood. The nostrils of the feasters were filled with the rich odor of sacrifices offered on earth, and their ears charmed by the songs the Muses sang to the accompaniment of Apollo's lyre.

In the place of honor sat Zeus on his golden throne, and Hera, his sister and wife, sat beside him, while about them assembled the other ten Olympians, all brothers, sisters, sons, or daughters of the " father of gods and king of men." For after his victory over the Titans Zeus ruled supreme over heaven and earth. He challenges the other Olympians to dispute his power:

Zeus
(Jupiter).

Go to now, ye gods, make trial that ye all may know. Fasten ye a rope of gold from Heaven, and all ye gods lay hold thereof and all goddesses; yet could ye not drag from Heaven to earth Zeus, counselor supreme, not though ye toiled sore. But once I likewise were minded to draw with all my heart, then should I draw you up with very earth and sea withal. . . . By so much am I beyond gods and beyond men. (*Iliad*, VIII. 18 ff.)

As sky-god he drew the clouds over the face of heaven, sending storm and rain upon the earth, or he dispersed them and looked down over all as a benignant father. The weapon of his anger was the thunderbolt; Victory stood at his right hand. Yet his rule was not one of arbitrary violence; he was the author and promoter of law and order, of a civilized and regulated intercourse between men, of hospitality and just treatment of man by man. Hesiod calls upon the Muses to sing of him in words that recall the song of the Virgin Mary:

> Muses of Pieria, who glorify with song, come sing of Zeus your father, and declare his praise, through whom are men famed and unfamed, sung and unsung, as Zeus Almighty will. Lightly he giveth strength, and lightly he afflicteth the strong; lightly he bringeth low the mighty and lifteth up the humble; lightly he maketh the crooked to be straight and withereth the proud as chaff; Zeus, who thundereth in Heaven, who dwelleth in the height. (Hesiod, *Works and Days*, 1 ff.)

His marriage with Hera. Zeus was married to his sister, "Hera of the golden throne," a beautiful, queenly goddess, yet, as Homer portrays her, a very human woman, implacably jealous of Zeus's other loves, intriguing to get her own way, using against her lord all the traditional weapons of a woman. For all his power and majesty, Olympian Zeus went in dread of his wife's reproaches and persistency and drew the thickest of clouds between them when he indulged in any pleasure of which she would not approve. Though she had no choice but to yield when he asserted his will, she reserved to herself the compensation of taunts and a sullen demeanor. On one occasion when he had promised a favor to another of the goddesses, this altercation took place:

Anon with taunting words spake she to Zeus, the son of Cronus, "Now who among the gods, thou crafty of mind, hath devised counsel with thee? It is ever thy good pleasure to hold aloof from me and in sweet meditation to give thy judgments, nor of thine own good will hast thou ever brought thyself to declare unto me the thing thou purposeth."

Then the father of gods and men made answer to her: "Hera, think not thou to know all my sayings; hard are they for thee, even though thou art my wife. But whichsoever it is seemly for thee to hear, none sooner than thou shalt know, be he god or man. Only when I will to take thought aloof from the gods, then do not thou ask of every matter nor make question."

. . . He said, and Hera the ox-eyed queen was afraid, and sat in silence, curbing her heart. (*Iliad*, I. 539 ff.)

Though Hera was Zeus's queen and lawful wife, he united himself with many other goddesses and mortal women. Many of these unions originated as symbols of natural facts, others as symbols of philosophic truths. Thus as sky-god, god of sun and rain, Zeus must join in marriage union with De me'ter, the grain-goddess, that Per seph'o ne, the young corn of the new year, may be born. Again, as the great, creating, regu-

lating mind, he must unite with Mnemosyne
(ne mos'i nē) or Memory, that the Nine Muses,
the goddesses of poetry, music, and science, may
draw from father and mother what is needed for
all great creative work. But the extraordinary
number of Zeus's unions was due to the fact that
Greek mythology was not the creation or inheritance of one land and people, but was drawn
from the religion and traditions of Greeks in
many different lands and under many different
conditions. The religious traditions of many
peoples with whom the Greeks had intercourse
were incorporated by them into their own
mythology. Moreover, each Greek state had its
own local hero, the ancestor or early king of that
group, and these heroes were always of divine
origin, very many of them the sons of Zeus by
mortal women. Thus the Arcadians traced their
descent from Arcas, a son of Callisto by Zeus, of
whose love the following story is told.

Callisto.3   Cal lis'to was a nymph, a favorite companion
of the huntress Ar'te mis. One day, wandering
alone in the woods, she lay down upon the ground
to rest. Zeus saw her there, and thinking himself quite safe from the jealous eyes of Hera,
came down secretly and wooed her. Callisto
would gladly have escaped the attentions of the

3 Following the story as told by the Latin poet Ovid
(*Metamorphoses*, II. 410 ff.), but retaining the original
Greek names.

god and gone to rejoin Artemis and her nymphs; but who could withstand Zeus! Artemis, who, as herself a maiden, would have none but maidens in her company, turned Callisto away when she would have rejoined her. Solitary and sad the nymph lived in the woods until she bore to Zeus a son, Arcas. Now Zeus's love for Callisto was known to Hera. "You shall not go unpunished," said she to the nymph, "for I shall take away that beauty by which you charmed my husband's love." In vain Callisto begged for pity. Her arms began to be covered with coarse black hair; crooked claws grew from her hands, which now served as forefeet; that face which once aroused Zeus's love was deformed by huge ugly jaws. When she would have prayed for mercy, the power to speak was taken from her, and an angry frightened growl was all that she could utter. But under her bear's form her human heart, her grief and her love remained. How often in her solitary anguish, fearing to rest in the dark woods, she sought her old home! How often she was driven away by the barking dogs! Once herself a huntress, she was now the hunted. Often she hid from the bears she met in the mountains, forgetful that she was now of their kind. So fifteen troubled years passed. One day her son Arcas, out hunting wild beasts, met with his mother in the forest. She recognized her child and ran to greet him. Terrified by the rush of

the great bear, he aimed at her his hunting-spear.
Zeus checked his blow and raised Callisto to the
heavens, where he set her as the constellation of
the Great Bear.   Hera's jealousy was not at all
satisfied by this.   "Behold I took from her her
human form and now she is made a goddess!
Is this the punishment for a guilty woman!   Is
this my power!"   She went to the sea-gods and
prayed that they would never permit Callisto to
dip below their waves.   The prayer was granted,
and thus it is that the Great Bear can always be
seen in the heavens and never sinks below the
waters.

Another story that shows the unrelenting
hatred with which Hera pursued those favored by
Zeus is that of Io.

Io was the daughter of In'a chus, a river-god.
Zeus loved and wooed and won her, coming to
her secretly under cover of a cloud spread between their meeting-place and Hera's watchful
eyes.   But the jealous queen, looking down upon
the realm of Argos, and wondering to see the
low-lying cloud under a clear sky, at once suspected some wrong-doing on her husband's part.
She glided down from heaven and bade the cloud
recede.   Zeus, however, had foreseen the coming of his wife and had changed the daughter of
Inachus into a beautiful white heifer.   Suspecting the trick, Hera requested the heifer as a gift,

* Following Ovid, *Metamorphoses*, I. 583 ff.

and Zeus was constrained to yield or acknowledge
his love. Io was given by her mistress in charge
of Argus, a monster of whose hundred eyes but
two were closed at one time. When she would
have held out supplicating hands to Argus, she
had no hands to hold out. When she tried to
speak, she was terrified by her own lowing. She
came to the banks of the river Inachus where she
was wont to play; when she saw the reflection
of her great mouth and new-formed horns, she
fled from her own image in terror. The Naiads
did not know her; her own father Inachus did
not know her. She followed her father and sisters and offered herself to be petted and admired.
She licked their hands and kissed her father's
palms, nor could she keep back the big tears from
rolling down her nose. At last with her hoof
she traced in the sand the letters of her own name,
Io. "Woe is me!" cried her father, and fell
upon the heifer's neck. "I have sought you
through all lands. Better were it that I had never
found you." Hundred-eyed Argus parted them
as they lamented, and put her in a new pasture.
But Zeus could not endure to see her so unhappy.
He sent Hermes, his son and messenger, most
wily of gods, to destroy the ever-watchful Argus.
Laying aside his winged sandals and disguised
as a shepherd, Hermes approached Argus, who,
weary of his lonely and tedious watch, called to
him to come and share the shade of his tree.

Seated beside Argus, Hermes piped to him charmingly on his shepherd's pipes, varying with song the long stories with which he beguiled the hours. Two by two the hundred eyes were closed, until at last no eye was awake to watch his charge. Hermes at once slew him and set Io free. The hundred eyes Hera took and placed in the tail of her sacred peacock, where they may be seen to-day. But her jealous wrath still pursued unfortunate Io. She sent a gad-fly to torment her and drive her from land to land. In her weary search for peace, the heifer passed over the strait that divides Europe from Asia, whence it derives its name, Bosphorus, the way of the cow. Over the sea, too, that bears her name, the Ionian Sea, she wandered, until at last she arrived in Egypt, where she was restored to her natural form and gave birth to a son, the ancestor of the Ionian Greeks.

Antiope.　An ti′o pe was the daughter of the king of Thebes. By Zeus she became the mother of two sons Am phi′on and Zethus. Immediately after their birth the babies were taken from her and exposed on Mt. Cithæron, where they grew up among the shepherds. Antiope fell into the power of her uncle Lycus, whose wife Dirce treated her with the greatest cruelty. After some years she made her escape and fled to Mt. Cithæron, where she happened to take refuge in the hut where her sons lived. As one of a company of

Bacchantes, votaries of the wine-god Bacchus, Dirce came, by chance, to the same place, and finding the hated Antiope, she ordered Amphion and Zethus to kill her by tying her to the horns

Fig. 4. Dirce tied to the bull.

of a fierce bull. They were about to carry out this barbarous command when the shepherd informed them that the victim was their own mother. Releasing her, they now executed the

same sentence on Dirce, who was instantly torn
in pieces by the angry bull. Lycus, too, was
killed, and the brothers became kings of Thebes.
It is said that when they were building walls
about the city Zethus' strength enabled him to
lift huge stones into place, but that Amphion's
skill as a musician was so great that when he
played his lyre stones yet more huge rose of
themselves and took their places in the wall.

The story of Baucis and Phi le'mon shows how
Zeus could reward those who respected the law
of hospitality and punish those who violated it.

Baucis and
Philemon.[5] In a certain place where now is a marsh fre-
quented by wild birds was once a village.   Here
Zeus came in the guise of a mortal, and with him
his son Hermes, winged sandals laid aside.   They
went to a thousand dwellings seeking rest and
refreshment; all were barred against them.   Yet
one, a little house thatched with reeds, received
them.   Here good old Baucis and her husband
Philemon had grown old together, making happiness even out of their poverty by bearing it
together with contented hearts.   Here then came
the Immortals, and bending down their heads entered the low door.   The old man placed a seat
and bade them sit down, while Baucis bustled to
throw over it a coarse covering.   Then she gathered together the dying embers, added dry leaves
and fuel and blew it into a flame with her feeble

[5] Following Ovid, *Metamorphoses*, VIII. 620 ff.

breath.   Her husband brought in a cabbage from
the little garden, cut a fat piece from the long-
cherished flitch of bacon, and put them over the
fire to cook.   They shook up their cushion of
soft sedge-grass, laid it on the dining-couch, and
put over it a covering that, poor and patched
though it was, they used only on great festivals.
While the gods reclined on the couch, the trembling old woman, with skirts tucked up, set out
the table.   One foot of the table was uneven;
a brick steadied it, and a handful of greens cleaned
off the top.   The feast began with olives, stewed
berries, endive, radishes, cottage-cheese, and eggs
carefully fried, all served in earthenware dishes.
After this the mixing-bowl and cups, made of
beech-wood lined with smooth wax, were set out
for the wine — not rich old wine, but the best
they had.   There were nuts, figs, dried dates,
plums, and fragrant apples served in baskets, and
purple grapes gathered from the vines, and in
the middle of the table the honey-comb.   Above
all there were cordial looks and eager good-will.
And now the astonished couple began to notice
that the mixing-bowl, as often as it was emptied,
filled up again of its own accord.   They trembled, and holding out their hands in supplication,
asked forgiveness for the humble fare.   There
was one single goose, the guardian of the little
farm; this its masters now prepared to slaughter
for their divine guests.   It escaped them, and

flapping its wings, dodged about the little room and at last took refuge at the feet of the gods. The Immortals forbade its slaughter. "We are gods," said they, "and while this neighborhood pays the penalty for its inhospitality, you shall be free from misfortune. Leave your house and follow us." The two old people obeyed and, hobbling along with their sticks, climbed the hill. When a little way from the top, they looked back and saw all the village covered by a marsh; only their own house was left. While they wondered and bewailed their neighbors' fate, that little old hut of theirs was transformed. In place of the forked sticks supporting a roof thatched with reeds, rose marble columns crowned with gilded beams; the doors were of embossed metal, and the pavement of marble. Then the son of Cronus spoke: "Ask, righteous old man and worthy woman, what you will." Philemon consulted a moment with Baucis and then answered: "We ask to be priests and to keep your shrines; and since we have lived happily together, let the same hour take us both, and let me never see the grave of my wife nor have to be buried by her hands." Their prayer was granted; they were guardians of the temple as long as they lived. One day as they stood side by side before the temple each saw a change come over the other. Now their forms, bent with age, grew straight and strong and rooted firmly in the earth. Then as the wav-

ing tree-tops grew over their heads, each said:
" Farewell, O Wife! O Husband!" and then
the bark covered their mouths.   And so, in after
years, the shepherds pointed out the oak and the
linden growing side by side, and said: " The

Fig. 5.   Head of Zeus.

gods care for the godly, and protect those who
do them service."

Zeus was represented in art as a man of generous build and majestic bearing, usually draped
from the waist down.   His head was massive,
his brows heavy, his hair and beard extremely

Zeus: his
appearance
and worship.

thick, as though his face looked out from masses of piled thunder-clouds. Beneath his overhanging eyebrows gleamed those eyes whose glance was lightning, and the heavily lined forehead foreboded that frown at which the heavens shook. His whole appearance was that of the majestic and powerful god of heaven and earth. He was generally represented as seated upon a throne, holding in one hand his scepter or a spear, and in the other his weapons, the winged thunderbolts. With him often appeared the eagle, the bird that by his bold heavenward flight and lightning-descent upon his prey was associated with the sky-god. On his scepter or beside him appeared a winged female figure, Victory, for he held the balances of fate and gave victory to this or that warrior as he willed. Among the Greeks themselves the statue most admired was that of gold and ivory set up in the temple at Olympia, in southern Greece. Before this representation of the greatest of their gods, Greeks from all parts of the Hellenic world met once in every four years to offer sacrifice and to compete in athletic contests, honoring their divinity by the exhibition of perfect bodies under perfect control. So great was the honor paid to successful contestants that the most famous lyric poets of Greece devoted their genius to celebrating them in hymns, which were sung by choruses to the accompaniment of

Fig. 6. View of ruins at Olympia.

the lyre or flute when the victors returned to their
own cities in triumphal state. Moreover, the
greatest sculptors joined to do them honor; for
the proudest glory of an Olympic victor was the
right he gained of having his statue set up in the
precinct of the god.   As one walks now through
the ruins at Olympia, here he can make out the
plan of the palestra in whose wide spaces Greek
youth wrestled, ran races, rivaled one another in
throwing the discus.   Here was the long colon-
nade or stoa beneath whose shade poets read
their works; in front, long rows of statues of
youths, nude as they appeared when winning their

victories.   Here was the line of treasuries of all the states of Greece, and in the center, even now impressive for the great drums of its columns, fallen and piled in confusion by the earthquakes of centuries, rise the high foundations of the great temple of Olympian Zeus.

At Do do'na, in Epirus, was a famous oracle of Zeus, one of the oldest holy places in all Greece. Here the priestess read the will of the god from the sound of the rustling leaves of the great oak, a tree especially sacred to Zeus.   In every part of the Greek world were places set apart for his worship, and each state claimed his favor for some special reason.   As late as early Christian times in Crete the grave of Zeus was pointed out, for conceptions of immortal gods were strangely combined with thoughts of death.

Jupiter.   Zeus was identified by the Romans with their old Latin god, Jupiter or Jove, and the stories told of the one were transferred to the other. Jupiter was originally a sky-god, as Zeus was, and king of gods and men.   Temples in his honor crowned many high hills in Italy, and he was called upon to send rain in time of drought. On the Alban Mount the temple of Jupiter Latiaris was the religious center of the Latin Confederacy.   Jupiter Optimus Maximus was worshiped on the Capitoline Hill at Rome as guardian of the state and giver of victory in war, and to him generals returning victorious to celebrate a triumph offered the best of the spoils of war. Like Zeus, the Roman Jupiter was protector of right and truth and the sanctity of oaths.

CHAPTER III

HERA, ATHENA, HEPHÆSTUS

I. HERA (JUNO)

I sing of golden-throned Hera, whom Rhea bore, an immortal queen, in beauty preëminent, the sister and the bride of loud-thundering Zeus, the lady renowned, whom all the Blessed throughout high Olympus honor and revere no less than Zeus whose delight is in the thunder. (*Homeric Hymn to Hera*. Translation by Andrew Lang.)

The wife of Zeus. As wife of the supreme god, Hera was naturally the guardian of the marriage state. The bride sacrificed to her, and matrons of the city were the priestesses of her temple. At Samos the annual celebration of her marriage with Zeus was the greatest of festivals. By Zeus she had three children, Ares (Mars), god of war, Hephæstus (Vulcan), god of the forge, and Hebe, goddess of youth. Though Hebe was originally also cup-bearer to the gods, for some reason, perhaps because she slipped one day when pouring the nectar, she was displaced by Gan'y mede, a Trojan prince. Zeus saw the boy on earth and loved him for his boyish charm and beauty. Assuming the form of his royal eagle, the god came

36

Fig. 7. Hera.

upon Ganymede when he was watching his flocks on Mt. Ida, and carried him off to Olympus to be his cup-bearer. This aroused Hera's anger, not only against her husband but against the whole race of Trojans, whom ever after she pursued with relentless hatred. Indeed all Zeus's favor-

Fig. 8.   Ganymede and the Eagle.

ites among mortals and his children by mortal wives were objects of jealous hate to Hera.

Iris was the wind-footed, fleet messenger of Hera, who bore her commands to other gods and to mortals. As she flew down from Olympus men knew of her coming by the many-colored trail she left behind her; for Iris was the rainbow, the symbol of connection between earth and heaven.

Appearance and emblems. Greek artists conceived of Hera as a woman in the full bloom of her age, of majestic form

Fig. 9. Head of Hera.

and carriage, with a serene and beautiful face, a conception inspired by the ideal for which she stood, the queenly protector of wifehood and motherhood. As a matron she was portrayed clad in a long full garment, and on her head a crown. Often she held a scepter, sometimes a pomegranate, the symbol of fertility for women and plants. Beside her often appears the peacock, his tail adorned by the hundred Argus eyes. (See p. 26.)

Juno. Corresponding to Hera as wife of Zeus, in Roman worship stood Juno, the wife of Jupiter. She too in old times had been the special guardian of women and the marriage-tie.

II. ATHENA (MINERVA)

The Birth of Athena. Of all the children of Zeus the one who most resembled her father in nature and power and who most enjoyed his respect and confidence was the maiden goddess, Pallas Athena. The story

Fig. 10. Athena (known as "Lemnian Athena").

of her birth is consistent with this special relation, since she sprang, fully grown and fully armed, from the head of Zeus.

Her did Zeus the counselor begot from his holy head all armed for war in shining golden mail, while in awe did the other gods behold it. Quickly did the goddess leap from the immortal head, and stood before Zeus, shaking her sharp spear, and high Olympus trembled in dread beneath the strength of the gray-eyed maiden,

Fig. 11.   Birth of Athena from the head of Zeus.

while earth rang terribly around, and the sea was boiling with dark waves, and suddenly brake forth the foam.   Yea, and the glorious son of Hyperion checked for long his swift steeds, till the maiden took from her immortal shoulders her divine armor, even Pallas Athena; and Zeus the counselor rejoiced. Hail to thee, child of ægis-bearing Zeus. (*Homeric Hymn to Athena.*)

The birth of Athena is a favorite subject with Greek artists.   Zeus is represented seated upon his

Her origin and nature.

throne, while about him are others of the Olympian divinities. Before him stands the god of the forge, Hephæstus, still grasping in his hand the ax with which, to assist the miraculous birth, he has cleft the skull of Zeus. Athena stands beside her father, triumphant, brandishing her spear, her breast protected by the ægis, or sacred breast-plate, adorned with the head of the Gorgon Medusa. (See p. 209.) Originally, in the ancient nature myth, Athena seems to have represented the waters of heaven let loose from the clouds (represented by the head of Zeus) when the thunderbolt (the ax of Hephæstus) cleaves them. The dreadful Gorgon's head with its snaky locks, on the breast-plate, suggests the thunder-cloud and the forked lightning. At an early time, however, Athena ceased to be regarded as a nature goddess and was worshiped as goddess of reason and practical wisdom, and as patroness of arts and crafts. On the other hand, she was the goddess of war-strategy, the defender of cities, especially her own city of Athens. As champion of civilization and justice, the almighty father granted it to her to wear his ægis. Thus she represents, as has been well said, " the warlike courage that gives peace, and the intellectual activity that makes it fruitful."

The Parthenon. To Athena, as guardian of the city of Athens, was dedicated the Parthenon, the temple that crowns the height of the Acropolis. Here was the great gold and ivory statue by the sculptor Phidias, and hither each year the Athenians came in procession to offer to the goddess the new peplos or robe, woven by the women of Athens as an offering to the goddess of handicrafts.

Athena is represented as of strong and noble form, dressed in a long flowing garment. Her finely molded features express courage and high intellectuality. In addition to the ægis she usually wears a helmet, surmounted by a sphinx and griffins, and she holds in her hand a spear, or, frequently, a small winged figure of Victory. Other emblems are the snake and the owl. The emblem of the olive is given her as guardian of the city of Athens.

Fig. 12.   Athena (known as "Minerva of Velletri").

When the great city, of Athens was founded all the gods desired to have it as their own. Athena and Poseidon (Neptune) were recognized as having the best claim to it, and it was determined that of the two that one should be chosen who should give the best gift to the city.

The twelve gods assembled to act as judges, and Cecrops, the king of Athens, served as a witness. The scene of the contest was the height of the Acropolis. Poseidon struck the rock with his trident and a salt spring gushed forth. Then Athena advanced and struck the rock with her spear; an olive tree sprang up. To Athena was adjudged the victory, for the olive was always a great source of wealth to the Athenian state. The sacred olive tree was preserved in the temple precinct, and the story of its miraculous sprouting in a night, when the Athenians returned to rebuild their citadel after its burning in the Persian Wars, is told by Greek historians. To this day one may see, also, the mark of Poseidon's trident in the rock below the ancient temple. Some say that Poseidon's gift was not a spring, but a horse.

In the story of A rach'ne, Athena appears as goddess of handicrafts.

Arachne. a   Arachne was a mortal who excelled all other maidens in weaving. Her work became so famous that the very nymphs deserted their woods and streams to see it. Nor was it more the finished work that excited this admiration than the grace and skill of the maiden while she wove. One would think that she had been taught by Pallas. Yet she herself denied this and challenged the goddess to compete with her. Angry

a Following Ovid, *Metamorphoses*, VI. 1 ff.

at this presumption, the goddess determined to humble her. She put on the form of a white-haired old woman, her feeble limbs supported by a stick. "Take the advice of an old woman," she said to Arachne, "you wish to be called more skilful than all mortal women; yield at least to the goddess, rash girl, and ask forgiveness for your boastful words." The maiden angrily eyed her visitor and answered rudely: "You have grown weak-minded with old age. If you have any daughters, bestow your advice upon them! I can attend to my own affairs. Why does not the goddess come herself? Why does she avoid a trial of skill?" "She has come," said the goddess, and threw aside her disguise. The nymphs and all the bystanders worshiped, only the maiden was unterrified, and obstinately insisted on the contest. The daughter of Zeus did not refuse. Arachne began to weave; she wove a web as fine as a spider's. A thousand colors were there, so finely shaded that each faded into the other until the whole was like the rainbow. Pallas wove the scene of her contest with Poseidon. There sat the twelve gods in august assembly, kingly Zeus in their midst. There was Poseidon with his trident, and Athena herself, her breast protected by the ægis, and beside her the newly-sprung olive tree. Then, that the presumptuous girl might learn by example, Athena wove the stories of mortals who had dared to compete with gods and had suffered punishment. But Arachne was not daunted. She wove into her web stories of the weaknesses and strifes of the gods, Zeus and his loves, and jealous Hera — many were the foibles there held up to derision. Then about it she wove a lovely border. Athena herself could not but wonder at the maiden's skill, but her arrogance aroused her resentment. She struck the delicate web with her shuttle, and it crumbled into bits; then she touched Arachne's forehead. A sense of her impiety rushed over the girl; she could not endure it, and hanged herself with a skein of her own silk. But Athena did not wish that so skilful a worker should die; she cut the skein and, sprinkling upon her the juice of aconite, transformed the maiden into a spider, that through all ages she might continue to spin her matchless webs.

Minerva. Minerva was an old Etruscan goddess whom the Romans worshiped as patroness of handicrafts and goddess of practical wisdom. Her festival was celebrated by guilds of artisans and physicians, and on it school-children were given a holiday. By her later identification with the Greek Pallas Athena she became known as goddess of military strategy and as protectress of cities. Jupiter, Juno, and Minerva formed a divine triad worshiped on the Capitoline Hill.

III. HEPHÆSTUS (VULCAN)

Half-brother of Athena, and son of Zeus and The god of fire. Hera, was He phæs′tus, the lame god of fire, the forge and metal-work, and as such, together with his great sister, a mighty helper of men in their struggle for civilization. He is thus addressed in the *Homeric Hymn:*

Sing, shrill Muse, of Hephæstus, renowned in craft, who with gray-eyed Athena taught goodly works to men on earth, even to men that before were wont to dwell in caves like beasts; but now, being instructed in craft by the renowned craftsman, Hephæstus, lightly the whole year through they dwell happily in their own homes. (*Homeric Hymn to Hephæstus.*)

He was born lame, but two stories are told of his fall from heaven that would more than account for any such deformity. According to the one, Hera, chagrined at finding her son physically imperfect, threw him out of heaven. To avenge himself for this cruelty on his mother's part, Hephæstus cunningly constructed a golden chair and brought it as a present to Hera. When she had taken her seat upon it, invisible chains held her fast, nor could she be freed. The gods pleaded with Hephæstus in vain, until Di o ny′sus (Bacchus), the wine-god, made him drunk and so brought him to Mt. Olympus and induced him to undo his own handiwork. According to the other story Zeus, resenting his championship of

his mother in one of the many quarrels between
the royal pair, seized him by the foot and hurled
him from Olympus.

> All day I flew, and at the set of sun I fell in Lemnos,
> and little life was in me.   (*Iliad*, I. 592.)

**Appearance
and emblems.**
Hephæstus made the glorious palaces of the
gods on Olympus; he made the scepter of Zeus

Fig. 13.   Hephæstus and the Cyclopes preparing the shield
of Achilles.

and the shield of Achilles; he helped to mold
Pandora.   His workshops were under the earth,
where volcanoes gave an outlet to the fires of his
forge.   Thus the Greeks saw his home in the
volcanic island of Lemnos, and the Greeks of
South Italy and Sicily, under Mt. Ætna or on

one of the Lipari Islands. On the latter, it was the popular belief that if the metal were left over-night near the crater, and due prayer and sacrifice made to the god, a marvelously forged sword would be found in the morning. To aid him in his work he had wonderful maidens of gold. He is described in his workshop by Homer:

He said, and from the anvil rose limping, a huge bulk, but under him his slender legs moved nimbly. The bellows he set away from the fire, and gathered all his gear wherewith he worked into a silver chest; and with a sponge he wiped his face and hands and sturdy neck and shaggy breast, and did on his doublet, and took a stout staff and went forth limping; but there were handmaidens of gold that moved to help their lord, the semblance of living maids. In them is understanding at their hearts, in them are voice and strength, and they have the skill of the immortal gods. (*Iliad*, XVIII. 410 ff.)

Ever friendly and helpful, often a peacemaker, Hephæstus was beloved of men and gods, though his limping gait subjected him to ridicule.

Then he poured forth wine to all the gods, from right to left, ladling the sweet nectar from the bowl. And laughter unquenchable arose among the blessed gods to see Hephæstus bustling through the palace. (*Iliad*, I. 597 ff.)

Hephæstus is not a favorite subject in art, but when he appears it is as a strongly-built man. his lameness only hinted at. He is dressed in a workman's short tunic and wears the workman's cap. Probably he originally represented the lightning; hence the story of his fall from heaven.

Vulcan, the fire-god, was more feared than courted in Rome, with its close-built streets, so subject to destructive fires. His worship, therefore, as originally that of the war-god Mars, was kept outside the city.

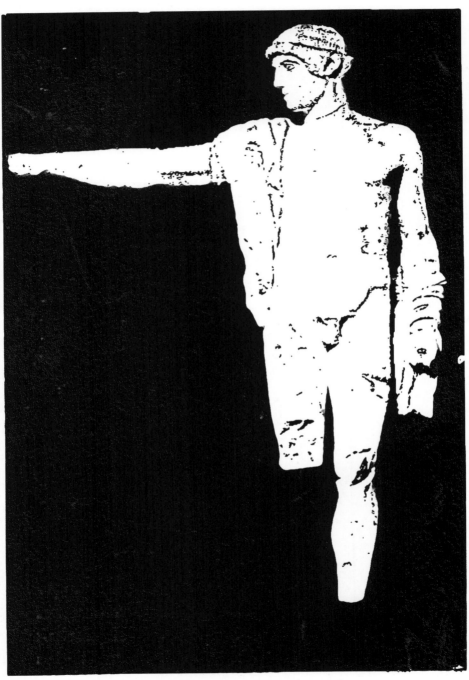

Fig. 14. Apollo, from Olympia.

CHAPTER IV

APOLLO AND ARTEMIS

I. APOLLO

THE purest and highest worship of the Greeks The god of light and healing. was perhaps that offered to Phœbus Apollo, the glorious god of light, who in later mythology took the place of the Titan Helios. In his chariot he drives across the heavens, attended by the Hours and Seasons, and at evening stables his horses in the golden west. Nothing false or impure might be brought near to him; his was a cleansing and enlightening power. With his arrows, the rays of the brilliant Greek sun, he destroyed his enemies and brought pestilence and death upon those that had fallen under his displeasure. But he was a destructive god only when provoked to anger; he was preëminently the god of healing and medicine. It was he that inspired physicians to divine the hidden cause of disease; he was their patron. This healing gift was especially exercised by Apollo's son, the divine physician As cle'pi us, who incurred Zeus's wrath by even restoring the dead to life.

But Apollo's greatest importance in the Greek The Oracle at Delphi. world was as god of prophecy, the giver of the prophetic gift. The most famous of all oracles was that at Delphi, a town of central Greece situated on the slopes of Mt. Parnassus. Here the priestess, seated on a tripod over a cleft in the rock, was thrown into an inspired frenzy by the

Fig. 15. The Sun-God in his Chariot.

vapors that rose about her. Her incoherent utterances were interpreted by the priests of the shrine. Hither came those seeking guidance, not only from all the Greek world, but from distant and non-Hellenic lands. No great undertaking might be entered upon without the sanction and

Fig. 16. Foundations of Apollo's Temple at Delphi.

guidance of the god; especially those seeking to found a new colony must first consult the oracle of Apollo. Thus the god was the founder of cities, the promoter of colonization, the extender of just and civilized law.

In all his manifestations Apollo stands for the Greek ideal of manly strength and beauty, of the highest and purest development of body and intellect. He inspires not alone physicians with their art and prophets with their power, but to him all poets and musicians owe the divine spark. He is the giver of all beauty and harmony. On Mt. Parnassus he led his chorus of the Nine Muses, and at the banquets of the gods he charmed the Olympians by the music of his golden lyre.

The god of beauty and music.

Apollo is always represented as in the prime of youth, with smooth face and refined (in later art almost feminine) features. As the archer he is usually entirely nude and holds the bow. As sun-god he appears in his chariot drawn by winged horses, while "rosy-fingered Dawn" throws open before him the gates of the East and the Hours and Seasons accompany the chariot. As god of music and leader of the Muses, he is dressed in the long flowing garment of the Greek bard and holds the lyre. About his forehead he wears the wreath of laurel, sacred to him and always the reward of the poet.

Appearance and emblems.

Apollo was the son of Zeus and the goddess

The Birth of Apollo.

Leto (La to'na). The story of his n
wanderings, driven by the cruel jealousy (
to seek a birthplace for her children, and
at last the little rocky isle of Delos [7] offere
refuge, is told in the *Homeric Hymn.*

Fig. 17. Apollo as leader of the Muses.

But the lands trembled sore and were adr(
none, nay not the richest, dared to welcome Pho
till Lady Leto set foot on Delos, and speaking

[7] Delos had up to that time been a floating is
return for its hospitable reception of Leto, Zeus
it to the bottom with adamantine chains.

words besought her: "Delos, would that thou wert minded to be the seat of my son, Phœbus Apollo, and to let build him therein a rich temple. . . ." And forth leaped the babe to light, and all the goddesses raised a cry. Then, great Phœbus, the goddesses washed thee in fair water holy and purely, and wound thee in white swaddling bands, delicate, new-woven, with a golden girdle around thee. Nor did his mother suckle Apollo, the golden sworded, but Themis with immortal hands first touched his lips with nectar and sweet ambrosia, while Leto rejoiced, in that she had borne her strong son, the bearer of the bow. (*Homeric Hymn to the Delian Apollo.*)

After the birth of the twins, Apollo and Artemis, the story tells how once in Lycia Leto came, weary and parched with thirst, to a pond where some countrymen were gathering reeds. The boors refused her the privilege she entreated of quenching her thirst, and threatened the fainting goddess with violence. They even waded into the pond and stirred up the mud to make the water undrinkable. In just anger at their boorishness and cruelty the goddess prayed that they might never leave that pool. There they live still, often coming to the top to breathe, or squatting on the bank, croaking their discontent with hoarse voices. Their backs are green and their bellies are white; their heads grow out of bloated bodies; their eyes bulge. You can see cold-blooded creatures like them in the nearest frog-pond.

Python. At Delphi, before the coming of Apollo, the site of the oracle was guarded by a pestilential earth-born serpent, Python, who laid waste all the land. This monster of disease and darkness the god of light killed with his golden shafts and made the oracle his own. Exulting in his victory, he now sang for the first time the Pæan, the song of triumph and thanksgiving, and on the scene of his victory he planted his sacred laurel tree.

How the laurel came to be sacred to Apollo is told by the Latin poet Ovid as follows:

Daphne. 8 Eros (Cupid) was responsible for Apollo's unhappy love for Daphne. Once the sun-god saw him fitting an arrow to the string, and being haughty because of his recent victory over Python, he taunted the little god of love. "Mischievous boy, what have you to do with such weapons! These are arms that become my shoulders — I, who lately with my arrows laid low swelling Python. Be you content to track out love-adventures with your torch; do not aspire to my honors!" Aphrodite's son answered him: "Your arrows pierce all things, Phœbus; mine pierce you." As he spoke he drew from his quiver two arrows; the one with point of gold inspires love, that tipped with lead repels it. With the first he wounded Apollo; with the second he pierced Daphne, the daughter of a river-

---

8 Following Ovid, *Metamorphoses*, I. 452 ff.

god. Straightway the god loved, but the nymph
hated the very name of lover and gave herself,
like the maiden goddess Artemis, to hunting wild
things in the woods. Many suitors sought her,
but she refused them all and persuaded her father
to permit her always to live a maiden. But
Apollo loved. He saw her hair in charming confusion about her neck; he saw her eyes beaming
like stars; he saw her lips and longed to kiss
them. He praised her hands and her shapely
arms; he thought her all beautiful. She fled
from him more elusive than the light breeze, nor
did she stay to hear his entreaties: "Nymph,
I pray you, stay! I who pursue you am no
enemy. Nymph, stay! love is the cause of my
pursuit. Alas! what if you should fall! What
if the horrid thorns should wound your innocent
ankles, and I should be to you the cause of pain!
The ground is rough; run not so fast! I, too,
will follow more slowly. · I who love you am no
boorish mountaineer; I am no rough shepherd.
Rash girl, you know not whom you flee. Jupiter
is my father. Through me what was and is and
will be is disclosed; through me the notes ring
harmonious on the strings. My arrow is sure,
yet one arrow is surer; it has wounded my heart.
Medicine is my invention; I am called savior
through all the world. Alas! no medicine can
cure my love, nor can the skill that saves all
others save its master."

But the nymph still fled and the god still pursued, she swift through fear, he swifter yet as winged with love. Now he drew so close upon her that she felt his breath upon her neck. She felt her strength go from her and in her despair called upon her father, the river-god: "Help me, O Father! Let the earth open for me, or else change this form that has been my ruin!" As she ceased her prayer a heaviness seized her limbs; her soft bosom was inclosed in a delicate bark; her locks became leaves, her arms branches. The foot, lately so swift, was rooted in the ground; only her beauty remained. Phœbus still loved her, and placing his hand upon the trunk, he felt her breast tremble beneath the new-formed bark. He put his arms about it and kissed the wood; the wood shrank from his kisses. Then said the god: "Since you cannot be my wife, you shall surely be my tree, O Laurel, and ever shall you adorn my head, my lyre, and my quiver. And as my head is ever crowned with youth and beauty, so shall your branches ever be crowned with green and glossy leaves."

As the ever-green laurel recalls the story of Apollo's unrequited love for a nymph, so the fragrant hyacinth springs from his unhappy attachment to a mortal youth snatched away by an untimely death.

Hyacinthus. 9   There was a time when even Delphi was de-

9 Following Ovid, *Metamorphoses*, X. 162 ff.

serted by Apollo, when the bow and the lyre lost
their charm for him. He spent all his days with
Hy a cin'thus, carrying his hunting-nets, holding
in his dogs, accompanying him on the hunt or
in his sports. One day the friends, having taken
off their clothes and been rubbed with oil, were
amusing themselves throwing the discus. Apollo
threw it high and far, exhibiting skill and
strength in the sport. Hyacinthus rushed forward to get the discus, not counting for the strong
rebound from such a throw. It glanced upward
and struck the boy full in the temple. The god
caught him in his fall and held him close, trying
to staunch the wound and applying medicinal
herbs. For once his art failed him. For as a
lily when the rays of the sun have struck hot
upon it droops its head towards the earth and
faints and dies, so the mortal youth drooped
his head upon his breast and fell lifeless from
the god's embrace.

In his grief Apollo upbraided himself as its
cause, and, since he could not restore the boy to
life, declared that at least his name should live forever, celebrated by him in song. And lo! where
the red blood had flowed out upon the earth,
there sprang up a splendid purple flower with
a form like a lily. It bore on its petals " Ai,
Ai " (Alas, Alas), a memorial of the sun-god's
mourning. And · as often as the fresh young
spring drives away the winter, so often are these

flowers fresh in the fields. Hyacinthus rises again.

Marpessa. There was an occasion when Apollo presented himself as rival to a mortal and was rejected. Mar pes'sa was a beautiful maiden, loved by Idas, who, with the help of winged horses given him by Poseidon, stole her from her father. Apollo overtook the runaway couple and seized the maiden for himself. But Idas, fearing not even the god in defense of his beloved, drew his bow against him. To prevent the unequal contest, Zeus gave Marpessa her choice between the two. On the one side stood the glorious sun-god, offering immortality, power, glory, and freedom from all earthly trouble. On the other stood Idas, offering only faithful love and partnership in his life with its mingled joy and sorrow. The woman chose the mortal, fearing unfaithfulness on the god's part, since immortal youth was not granted her with immortal life, and preferring to live, love, grow old, and die, with one capable of a like love and destined to a like fate.

Niobe. [10] In the tragic fate of Ni'o be and her fourteen children, Apollo with his sister Artemis appears as his mother's avenger, and his golden arrows bring destruction.

The story of Arachne's punishment for her presumption towards Athena should have been a warning to all. But Niobe was too haughty

[10] Following Ovid, *Metamorphoses*, VI. 146 ff.

to heed it. Many things made her proud. Her husband was a celebrated musician; on both sides of her family she was descended from the gods, and she ruled over a great kingdom. More than all, she was proud of her children, seven sons and seven daughters.

The Priest of Leto had cried through the city: "Come, all ye people, offer to Leto and the children of Leto the sacrifice of prayer and incense! Bind your heads with laurel! Leto bids it by my lips." All the people obeyed and offered sacrifice. Then came Niobe, dressed in purple and gold, moving stately and beautiful among her subjects and casting haughty looks about. "What madness," said she, "to place celestial beings of whom you have only heard above those seen! Why is Leto worshiped at the altars, while no incense rises in my honor? My grandfather is Atlas, who bears on his shoulders the starry heavens. My other grandfather is Zeus. Wide kingdoms own me as queen. Moreover, my beauty is worthy of a goddess. Add to all this my seven sons and seven daughters, and see what cause I have for pride! I know not how you dare to prefer Leto to me — Leto, who is the mother of but two! I am beyond the power of Fortune to injure. Go! enough honor has been paid to her and her offspring. Put off the laurel from your heads!" Niobe was obeyed; the worship of Leto was neglected or celebrated in secret. The goddess was indignant and said to her two children: "Lo, I, your mother, proud of having borne you, and second to no one of the goddesses, unless it be Hera, am brought to doubt whether I am a goddess. I am cut off from the honor due, unless you help me. Moreover, this woman adds insults and has dared to set her children above you." Apollo and Artemis heard her. Hidden in clouds they came to the city of Thebes.

Two of Niobe's sons happened to be practising their horses on the race-course near the city. The elder was just nearing the end of the course when he received Apollo's arrow full in the breast. Dropping the reins from his dying hand, he fell from his chariot in the dust. His brother, hearing the whizz of the arrow and seeing no man, gave free rein to his horses, hoping to escape. Apollo's unescapable shaft overtook him, and his blood reddened the earth. Two others of the sons were wrestling in the palestra. One arrow pierced the two, locked as they were in one another's arms. As they fell, another brother rushed up to save them; he fell before he could reach them. A sixth met his death in the same way. The youngest raised his hands in prayer: "O all ye gods, spare me!" Apollo might have been moved, but the arrow had already left the string.

Chance report and the prayers of those about

her first told Niobe of her calamity. Her husband, unable to bear his grief, had fallen on his
own sword. How different was Niobe now from
her who had lately driven the worshipers from
Leto's altars and had passed in haughty state
through her city; envied then by all, now pitiable
even to her enemies. With her seven daughters

Fig. 18. Niobe and her Daughter.

she came to the place where the bodies lay and,
throwing herself upon them, cried: " Gloat over
my grief, Leto, satisfy your cruel heart! Yet
are you the victor! More remains to me in my
wretchedness than to you in your vengeance."
Hardly were the words spoken than the cord of
Artemis' bow twanged. One by one six of the
daughters fell dead beside their brothers. But

one remained, the youngest; her mother tried to shield her with her own body. "Leave one, and that the youngest!" she cried; but she for whom she prayed fell. Niobe sat, childless and a widow, among the corpses of her sons and daughters. In stony grief she sat there; no breeze stirred her hair; her cheeks were pallid, her eyes unmoved; her blood was frozen in her veins; she was turned to stone. Magically borne to her fatherland in Asia, there she still sits on the mountain, and from her marble cheeks the tears still flow.

Phaëthon.[11]   Pha'e thon was the son of Apollo by a nymph, Clym'e ne. When one of his playmates mocked him for believing that Apollo was really his father, Phaëthon made no answer, but, coming home, asked his mother to give him some assurance of his parentage. Clymene swore to him by all that was sacred that she had told him truly, but suggested that if he was not satisfied, he should go and put the question to his father himself.

The boy eagerly traveled toward the sunrise, beyond the borders of earth, and came to the palace of the sun. Phœbus, dressed in a purple robe, was seated on a throne glittering with gems. To right and left stood the Days, the Months, the Years, and the Ages. There too were the Seasons; young Spring, crowned with

[11] Following Ovid, *Metamorphoses*, I. 750 ff.

fresh flowers; Summer, nude but for her wreaths
of grain; Autumn, stained with trodden grapes;
and icy Winter, rugged and hoary-haired. Before this company appeared the boy Phaëthon,
and stood hesitating near the door, unable to
bear his father's brightness. But the sun, looking at him with those eyes that see all things,
greeted him kindly and asked the reason of his
coming. Phaëthon, encouraged by his recognition, answered: "O light of the vast world,
Phœbus, my father, if that name is permitted, I
pray you to give me some pledge that I may be
recognized as your very son." In answer the
father embraced him and promised to grant whatever he should ask; he swore it by the Styx, an
oath no god might break. But when Phaëthon
asked for the privilege of driving for one day
the chariot of the sun, Phœbus did all in his
power to dissuade him, telling him the dangers
of the way, and that not even Zeus, who wields
the thunder, could drive that chariot. Surely it
was no task for a mortal! But Phaëthon was
obstinate in his demand, and Apollo had sworn
by the Styx.

The chariot was Hephæstus' work, all of gold
and ivory, set with gems, and marvelously
wrought. As Phaëthon wondered at the work,
wakeful Aurora threw wide the golden gates and
opened the courts full of rosy light. The stars
fled away. When Phœbus saw the earth grow

red and the pale moon vanish, he bade the Hours
harness the fiery horses. Then he touched his
son's face with sacred ointment that it might
bear the scorching flame, and on his head he
placed the rays, giving him this last advice. "If
you can still heed your father's words, my boy,
spare the whip and firmly hold the reins! Keep
to the middle course, where you will see the
tracks of my wheels; for if you go too high you
will burn the homes of the gods, if too low, the
earth. I commit the rest to Fortune. As I
speak, damp Night has reached its western goal:
we may no longer delay; we are demanded, and
Dawn has put the shades to flight. Take the
reins, if you are still resolved."

The boy joyfully mounted the chariot and
thanked his father. The fiery horses sprang forward, outstripping the wind that rose at dawn
from the east. But the chariot seemed light without the accustomed weight of the mighty god,
and the horses bolted and left the trodden road.
Phaëthon neither knew which way to turn, nor,
had he known, could he have guided the horses.
When from his dizzy height he looked down on
the lands lying far below him, he grew pale and
his knees trembled in sudden fear; his eyes were
blinded by excess of light. And now he wished
that he had never touched his father's horses:
he wished that he had never even known of his
high birth. What should he do? He looked at

the great expanse of sky behind his back; yet more was before him. He measured the two with his eye. Trembling, he saw about him the monsters of which his father had warned him. The Serpent, roused from his age-long lethargy by the too near approach of the sun's chariot, hissed horribly; there Scorpio, curving menacing arms, threatened death with his poisonous fangs. At sight of this monster Phaëthon's heart failed him and he dropped the reins. The horses ran wild. The Moon wondered to see her brother's chariot running nearer the earth than her own, and the clouds all on fire. Then all the moisture in the earth was dried up and the ground cracked. Trees and crops, cities with their inhabitants, all were turned to ashes. They say that this was how the people of Africa were turned black, and how Sahara became a sandy waste. The nymphs pined away, seeing their fountains dried up about them, and the river-beds were dusty hollows. The ground cracked so wide that the light penetrated even into Tartarus and startled Hades and his queen. The seas shrank and the fishes sought the bottom. Three times Poseidon dared to raise his head above his waters, and each time the heat forced him back. At last Earth, the mother of all, faint and scorched, appealed to Zeus for help, calling him to witness her own undeserved distress, and the danger to his own realm of heaven if this wild conflagration continued.

Then Zeus hurled his thunder-bolt against Apollo's son. The horses tore themselves loose and left the chariot a wreck. Phaëthon fell, like a shooting star, leaving a trail of fire behind him, until the waters of the river Po in Italy closed over him. Then Apollo hid his face in grief, and they say that one whole day went by without a sun. The raging fires gave light. The water-nymphs found Phaëthon's body and buried it, raising over it a tomb with this inscription: "Here lies Phaëthon, who drove his father's chariot; if he could not control it, yet he fell nobly daring."

Asclepius. Another son of Apollo, As cle'pi us, the divine physician, has already been mentioned. Asclepius was widely worshiped as god of medicine, and at his temple in Epidaurus marvelous cures were wrought. Here his priests cared for the sick, and about the shrine rose a great establishment to which flocked those needing his ministrations. The god appeared by night to the patients, not so often in his own form as in that of the serpent sacred to him. It was in this form that Asclepius (called by the Romans Æs cu la'pi us) was brought to Rome at the time of a plague. It is said that the serpent left the ship before it came to land and swam to an island in the Tiber. There his worship was established, and it is interesting to know that at this day a city hospital is still there.

Fig. 19. Asclepius.

When Zeus, in anger at Asclepius' presumption
in restoring the dead to life, struck and slew him
by a thunderbolt, Apollo rashly attempted to
avenge his son's death by shooting with his arrows the forgers of the thunderbolt, the Cyclopes. In punishment for this insubordination,
Zeus compelled him for one year to serve a mortal. During this time of exile he kept the sheep
of the just Ad me'tus, a prince of Thessaly.
Al ces'tis, the wife of Admetus, gained a place
among the women famous in story by an act of
noble self-sacrifice.

When the day approached that was destined   Alcestis. 12
for Admetus' death, that prince won the reward
for his just and wise treatment of his divine
shepherd; for Apollo gained for him the promise of a postponement of that evil day, on condition that he could induce some other to take his
place. With full assurance that some one of his
devoted friends and servants, or, most certainly,
one of his parents, would feel disposed to offer
his life as a ransom, Admetus appealed to one
after another. All refused; even his father,
though reminded by his son that in any case he
had not long to live, and that he should feel quite
content to die since he would leave a son to carry
on the family, quite obstinately refused. It almost seemed that Death must have his own, and
Apollo's promise be unfulfilled. Then Admetus'

12 Euripides, *Alcestis*.

young wife, Alcestis, took his fate upon herself, and for love of her husband, offered to go to the dark home of Hades in his place.

The day of the sacrifice came, and Apollo, whose brightness and purity might not be polluted by nearness to the dead, prepared to leave the house of his servitude. Meeting Death by the way, he vainly tried to persuade him to spare Alcestis too, but that relentless enemy passed inside the house to cut from his victim's head the lock of hair that consecrated her to the gods of the lower world.

Meanwhile Alcestis had been preparing herself for her terrible visitor. She put on her finest robes and her ornaments, she decked the house with garlands, and before the shrine of Hestia, the guardian of the home, she prayed that her two little children might find in the goddess a protectress loving as a mother. And when the children came running to her and the servants sadly crowded round her, she bade them each one a loving and courageous farewell. Admetus came and with tears entreated her not to leave him forlorn. He did not offer to meet Death for her. Only one request she made as her strength ebbed, let her husband bring no stepmother to tyrannize over her children.

To the house of mourning the hero Heracles (Hercules), on one of his many adventurous journeys, came and begged entertainment. The servants would have turned him away, unwilling that their attentions to their dead mistress should be interrupted, but Admetus, true to the Greek law of hospitality, concealed his trouble and ordered a feast to be prepared for his guest. The hero, warmed by food and wine, became so noisy in his enjoyment of it that the servants could not contain their indignation and reproached him with his inconsiderate behavior. Great was Heracles' mortification at finding that it was a house of mourning he had unwittingly invaded, and swearing that the courteous Admetus should never regret his kindness, he hurriedly left the house.

The funeral ceremonies were over and Alcestis had been committed to the tomb. Her husband returned to his widowed home, bowed with grief and half awakened to the selfishness of his own choice. At this moment Heracles reappeared, leading with him a veiled woman whom he urged the prince to keep for him for a time. Admetus, remembering his promise to Alcestis, was unwilling to admit any woman to his roof, wishing to avoid even the appearance of setting up any one in his wife's place. Only by much insistence could the hero induce him to take her by the hand and lead her in. Then Heracles drew off the veil and disclosed Alcestis herself, whom he had rescued by wrestling with and overthrowing Death.

Apollo in Rome. The worship of the Greek god Apollo was early introduced into Rome under the same name. With the introduction of his worship was associated the acquisition of the Sibylline Books, sold, according to the legend, to King Tarquin by the Sibyl of Cumæ. These precious books of prophecy were kept beneath the temple on the Capitoline Hill and in time of danger to the state were solemnly consulted by those ordained for that purpose.

II. ARTEMIS (DIANA)

The goddess of the moon and the chase. Artemis was the child of Zeus and Leto, twin sister of Apollo. As Apollo took the place of the Titan Helios as god of the sun, so Artemis took the place of Se le′ne as goddess of the moon. In her chariot she too drove across the heavens; her weapons, like his, were the bow and arrows. But Artemis was more generally known as goddess of the chase and of all wild things in nature. Dressed in the short hunting-dress, pulled up through her belt to give her freedom of motion, with quiver and bow over her shoulder she scoured the forest in pursuit of game. Her companions were the mountain nymphs and the spirits of the woods and streams. To her the huntsman made his prayer and to her he offered the first fruits of his game on rough stone altars. But though a huntress, she was yet the friend and protectress of beasts, both wild and do-

Fig. 20. Artemis of Versailles.

mestic, and their young were under her special
care.

Artemis is represented as a graceful, active
maiden, dressed in a short hunting-dress coming
only to the knee, and armed with bow and quiver.

When represented as
moon-goddess she ap-
pears in her chariot.
Her emblems are the
crescent, and the bow
and quiver, and she of-
ten has beside her a
deer or some other
animal of the chase.

As Apollo stood for
the ideal of youthful
manly beauty, so Arte-
mis was the ideal of
maidenhood, of mod-
esty, and of graceful
activity. She was the
patron goddess of
young girls and her
worship was served by

Fig. 21. Artemis of Gabii.

them. Before marrying, Greek girls offered in
sacrifice a lock of hair, together with their dolls
or other toys; when in trouble it was to her they
called for help.

Ar e thu'sa, now a fountain in the Sicilian city

13 Following Ovid, *Metamorphoses*, V. 577 ff.

of Syracuse, was once a nymph, a follower of Artemis, and lived in southern Greece. She cared nothing for admiration and love but was wholly devoted to the chase. One day when she was tired and hot, she came upon a clear, cold stream, flowing silently through the woods. She drew near and dipped in, first her toes, then as far as her knees; the cold water was so refreshing that she took off her clothes and plunged into the stream. While she was enjoying her bath, she heard a murmur under the water, and as she hastened to the bank in sudden fear, the hoarse voice of the river-god Al phe'us: "Whither are you hastening, Arethusa?" She fled and the eager god pressed hard upon her. Through fields and pathless woods, over rocks and hills she ran, and ever the sound of his pursuing feet grew nearer. At last she was exhausted and cried to Artemis, the protector of maidens. The goddess heard and threw about her a thick mist to hide her from the eyes of her pursuer. Though baffled, the god still sought her. A cold sweat poured from the maiden's limbs, drops fell from her hair; she was transformed into a spring. But even in this form Alpheus recognized her and, to mingle his waters with hers, laid aside the human form he had assumed. Then Artemis opened the earth, and Arethusa flowed down through black underground ways until she rose again across the sea in Sicily. But the river-god endured even the darkness of the under-world in pursuit of his love, and in that bright Sicilian land at last joined his waves with hers.

That Artemis could be cruel in punishing one who offended her maiden modesty is seen in the story of Ac tæ′on. Actæon.[14]

In a valley thickly wooded with pine and pointed cypress trees was a natural cave, wherein bubbled a spring of clearest water. Here Artemis, when tired with hunting, used to bathe. She would enter the cave, hand her hunting-spear to one of her attendant nymphs, her bow and quiver to another, to a third her mantle, while others took off her hunting-shoes. Then she would step into the spring, while the nymphs poured water over her.

It was high noon, hot with the heat of the dog-days, and Actæon, satisfied with the morning's sport, had left the other hunters and wandered innocently into the grove. Hoping to find water he entered the cave. At sight of him the nymphs raised a shrill outcry and crowded about Artemis to hide her from his profane eyes. Insulted by the intrusion, unintentional though it was, Artemis protected herself even better. She splashed water from the spring in Actæon's face, saying as she did so: "Now, if you can, boast that you have seen me unappareled!" At touch of the

[14] Following Ovid, *Metamorphoses*, III. 138 ff.

water his human form was changed to that of a
stag; and not his form alone, for trembling fear
entered his once bold heart and he fled, dreading
alike the woods and his own home and former
companions.   As he fled, his own dogs, driven
mad by Artemis, saw him and gave chase, all
fifty of them.   Over hills and rocks he fled and

Fig. 22.   Actæon killed by his Dogs.

longed to stop and cry: "I am Actæon; know
your master!"   But the words would not come,
and all the air resounded with the baying of the
dogs.   They closed in on him and tore him to
pieces, while the hunters, who had urged them
on, called loudly for Actæon, eager that he should
have a share in such good sport.   It is said that

when the dogs recovered from their madness, they ran howling through the woods, seeking their master.

Once even the maiden Artemis loved a mortal. **Endymion.** En dym'i on was a shepherd who kept his flocks

Fig. 23.   Sleeping Endymion.

on Mt. Latmos, in Asia Minor.   As she drove her chariot across the sky by night, Artemis looked down and saw the youth sleeping.   His beauty as he lay drew the moon-goddess to him in love.   Each night she left her course to descend to the mountain-top and kiss the shepherd.   Her long absences and her paleness when she returned aroused the suspicions of the other Olympians, only too glad to detect a sign of weakness in the cold maiden. Wishing to remove temptation from her way, Zeus gave Endymion his choice between death in any form and perpetual youth with perpetual sleep. Endymion chose the latter, and still he sleeps in his cave on Mt. Latmos, visited each night by the moon-goddess, who silently and sadly kisses his pale cheeks. Nor do his flocks suffer, for Artemis drives them by night to rich pastures and watches over their increase. This story was originally told of Selene, but later the Greeks transferred it to the younger goddess.

The giant O ri'on, too, won the affection of Artemis, though perhaps, in this case, she looked upon him rather as a congenial companion in hunting than as a lover. He was a son of Poseidon and had from his father the power of walking through the sea as easily as he walked on the land. Because he was too hasty in his wooing of a certain girl, her father made him drunk and then put out both his eyes. Finding his way by the sound of the hammers to Hephæstus' forge in Lesbos, he borrowed one of the lame god's assistants to act as his guide, and so came to the far east where the sun rises. The brightness of the sun-beams restored his sight, and Orion became a constant companion of Artemis. Apollo disapproved of the friendship,

and one day he challenged his sister to hit with
her arrow a dark speck that was moving on the
water; it was too late when she learned that the
mark was Orion's dark head. As she could not
restore him to life, she put him in the heavens
as a constellation, one of the brightest and most
beautiful that we can see. All the winter nights
he races across the heavens with his dog, Sirius,
at his heels, or he pursues the seven Ple′ia des,
maidens changed to stars that one sees all
crowded together and pale with fright as they
flee. In the summer, Orion appears in the east
at dawn, for he loves the dawn-goddess and,
great and brilliant as he is, grows pale before her.

Artemis appeared under quite a different character as Hec′a te, for that mysterious deity, who
is associated with witchcraft and the horrors of
night and darkness, is but another form of the
bright moon-goddess. Her dark and mysterious
knowledge, such knowledge as sorceresses and
witches made use of in their evil charms, came
from her association with grave-yards and from
the celebration of her worship by night at cross-
roads, a time and place that open the supersti-
tious mind to impressions of terror and the presence of mysterious powers.[15] She was a goddess

Hecate.

[15] In New England, at the time of the witchcraft panics,
those people suspected of being in league with the Devil
were believed to hold their dark and hateful assemblies by
midnight at the cross-roads.

of triple form; her three faces looked down the three forks of the roads where her statue was often set up.   The baying of dogs on moonlight nights was thought to be a warning of her approach.

The Latin goddess Diana was originally a special deity of women.   A temple was dedicated to her in a lonely wood beside the lake of Nemi, in the Alban Hills.   Here all the towns of the Latins united in her worship.   This shrine is famous because of the gloomy legends connected with it.   It was said that in the wood grew a tree on which was a golden bough, and that he who could pluck this bough and slay the priest who kept the shrine thereby succeeded to his honor and retained it until he himself was slain by another.   Diana, as a goddess of women and of nature, became identified with the Greek Artemis and was then worshiped as goddess of the moon and the chase.

CHAPTER V

HERMES AND HESTIA

I. HERMES (MERCURY)

HERMES was the messenger of Zeus, the conductor of souls to the lower world, the guardian
of ambassadors, of travelers and merchants, the
patron of trade, skilled in all wiles, deceit and
trickery, the mischievous thief; on the other hand,
a shepherd and patron of shepherds. He was
the son of Zeus by Maia, "a fair-tressed nymph,"
who gave him birth in a cave in Arcadia "rich
in sheep." [16]   In the morning he was born, and
by mid-day he stealthily left his cradle and set
forth to seek adventure. On the threshold of
the cave he met a tortoise, waddling along on the
grass.   At once the ingenious boy saw what use
he could make of it.   "'Hail darling and dancer,
friend of the feast, welcome art thou!   Whence
gottest thou that gay garment, a speckled shell,
thou, a mountain-dwelling tortoise?'"   Then he
scooped out the flesh of the tortoise, bored holes
through its shell, covered it with ox-hide, put on
it two horns, and stretched across it seven strings.

The wind-god's infancy

[16] Following the *Homeric Hymn to Hermes*. Quota-
tions from the translation by Andrew Lang.

Touching the strings he sang gaily to the accompaniment of the newly-invented lyre. When the chariot of Apollo had sunk into the waves of Ocean, this nimble infant left his cave and lyre, and ran to the shadowy hills, where fed the cattle of the sun. From the herd he separated fifty cattle and drove them hither and thither to confuse their tracks. Next, he made sandals of woven twigs and fastened them on his own feet to obscure his tracks, and so drove the cattle backward to the river. Then he made a great fire and roasted two of the beasts. Carefully covering up the marks of the fire and the feast, and throwing aside his sandals, back to his mother's cave he flew, before the sun-god should rise in the east and catch the thief at his work. Through a hole, like a breath of wind, he entered the cave, and treading noiselessly, climbed into his cradle and wrapped about himself the swaddling-clothes. But Apollo, when morning rose from the stream of Ocean, missed the cattle and questioned an old man who was digging in a vineyard on the hillside. From the old fellow's account of the marvelous child who had stolen the cattle Apollo at once recognized his newborn brother. When that little thief saw Apollo, bent on vengeance, enter the cave, " he sank down within his fragrant swaddling-bands and curled himself up, feet, head, and hands, into small space, though really wide awake, and his tortoise-shell

Fig. 24. Hermes in Repose.

he kept beneath his arm-pit." But Apollo saw through the wiles of the cunning baby and angrily threatened to throw him into Tartarus. In vain did Hermes plead that he knew nothing of the cattle: "'Other cares have I, sleep and mother's milk, and about my shoulders swaddling-bands, and warmed baths.'" He dared even to add a great oath that he was innocent. As Apollo was far from satisfied, there was nothing for it but to go to Olympus and put their dispute before their father Zeus. Even there the crafty little thief dared to repeat his lies, adding submissively: "'The Sun I greatly revere, and other gods, and *Thee* I love, and *him* I dread . . . but do Thou aid the younger.'" But perhaps because the infant could not refrain from adding a wink to his innocent tale, "Zeus laughed aloud at the sight of his evil-witted child," and bade the brothers be reconciled and Hermes show Apollo his cattle. When Apollo was again roused to anger by the sight of the hides of the slain cattle, Hermes drew forth his lyre and played and sang so bewitchingly that Apollo was pacified and gladly formed a compact with his clever little brother; Hermes was to be keeper of the cattle and give to Apollo the lyre, which was ever afterwards his favorite instrument. In this myth, on the nature side, we see Hermes, a wind-god, driving off the clouds, the cattle of the sun-god. We see, too, Hermes as the herdsman, the inventor and the cunning thief; perhaps also, in his compact with Apollo, we see him as the trader.

The patron of athletes, traders and travelers.

Clever and agile, good-humored and young, Hermes was the patron of young men, and to him they prayed, especially for success in athletic contests. His statue was set up in gymnasia; he presided, too, over games of chance. Both by his speed in hastening from land to land, and by his smoothness of address and his nimble wit, he was the natural patron of traders. In the market-place, the commercial and financial center of Athens, statues of Hermes had a prominent place. As he was the guide of travelers, square blocks topped by a head of Hermes marked the cross-roads and the important street-crossings in the city. It was the mutilation of these Hermæ that caused such a panic at the time of the Athenian expedition against Sicily. Alcibiades was recalled from the war to answer to the charge of having impiously destroyed them.

The herald of Zeus and conductor of souls to the lower world.

Hermes is best known as herald of the gods. At Zeus's bidding he binds on his winged sandals, takes his herald's staff in hand, and flies swiftly to earth to carry to men the commands of the father. It is he who conducts to Hades the soul when it leaves the body, and gives it into the charge of the gods of the lower world.

Appearance and emblems.

Hermes is represented as a young man with close-cropped curly hair, vivacious look, and agile, vigorous frame. He wears his winged sandals, often a traveler's hat or a winged cap; otherwise he is usually nude. In his hand he carries his caduceus, or herald's staff, winged at the top, with two serpents twined about it. He most fully expresses the character of the Greek peo-

Fig. 25. Hermes from Olympia.

ple, as a French writer (Collignon) says, "the inventive genius, the alert intelligence, the physical vigor, developed and made supple by the training of the palestra."

The worship of Hermes under the name of **Mercury.** Mercury was introduced into Rome at a time when there was anxiety about the grain trade with South Italy. His function as patron of commerce was, therefore, his most important one in Rome.

II. HESTIA (VESTA)

The goddess of the hearth-fire. While the fire of the forge is typified by Hephæstus, Hes'ti a represents another aspect, the fire on the hearth, the natural altar and the spiritual center of family life. About the hearth the gods of the family had their places; here the family celebrated their festivals; here the stranger found protection, and about it every new-born infant was carried as a symbol of his admission to the family life. So, too, the city, as the larger family, had its common hearth whereon the holy fire of Hestia must always be kept lighted. And when a group of citizens, self-exiled from their home, set out under Apollo's sanction to found a colony, the hearth of the new home on the foreign shore must receive a fire kindled at the hearth of Hestia in the mother-city. Thus the spiritual bond between the parted kinsmen remained unbroken, and the same goddess held the new homes under her protection. Moreover, the essential brotherhood of all true Hellenes was symbolized in the great hearth-fire of Hestia at the center of the Greek world, Delphi. So closely is Hestia identified with the fire of the hearth that no further outward form was needed — statues of her are rare. As eldest sister of Zeus she is, however, represented as a woman of stately form and calm, benign expression, dressed in the double

Fig. 26. Hestia.

chiton or tunic of a Greek lady, her head covered with a veil.

A passage in the *Homeric Hymn to Aphrodite* shows the respect that Hestia enjoyed among the gods of Olympus:

Nor to the revered maiden Hestia are the feats of Aphrodite a joy, eldest daughter of crooked-counseled Cronus, that lady whom both Poseidon and Apollo sought to win. But she would not, nay stubbornly she refused; and she swore a great oath fulfilled, with her hand on Father Zeus of the Ægis, to be a maiden forever, that lady goddess. And to her Father Zeus gave a goodly mede of honor, in lieu of wedlock; and in mid-hall she sat her down, choosing the best portion; and in all the temples of the gods is she honored, and among all mortals is chief of gods.

The Roman Vesta is identical with Hestia of the Greeks. At Rome the small round temple of Vesta in the Forum was the religious center of the community. Here no image of the goddess was needed, but her fire, kindled yearly on June 15th from the rays of the sun by means of a burning-glass, was kept always lighted by the Vestal Virgins. These maidens were drawn from the noblest families of Rome, and served the goddess for thirty years under a vow of virginity. Every honor was paid them, and they could extend their protection over whom they would; even a criminal who met a Vestal on his way to execution might thus gain his freedom. Any disrespect to a member of the order was punished by death, and their influence on state affairs was often considerable. On the other hand, as any breaking of the vow of virginity brought pollution to the city hearth and evil to

the community, such unfaithfulness was pitilessly
punished; the guilty priestess was buried alive.
When the Roman emperor wished to demonstrate
that he was the center as well of the religious as
of the political life of Rome, he transferred the

Fig. 27. Genius and Lares.

hearth of Vesta from the Forum to the Palatine
Hill, where his palace was.

Associated with the worship of Vesta at the
family hearth was the worship of the Lares and
Penates, the gods of home and of the household
store. Their images must be guarded jealously

Other Roman
gods of the
family.

by the householder, and must go with him, should he be forced to leave his old home for a new one. So Æ ne'as, when fleeing from Troy, bids his father on the flight to hold fast to the penates. (*Æneid*, II. 717.)

Fig. 28. Ares with Eros.

CHAPTER VI

ARES AND APHRODITE

I. ARES (MARS)

IF Athena, as the warlike defender of right and justice, the protector of cities, enjoyed the honor of all men and the fullest share in her mighty father's confidence, it was far otherwise with Ares, the god of war and battle. Zeus declares in his anger,

"Most hateful to me art thou of all the gods that dwell on Olympus; thou ever lovest strife and wars and battles." (*Iliad*, V. 890.)

Athena addresses him as,

"Ares, Ares, blood-stained bane of mortals, thou stormer of walls." (*Iliad*, V. 31.)

He was the personification of battle, always thirsting for blood; his worship originated among the savage tribes of Thrace. He was drawn in his chariot by his fiery horses, Fear and Dread, borne by a Fury to the North Wind, and was attended by Strife, Rout, Terror, and Battle-din.

In art, however, this blood-stained Ares gave

place to a much milder conception.   In the fourth
century B.C. he appears as a young man with spirited but somewhat thoughtful face, and slender,
graceful, nude form.   Often he has no arms

Fig. 29.   Bearded Mars.

other than a helmet and a shield or club.   He is
frequently seen with Aph ro di'te (Venus), goddess of love and beauty, or their child, Eros
(Cupid).   For Aphrodite, tired of her marriage
with the lame god of fire, Hephæstus, into which
she was forced by Zeus, yielded to the love of
Ares.   Homer tells how Hiphæstus, told of his
wife's infidelity by the sun -god, forged a net,
fine as a spider's web, wherein he insnared the

Fig. 30.   Aphrodite of Cnidos.

guilty lovers so that they could not move a limb. Here he held them prisoners, a laughing-stock to all the gods.[17]

From Ares was derived the name, A re op'a-gus, of the hill near the Acropolis in Athens, where cases of murder were tried in old times.

Worshiped as Mars, in Rome the war-god oc- **Mars.** cupied a much higher place than in Athens. To him was dedicated the Campus Martius, a field where the army met to be numbered, and to him, on the return of a victorious army, were dedi-cated the spoils of war. Through his son Romulus, the legendary founder of the city of Rome, the Romans claimed the special favor of the war-god. (See p. 348.) With Mars was associated Bel lo'na, a goddess personifying war.

II. APHRODITE (VENUS)

Aph ro di'te was the goddess of love and **Her birth and** beauty. According to one story she was the **marriages.** daughter of Zeus and the goddess Di o'ne; ac-cording to the better known story she sprang from the foam of the sea and was wafted gently over the crest of the waves to Cyprus, her sacred island.

Her did the golden-snooded Hours gladly welcome, and clad her about in immortal raiment, and on her deathless head set a well-wrought crown, fair and golden, and in her ears put ear-rings of orichalcum and

[17] *Odyssey*, VIII. 266

Fig. 31.   Birth of Aphrodite from the Sea.

of precious gold.   Her delicate neck and white bosom
they adorned with chains of gold, wherewith are be-
decked the golden-snooded Hours themselves, when
they come to the glad dance of the Gods in the dwelling
of the Father.   And when they had adorned her in all
goodliness they led her to the Immortals, who gave her
greeting when they beheld her, and welcomed her with
their hands; and each God prayed that he might lead
her home to be his wedded wife, so much they mar-
veled at the beauty of the fair-garlanded Cytherean.
(*Homeric Hymn to Aphrodite.*)

But Zeus gave her as wife to the lame fire-god
Hephæstus.   It has been already told how she
left him for Ares, and how Hephæstus avenged
himself and held them up to the ridicule of the
other Olympians.   Because of her beauty and
her power over the hearts of men and gods,
Aphrodite naturally aroused the jealousy of the

other goddesses. Hera never forgave the Trojan Paris for awarding her the famous golden apple.

To the marriage of Pe'leus and the sea-goddess Thetis all the gods were invited except Eris, the Goddess of Discord. To avenge herself for this neglect, Eris threw among the guests a golden apple bearing the inscription, " For the

Fig. 32. Judgment of Paris.

Fairest." Hera, Athena, and Aphrodite each claimed the apple. Unwilling to expose himself to the storm of wrath a choice among the three would raise, Zeus sent them to appear for judgment before Paris. This Paris, the son of the king of Troy, had been exposed as an infant and brought up among shepherds, and was now keeping his sheep on Mt. Ida. The three goddesses came before him, arrayed in all their charms, and each demanded judgment in her favor. As a bribe, Hera offered him power and riches; Athena, glory in war; and Aphrodite, the most beautiful woman in the world as his wife. Whether influenced by her promise or by the surpassing charms of golden-crowned Aphrodite, Paris decided in her favor, and she triumphantly bore off the golden apple. To Paris and the Trojans this judgment proved a curse, since the fulfilment of Aphrodite's promise in giving to Paris Menelaüs' wife, Helen, was the cause of the Trojan War, which ended in the utter destruction of the city.

Her appearance and emblems. In the figure of Aphrodite Greek artists tried to express their ideal of beauty and of womanly charm. She is less stately than Hera, with less of strength and intellectuality than Athena. Earlier artists represented her covered by a thin clinging garment, but the statues of a later date are usually quite nude. Her emblems are the apple and pomegranate, the rose and the myrtle, and the tortoise. Her chariot is drawn by sparrows or doves, or, on the waters, to betoken her birth from the sea, by swans.

Her powers. Not only men and gods, but all creation witness to Aphrodite's power. By her child Eros (or Cupid) all nature is given life and the power to reproduce itself. Through her power birds and beasts mate and give birth to their young; through her all green things grow and put forth

seeds.   And so her divine power is shown in the
spring, and when the gentle west wind breathed
over the land and all the earth grew green and
fertile, the Greeks sang songs of praise to violet-
crowned· Aphrodite and held a festival in her
honor.   But when the hot Greek summer came,
scorching the blossoms and robbing the fields of
their beauty, then a note of deep sadness came
into the worship of Aphrodite with the celebration of the Adonis feast.

A do'nis was a beautiful youth who grew up   Adonis.
under the care of the nymphs.   Aphrodite, victim of the same love that made her powerful over
all others, loved this youth and devoted herself
to the enjoyment of his company.   For his sake
she dressed herself like the huntress Artemis and
spent her days roaming over the hills with him
and following the chase.   Dreading his rashness.
she made him promise to hunt no dangerous
beasts, but to be content with deer and hares and
other· innocent game.   One day, after warning
him thus, she entered her chariot drawn by swans
and drove away to Olympus.   Adonis, on the
track of a wild boar, forgot his promise, entered
on the chase, and wounded the boar, which turned
on him and drove its white tusk into his
tender side.   As the boy lay dying, Aphrodite,
distraught with anguish, came to him.   Unable
to save her lover, she caused to grow from the
drops of his blood the anemone or wind-flower,

a delicate purple flower that grows plentifully in the Greek meadows in the spring of the year. In this story Adonis is the springtime, killed by the fierce heat of summer. Each year in commemoration of his death the people went through

Fig. 33.   Venus of Arles.

the city in procession, carrying a bier whereon lay a wax figure of Adonis, covered with flowers, while the women chanted the lament.

Low on the hills is lying the lovely Adonis, and his thigh with the boar's tusk, his white thigh with the boar's tusk, is wounded, and sorrow on Cypris (Aphrodite) he brings, as softly he breathes his life away. (Bion, *Idyl,* I. 7 ff. Translation by Andrew Lang.)

At dawn the image was thrown into the sea. Yet the mourning ended with joyful anticipation of Adonis' return from the lower world at the coming of the next spring.

Venus was an old Italian goddess, the giver of bloom and fruitfulness in nature, the protectress of gardens. The Romans identified her with the Greek Aphrodite, the bountiful goddess of love and beauty.

Aphrodite or Venus was always ready to help lovers who were wise enough to go to her. The following famous love stories are some of the many that witness to her power.

At a lan'ta had been warned by the gods that she should never marry; she therefore lived a maiden in the forests and devoted herself to the service of Artemis and the hunt. To the throng of lovers who sought her hand she always answered: " I am not to be won unless first vanquished in a race. Contend with me! My hand shall be the victor's reward, death the penalty of the vanquished." Yet so great was the power of her beauty that even on these hard conditions many entered the contest.

Hip pom'e nes had come as a spectator, and, despising women, had laughed at the folly of

Venus.

Atalanta's race. 18

---

18 Ovid, *Metamorphoses,* X. 560 ff.

those who entered the race. But when he saw the maiden the mocking laugh died on his lips. As she ran Atalanta grew continually more beautiful in his eyes; he hated his rivals and dreaded their success. The goal was reached, the crown of victory placed on Atalanta's head, and her suitors paid the penalty. Hippomenes was by no means deterred by their fate; he leaped into the race-course and facing Atalanta said: "It is an easy title to fame you seek against those slow runners! Contend with me, the grandson of Poseidon, and if you win you will gain a name worth winning!" Atalanta looked at him and seemed to doubt whether she would rather vanquish or be vanquished. "What god," said she, "wishes to destroy him and bids him to seek me as wife, at such a risk? I am not worth such a price. It is not that I am touched by his beauty — though I might well be touched by it — but he is still a boy; his youth moves me. Depart, stranger, while you can; some other maiden would be willing to be your wife. Yet why should I pity you, when I have let so many others meet their fate? But I wish that you should depart - or, since you are so foolish, I could wish that you were swifter!" So she hesitated; but the on-lookers demanded the race.

Then Hippomenes called upon Aphrodite to help a daring lover, and the goddess heard. From a tree of golden apples she picked three

and gave them to Hippomenes. The trumpeters
gave the signal; the racers darted forward. The
spectators shouted encouragement to the youth:
"Now, now is the time! Quick, quick, Hippomenes!" Many times when she could have
passed him the maiden delayed an instant; but
the goal was still far off, and averting her eyes
she darted ahead. Then Hippomenes threw one
of the golden apples. The maiden's eye was
caught by the gleam of the gold; she turned
aside and picked up the fruit. Hippomenes
passed by; the air resounded with applause. Atalanta made up for the delay by an effort and
was once more ahead. Delayed by the throwing
of a second apple, she again caught up and passed
her competitor. Only a short space remained.
"Now be with me and help me, Aphrodite!" he
prayed. Toward the side of the course with
all his strength he threw the last of the golden
apples. The girl seemed for an instant to hesi-
tate, but Aphrodite forced her to turn aside once
more. Hippomenes was victor and claimed his
reward.

In his victory, Hippomenes unluckily forgot
to give thanks to Aphrodite, and she, wishing in
her anger to destroy him, tempted him to profane the temple of Cybele (see p. 153), the great
mother of the gods. In punishment Cybele
changed the pair into lions and forced them to
draw her chariot.

Pygmalion and Galatea.

Pyg ma'li on was the king of Cyprus and a great sculptor. He made out of ivory a statue of Aphrodite, so beautiful that he fell in love with it. As if he had a living woman before him he spoke to the image, embraced and kissed it. He brought to her all sorts of presents such as please maidens, costly dresses, necklaces, and ear-rings. He called her his wife. At a festival of Aphrodite, who was especially worshiped on the island, he offered sacrifice and prayed the goddess to give him a wife exactly like the ivory image. When he came home and embraced the statue it seemed to him to return the pressure; the ivory cheeks glowed with a warm flush; the eyes answered his tender glances; the lips opened to respond to his endearments. The goddess had granted him more than he had dared to ask.

Hero and Leander.

In Abydos, on one side of the Hellespont (now the Dardanelles), lived a young man named Leander; on the opposite side in Sestos, a maiden named Hero lived in a tower by the shore and cared for Aphrodite's sacred swans and sparrows. At a festival of the goddess the two met and immediately fell in love. Though they were forbidden to see one another, every night Leander swam across the Hellespont and stayed with Hero until dawn began to break. One night the wind was high and the water dangerous, but the lover was not deterred. At first love bore him up, and the light his lady showed guided his way.

But the wind blew out the flame; his strength failed him and the waters closed over his head. Hero watched out the night in an agony of fear; at dawn she found her lover's body washed ashore.[19]

Pyr'a mus and Thisbe, living in adjoining Pyramus and Thisbe. 20 houses in Babylon, came to know one another, and in time the acquaintance grew into love. They would have married, but their fathers forbade it. They could speak only by nods and signs, but the more the love was kept secret the more ardent it became. In the high wall that separated the two gardens they had found a tiny crack, through which, without exciting suspicion, they might murmur endearments. "O hateful wall," they would say, "why do you stand in the way of lovers? How small a thing it would be for you to allow us to be united, or, if that is too much to ask, that you would at least open a way for our kisses! We are not ungrateful; we confess that it is to you we owe the chance to hear each other's voices." Speaking thus they said good-night and pressed their lips each to his own side of the unresponsive wall. One day, after indulging in these vain regrets, they came to a

[19] The English poet Byron, who swam the strait as Leander did, says that at this point the Hellespont is not more than a mile wide, but that the swimmer is carried down so far by the swiftness of the current that the distance covered is not less than four miles.

[20] Following Ovid, *Metamorphoses*, VI, 55 ff.

desperate resolve. When the silence of night had fallen they would escape their guardians' watchful eyes and go out from home. They agreed to meet at the tomb of Ninus, where a white mulberry tree grew beside a spring.

The long day wore away and at last night came. Thisbe cautiously opened the door and passed out unobserved. She had come to the tomb and seated herself under the mulberry tree, when lo! a lioness, her foaming jaws smeared with the blood of fresh-slain cattle, came to drink at the spring. By the rays of the moon poor Thisbe saw her, and with trembling feet she fled to a cave near by. As she fled she dropped her cloak. The lioness, having drunk her fill, was returning to the forest when she chanced to see the cloak where it lay. She tore it with her bloody jaws and so left it.

Pyramus, coming somewhat late, saw in the sand the tracks of the beast. He grew pale. He saw the garment stained with blood. "One night shall destroy two lovers," said he. "Unhappy girl, it is I that have been your death. I bade you come by night to a fearsome place, and came not first myself. Tear my body in pieces and devour my flesh, ye lions that live among the rocks! But it is the part of a coward only to wish for death." He raised Thisbe's mantle, and weeping, pressed kisses upon it. "Receive my blood!" he cried, and plunged his sword into his breast. The blood spurted high, and falling upon the mulberry tree stained the white berries a dark purple.

Thisbe, still trembling with fright, yet unwilling to fail her lover, returned to seek him. When she came to the spot the changed color of the berries made her uncertain whether she was right. While she hesitated in bewilderment, she saw the body lying on the ground. Shuddering, she recognized her lover and raised a cry of anguish, beating her breast and tearing her hair. She embraced the limp form and, raining kisses upon the cold lips, cried: "O Pyramus, what cruel fate has snatched you from me? Pyramus, answer! Your dearest Thisbe calls you. Hear me, and lift your drooping head!" At the name of Thisbe, Pyramus raised his eyes, already heavy in death, and having seen her, closed them. And she, recognizing her cloak and the naked sword, cried aloud again: "If your hand and your love have destroyed you, unhappy Pyramus, I too have a hand bold for this one deed. Love shall give me too strength for the blow. I shall follow you, at once the cause and the companion of your death. You who could be torn from me by death alone shall be torn from me not even by death." She spoke, and placing the point under her breast, fell upon the sword. The ashes of the lovers rest in one urn, and still the mulberry mourns in dark purple.

CHAPTER VII

THE LESSER DEITIES OF OLYMPUS

Of the twelve great gods and goddesses that made up the Olympic Council, ten have been already described. These are: Zeus, Hephæstus, Apollo, Hermes, Ares, Hera, Athena, Hestia, Artemis, Aphrodite. The two that remain are Poseidon, god of the sea, and Demeter, the grain-goddess, of whom later chapters will tell. Besides these greater gods there were many lesser deities. Those that had a place in Olympus are described in this chapter.

I. EROS (CUPID)

Eros, or Cupid, was the child of Aphrodite, some say by Ares. The conception of him as a little winged boy is later, originally he was conceived as a youth. Against his arrows no man or god was safe, for they inspired the passion of love. But once his weapons wounded their master himself and he fell under the spell of Psyche.

THE STORY OF CUPID AND PSYCHE [21]

There were once a king and queen who had three daughters. While the beauty of the two

Fig. 34. Eros or Cupid.

elder sisters was remarkable, that of the youngest was beyond the power of human tongue to ex-

[21] Apuleius, a Latin poet of the 2d Century A.D., tells this story in its fully developed form. It differs greatly in style and character from the mythological stories of early

press. The fame of her beauty drew people from the most distant lands to see her; men said that this was no mortal maid, but that Venus herself had deserted the heavens and come to dwell on earth. The shrines of the goddess were deserted, and the ashes grew cold on her altars; the worship due to her was paid to the maiden. Enraged at this transference of her honors to another, Venus called to her help her winged son Cupid, that pert and mischief-making boy. "I conjure you by your love for your mother," said she, "punish this rebellious beauty and avenge the insult to me. Inspire her with love for the lowest of beings, one so degraded that in the wide world is not his like."

Now while the two elder sisters were happily married to princes, the divine perfection of Psyche's beauty and the ill-will of the goddess had hindered suitors from aspiring to her love. Her parents, therefore, suspecting that in some way they had offended the gods, consulted the oracle of Apollo. The answer was given: "Hope for no mortal son-in-law; the maiden is destined to be the bride of a monster before whose flames and weapons Jupiter himself trem-

Greece, and has many of the features of the fairy tales of other European peoples. To omit the details would so detract from its interest and charm that it is here given at some length. Following Apuleius, Latin names are employed.

bles. To meet her husband the maiden must be led to the top of the mountain and there left." The king and queen, though overcome with grief, prepared to obey the oracle. Dressed as a bride and accompanied by a procession, funereal rather than bridal, Psyche was led to the destined spot. A day of mourning was proclaimed in the city, and the parents and friends were dissolved in tears.

Scarcely was Psyche left alone upon the mountain, when Zephyr (the west wind), tenderly lifting the trembling maiden, wafted her gently to a flowery valley below. Before her she saw a grove and in the midst of it a fountain. Near the fountain rose a wonderful palace — surely the home of some god! For the ceilings of cedar and ivory were supported on golden columns, while the walls were covered with silver wrought in marvelous designs. The pavement was a mosaic of precious stones. Filled with wonder and delight, Psyche plucked up courage to enter and examine the unguarded treasures of the place. No one appeared, but a voice spoke softly to her: "Why are you astonished, Lady? All these riches are yours. Yonder is your bed-chamber. When you have rested and refreshed yourself by the bath, we, your attendants, will wait upon you diligently, dress you and prepare for you a royal banquet." Her fears allayed by the gentle voice, Psyche did as she was bidden, and in due time partook of a feast exquisitely prepared and served by invisible attendants, while bodiless musicians sang to the accompaniment of an unseen lyre. That night the master of the place came to her and made her his wife, but before the light he disappeared. Thus it happened each night, and she learned to look forward to his coming and to love him for his sweet voice and his tender caresses, though she had never seen him. In the day, however, with only the bodiless voices to people her solitude, she felt lonely, and sorrowed to leave her family in ignorance of her fate. She told her trouble to her husband and entreated him to allow her to see her sisters. At last he unwillingly yielded to her caresses, warning her solemnly, however, that she must not listen to her sisters' persuasions and attempt to see or inquire about her husband's form. "Disobedience," said he, "will bring sorrow upon me and destruction upon you, sweet Wife."

The following day, when the two sisters came to the mountain and called upon Psyche by name, beating their breasts and lamenting her fate, obedient Zephyr carried them down to the valley and set them before the palace. After they had embraced and rejoiced together, and Psyche had showed them the beauties of the palace and had regaled them with the delicacies prepared by the invisible attendants, envy crept into the hearts of the sisters, and insatiable curiosity to know

Fig. 35. Cupid and Psyche.

the happy master of all these riches. Psyche told them that her husband was a beautiful youth, who passed his days hunting on the mountains. Then she loaded them with gifts and bade Zephyr carry them back to the mountain.

The more the sisters talked over their visit to the palace the more angry and envious they became. They complained that they were given over to old, bald-headed, stingy kings in foreign lands, while the youngest was married to a beautiful god and had control of untold wealth. Even the winds were her servants! They persuaded themselves that she had acted arrogantly toward them, and they resolved to bring about her downfall. On their third visit, therefore, assuming a tone of sisterly solicitude, they told her that her husband was well known to be a venomous serpent, who was often seen gliding down the mountain at daybreak. He was keeping her only until she was well fatted; then he would devour her. Let her conceal in the bed a lamp and a sharp knife, and when her husband was buried in sleep, let her kill him and so make her escape. The simple girl, though at first she indignantly rejected the suggestion, was at last persuaded. Night came, and with the darkness came her husband. As soon as he was asleep, Psyche, summoning all her courage, uncovered the lamp and seized the knife. But when by its light she saw no awful monster, but the gentlest and loveliest of all creatures, Cupid himself, the beautiful God of Love, overcome with delight and shame she fell upon her knees. So enchanted was she with the beautiful sight, the golden curls, the ruddy cheeks, the delicate wings that sprang from his shoulders, that she remained wrapped in admiration and forgot to extinguish the light. At the foot of the bed lay his bow and arrows. Curious to try how sharp they were, Psyche pressed the arrow point against her finger. Tiny drops of blood welled out, and thus did Psyche fall in love with Love. But while she pressed kisses on his face and hung over him, bewildered with delight, a drop of burning oil fell upon his shoulder. The god sprang up and, seeing the signs of his wife's faithlessness, tore himself from her frenzied embraces and flew away. Pausing for one instant in his flight, he turned and addressed her: "O simple Psyche, for you I was disobedient to my mother Venus, and when she bade me give you over to some base marriage, I chose instead to come to you myself as a lover. I, the most famous of archers, have wounded myself with my own arrow and have made you my wife. And you would believe me to be a monster and would cut off my head! It was of this that I so often warned you. As for those wicked plotters, they shall feel my anger; you will I punish by my flight alone." So saying he spread his wings and flew away.

When Psyche had recovered her senses, she set forth in search of Cupid. Towards evening she found herself close to the city where her eldest sister lived. To her she recounted what had happened, only that she changed Cupid's parting words. "Quit my house this instant," she quoted him as saying, "I will at once marry your sister." The wicked queen, goaded by love of gold and glory, left her home and her husband and hurried to the mountain. Then calling on Zephyr to waft her to the valley, she leaped from the rock and was dashed in pieces on the stones below. In the same way Psyche visited the second sister, and in the same manner she, too, suffered the penalty of her treachery.

In the meantime the sea-gull had brought word to Venus, who was bathing in the sea, that her son was lying at home grievously sick and likely to die. He added malicious gossip — that Cupid had been guilty of a disgraceful love affair with a mortal girl, and that, in consequence of his neglect, love had left the world. Hot with anger · the goddess hastened to her golden chamber, and finding him as she had been told, cried to him in a passion of rage: "This is fine behavior and becoming your birth and character! You trample upon the commands of your mother and take to wife that base girl whom I had sent you to torment with an ignoble love! But you were always troublesome and disrespectful, even to me;

and your father Mars you fear not at all, but are ever driving him into love affairs. You shall repent of it! I shall adopt one of the sons of my slaves and give to him the bow and arrows that you so little know how to use. I must have recourse to my old foe Sobriety; she will soon blunt your arrows and extinguish your torch!" So she turned her back upon her wounded son and left the house.

Meanwhile Psyche, still distractedly wandering in search of Cupid, came by chance to a temple of Ceres. Here was a confused heap of corn and grain, and near it scythes and other tools lying in disorder. Piously anxious to win the favor of any goddess that might help her, Psyche set to work to bring order out of the confusion. The goddess came to the temple while she was thus engaged. Throwing herself at her feet the girl besought her: " By thy plenty-giving hand, by the joyful rites of harvest, by thy secret mysteries, by thy dragon-drawn car, by the Sicilian fields and that thieving chariot and the descent of Proserpina (see p. 154) to a lightless wedlock, and the return of thy child to the world above, pity your suppliant, luckless Psyche! Amid this heap of grain let me hide for a few days, until the wrath of Venus is abated!" Ceres was moved but feared to offend Venus. Regretfully she drove Psyche from her temple. As she left the shrine of Ceres, Psyche saw in the valley beneath a shrine of Juno. Thither she turned her weary steps, and falling down before the altar, prayed the goddess to help her in her desperate need. Juno listened kindly but answered that she could give no protection to a fugitive slave of her daughter-in-law Venus. Then Psyche, convinced that no hope of help lay in any other, resolved to surrender herself to her mistress Venus and humbly to propitiate her.

Now Venus, repairing to heaven in her golden dove-drawn chariot, had asked and secured the help of the herald Mercury. He had cried the lost maiden through all the world: "If any one can seize in her flight or can discover the fugitive slave of Venus, a king's daughter, Psyche by name, let him repair to Mercury, the herald, at the temple of Venus; he shall receive as a reward from Venus herself seven sweet kisses." This proclamation further persuaded Psyche that the only course now open to her was one of sub-mission. She therefore hastened to the house of Venus, who, when she saw her, raised a joyful laugh. "At last," said she, "have you deigned to pay your respects to your mother-in-law? Or perhaps you came to visit your husband, who lies still in danger from the wound you gave him? But take courage! I shall receive you as a good mother-in-law should. Where are my servants, Solicitude and Sorrow?" These, immediately appearing, scourged and otherwise tortured the unhappy Psyche, and then brought her again before her mistress.

Venus next set the girl before a great heap of wheat, barley, millet, poppy, beans, and every other kind of grain and seed, and said scornfully to her: "You seem to me so deformed a slave that only by industry can you deserve your husband. I shall make trial of you. Separate the various grains in this heap, and see that the work is finished before evening!" So she left her. Despairing at the impossible task, Psyche sat still without moving a finger to the confused mass. But a little ant took pity on the wife of Cupid and called together the populous tribe from a neighboring ant-hill. In a very short time the grains and seeds were piled neatly into separate heaps. Then the little ants disappeared. Venus, returning from a feast, fragrant with perfumes and wreathed with roses, saw with anger the success of her hated slave. "Worthless girl," said she, "this is not the work of your hands but that of your wretched lover!" And throwing her a crust of dry bread she retired to rest.

At dawn Venus called Psyche, and pointing out to her a wood by the river, ordered her to get a lock of golden wool from the sheep that fed there. Psyche gladly set out, not hoping to secure the lock of wool, but intending to throw herself into the river. But a reed of the river spoke to her: "O sorrowful Psyche, pollute not my waters, nor dare to approach the sheep on the farther bank! For while the sun is hot, they are fierce and destroy any who come near them, but when at noon they go to rest under the trees, then with safety you may cross the river, and you shall find the golden wool caught on the bushes. So shall you accomplish the task safely."

Venus greeted her successful return with a bitter smile: "I know well," said she, "that you did not perform this task by yourself. Now I will make trial of your courage and prudence. Bring me from the fountain on yonder lofty mountain liquid dew in this crystal urn." Psyche hopefully received the urn and hurried to the mountain. But when she reached the top, she saw the impossibility of the undertaking. For the fountain rose from the top of an inaccessible rock and plunged down thence into a terrible chasm where fierce dragons kept perpetual watch. And the roaring waters called to her as they crashed down: "Depart, or you will perish!" As she shrank back in dismay, the eagle of Jupiter came to her: "Can you, a simple mortal, hope to steal one drop of the Stygian waters, terrible to Jove himself? Give me the little urn!" Psyche, therefore, receiving the full urn, joyfully returned to Venus.

The goddess was only the more enraged, and laid on her another task. "Take this box," said

she, "and direct your steps to the abode of
Pluto. There say to Proserpina that Venus begs
her to give her a little of her beauty in this box,
for she has exhausted all her own in anxious
attendance on her sick son. Return at once, for
I must dress for the theater of the gods." And
now truly Psyche saw that she was face to face
with destruction. She therefore ascended to the
top of a high tower, meaning to cast herself down
and so reach the infernal world by the shortest
way. But the tower spoke to her: "O wretched
girl, why do you seek to destroy yourself before
the last test of your endurance? Listen to me!
Near Lacedæmon in Achæa is the cavity through
which Pluto breathes. Here is the entrance to
the lower world. Go from thence by a straight
road to the palace of Pluto. Take with you two
pieces of bread soaked in honey, and in your
mouth two pieces of money to pay Charon (see
p. 188) for ferrying you across the river. The
bread will appease the fierce three-headed dog,
Cerberus. But be careful not to stop to listen to
the appeals for help from those you meet, for
Venus will send many wretched beings to induce
you to stop or lay aside the sop or the coin that
you need for your return journey. Proserpina
will receive you kindly and will offer you a soft
bed and a dainty banquet. Decline them both!
When you have received what you came for,
return at once to the upper world. On no ac-

count open or even look at the box that you
carry!"

Psyche started on her enterprise, and all fell
out as the tower had said. She obeyed his instructions resolutely until the danger were passed
and she was just about to emerge into the light
of day. Then she was seized with a rash curiosity and a longing to take for herself a little
of the divine beauty she carried so that she might
appear better in the eyes of her lover when she
should see him again. But when she opened the
box, there came forth no beauty but only a
Stygian sleep that instantly overpowered her, so
that she fell down where she stood and lay motionless.

Cupid, being now quite recovered of his
wound, had flown through the window of his
room and come to find Psyche. When, therefore, he saw her lying there motionless, he took
the sleep and shut it up again in its little box,
and arousing Psyche by the touch of one of his
arrows, said: "Unfortunate girl, a second time
you would have perished by that fatal curiosity!
But now fulfil your task to Venus; I will take
care of the rest." So saying he flew away and
Psyche carried the box to Venus.

Meanwhile Cupid flew straight to heaven, and
presenting himself before his grandfather Jupiter, asked his aid. The father of gods, smilingly
stroking the cheeks of Cupid, answered kindly:

"Though you, my child, presuming on your power, never pay me the reverence that is my due, and by your arrows cause me to act unworthily of my dignity and so injure my reputation, yet I will do all that you ask." He therefore sent Mercury to call the gods to a council meeting, and addressing them, he told them that he thought it best that Cupid should marry. Venus he bade submit, promising to make the marriage legal by raising Psyche to the order of the gods. Mercury brought the bride before him, and she received from Jupiter the nectar and ambrosia. "Take this," said he, "and be immortal; nor shall Cupid ever depart from your embraces, but this marriage shall be eternal." Then the wedding banquet was served. Cupid reclined beside Psyche, Jupiter by Juno, and so all the other gods and goddesses in order. Ganymede poured the nectar for Jupiter, and Bacchus for the other gods, Vulcan prepared the supper, the Hours scattered roses all about, the Graces scattered balsam, and the Muses sang melodiously, while Apollo accompanied them on his lyre and Venus danced to their music.

Psyche is the soul. By her own act she destroys her happy and innocent life with Love, endures in the world every trial and suffering, and even goes down to Hades, to be in the end reunited with Love and to live with him forever in heaven. The story as it is told here belongs to a late time. It is a philosophical fairy tale.

II. OTHER DEITIES OF OLYMPUS

The Graces (or Char'i tes) presided over the feast and the dance, all the gracious and festive side of social intercourse. For the Greek ideal demanded that men's everyday life, no less than their worship, should be ruled by grace and beauty, and the deities who brought this harmony to life were fittingly conceived as the daughters of no less a one than Zeus. They were three in number and were represented nude or in transparent drapery, adorned with spring flowers and roses. The Graces.

The Nine Muses, daughters of Zeus and Mnemosyne (ne mos'i nē, Memory), presided, each over a distinct form of poetry, art, or science. They formed the chorus of Apollo, the god of music, and with him haunted the heights of Parnassus or Helicon, or danced about the springs of Pieria. Their names, their functions, and their emblems are as follows: Clio, the muse of history, holds a roll of writing; Cal li'ope, the muse of epic poetry, holds a tablet and pen; Mel pom'e ne, the muse of tragedy, holds a tragic mask; Tha li'a, the muse of comedy, holds a comic mask or wears the distinctive costume of the actor of comedy; Terp sich'o re, the muse of the choral lyric and the dance, wears a long garment and The Nine Muses.

holds a lyre; Er'a to, the muse of love poetry, wears a thin garment and holds a lyre; Eu ter'pe, the muse of flute music, holds a double flute; U ra'ni a, the muse of astronomy, holds a globe; Po lym'ni a, the muse of religious poetry or the pantomime, is represented in an attitude of medi-

Fig. 36.   Clio.

tation.   To the Muses poets offered prayers and vows: "Fortunate is he whomsoever the Muses love, and sweet flows his voice from his lips." (*Homeric Hymn to the Muses.*)

The Three Fates.   The Three Fates held in their hands the thread of life, and when man's allotted life was spun, the shears of the fates cut it off.   Their names are given in the little verse from Lowell's *Villa Franca:* "Spin, spin, Clotho, spin!   Lach'e sis, twist! and At'ro pus, sever!"   They tell of the past, present, and future.

Fig. 37.   Thalia.

Nem'e sis, a darkly mysterious power that overshadowed even the gods themselves, for evil done or for excess of pride brought divine vengeance from which there was no hope of es- **Nemesis.**

Æolus. The winds were under the control of Æ'o lus, to whom Zeus gave the power to rouse or to quiet them.   In a vast cave in one of the volcanic Lipari Islands, he and his twelve boisterous children, the winds, lived a life of feasting and merri-

Fig. 38. Terpsichore.

ment. There they struggle against their prison doors and cause mighty rumbling of the mountain.   If let loose, Vergil says, they would sweep away earth and sea and sky in their destructive course.   Bo're as is the wild north wind; Zeph'y rus is the gentle west wind.

CHAPTER VIII

THE GODS OF THE SEA

PO SEI'DON was the son of Cronus and Rhea Poseidon (Neptune). and brother of Zeus. To him, after the overthrow of the Titans, was given control over all the waters, fresh as well as salt. He supplanted Oceanus of the older dynasty. The early Greeks thought that the waters were beneath the earth and held it up; earthquakes were due to them. Moreover the Ocean flowed all about the circle of the earth as a great salt river. Homer speaks of Poseidon as, "he that girdleth the world, the shaker of the earth." Though he was a member of the Olympic Council, he had his palace in the depths of Ocean.

There was his famous palace in the deeps of the mere, his glistering golden mansions builded, imperishable forever. Thither went he and let harness to his car his bronze-hoofed horses, swift of flight, clothed with their golden manes. He girt his own golden array about his body and seized the well-wrought lash of gold, and mounted his chariot, and forth he drove across the waves. And the sea-beasts frolicked beneath him, on all sides out of the deeps, for well they knew their lord, and with gladness the sea stood asunder. (*Iliad*, XIII. 21 ff.)

Beside him was seated his wife, " fair-ankled Am phi tri'te," the daughter of Nereus (see p. 148, while before and about his chariot swam the Tritons, half man, half fish, heralding their lord's approach by blasts on their shells.

In addition to his lordship over the waters Poseidon presided over horses and horsemanship. One version of his contest with Athena over Athens, as was said earlier, attributes to him the creation of a salt spring, but the other version attributes to him the creation of the horse.

The walls of Troy. After the overthrow of the giants, Apollo and Poseidon fell under the displeasure of Zeus, who therefore forced them to serve a mortal. They agreed with La om'e don, king of Troy, for a certain reward to build the walls of his city. When the work was completed, Laomedon refused to abide by his bargain and insolently dismissed the gods. Poseidon in his anger sent floods and a terrible sea-monster to ravage, the coast. To appease the monster no sacrifice was acceptable but that of He si'o ne, daughter of Laomedon. The princess was about to be devoured by the monster when Heracles, that friend of troubled mankind, appeared and rescued her. How he too was cheated of his reward by the faithless Laomedon, and how he avenged his wrongs, will be told later in the story of Heracles. (See p. 220.)

Fig. 39. Poseidon.

It <u>is</u> as god of horses and horsemanship that Poseidon appears in the story of Pelops and Hippo da mi′a. This Hippodamia was the daughter of Œn o ma′us, king of Elis. Many young men wished to marry her, but her father <u>had been</u> warned by an oracle to beware of his future son-in-law. As he <u>was</u> the owner of horses as fleet as the wind, he <u>made</u> the condition that he who would win the daughter must first contend with the father in a chariot-race, the reward of success <u>being</u> the hand of Hippodamia and the price of failure the suitor's life. Many had staked their lives on the venture, and the maiden re<u>maine</u>d unmarried. Pelops <u>had been granted</u> by Poseidon extraordinary skill in horsemanship; now he obtained in addition four winged steeds, and so offered himself for the perilous race. Nor was Poseidon Pelops' only divine helper, for, by the power of Aphrodite, Hippodamia's heart was so won at first sight that she <u>bribed</u> her father's charioteer Myrtilus to take out the bolt from his chariot-wheel before starting on the race. So Œnomaüs perished and Pelops led away Hippodamia as his wife. The lovers, however, by their ingratitude and treachery brought down upon their already accursed family the further displeasure of the gods, for Pelops, in a fit of rage, <u>hurled</u> Myrtilus into the sea. The tragic history of the race of Pelops is associated with the Trojan War and will be told in that connection.   (See p. 281.)

Neptune.   The Romans had from early times worshiped Neptune as god of moisture and of flowing water, when they identified him with the Greek Poseidon, they recognized him also as god of the sea.

Nereus.   Ne′reus, the wise and kindly "Old Man of the Sea," lived with his fifty charming daughters below the waters in a great shining cave.   He personifies the sea as a source of gain to men. the sea on whose calm and friendly surface merchants and sailors venture out in ships.   His fifty daughters, the Ne′reids, represent the sea in all its many phases.   They live together happily in their deep-sea cave, but often rise to the surface,

Fig. 40.   Marriage of Poseidon and Amphitrite.

and in sunlight or in moonlight may be seen sitting on the shore or on a rock covered with seaweed, drying their long green locks, or riding on the dolphins, or playing in the waves with the Tritons.   If a mortal comes near, they will slide down into the sea and disappear, for their bodies end in green fishes' tails and the deep water is their real home.   Three of the fifty are especially famous: Amphitrite, Poseidon's wife; Thetis (see p. 283), the mother of Achilles, and Gal a te'a, whom the Cyclops Pol y phe'mus loved.

A stranger and more mysterious "Old Man of **Proteus,** the Sea" was Pro'teus, the shepherd of Posei-

Fig. 41. Head of a Sea-God.

don's flock of seals. He had the gift of prophecy, and would tell the future if one could catch and hold him. But, like the sea itself, he continually changed his form, and when one had seized him as a roaring lion, he glided away as a serpent, or if one still held to that slippery form, suddenly he was a flame of fire, or as running water he slipped through the hands.

The Sirens.   Although from the earliest times the Greeks were a sea-faring people, they never forgot the perils that lurked in the deep, nor the uncertainty of trusting themselves to its waters. Especially in the west, near Sicily and Italy, fable told of the dangers that lay in wait for the rash voyager. Somewhere in that part of the sea was the island of the Sirens, beautiful maidens in face and breast but winged and clawed as birds. By the charm of their singing they lured mariners to drive their ships upon the rocks. He who heard their magic voices no longer remembered his dear native land, nor his wife and children, but only heard the charmer and cast himself into the sea. All the beach below where they sat and sang was white with the bones of men. Fair they seemed as the smooth bright surface of the sea that treacherously smiles over the bones of its victims. The much-enduring Odysseus was warned of these alluring maidens and passed by them safely only by having the ears of his companions stuffed with wax, while he himself was kept from the fatal leap by being fast bound to his own mast.

The Harpies.   Wholly terrible, without the malign charm of the Sirens, were the Harpies, with their huge wings and strong talons. They were goddesses of storm and death, who snatched and carried

away their booty as if on the wings of the wind.
When weary sailors had ignorantly landed on the
Harpies' shores, and, having prepared their feast,
sat down to enjoy it, down swooped these vile
birds and carried off the food in their claws.
Their coming brought not alone famine but the
mournful omen of approaching death.

The passage between the coasts of Sicily and Scylla and
Charybdis.
Italy was beset with danger. Here in the side
of a precipitous cliff was a cave where lurked
the monster Scylla. From out the dark cavern
she stretched her six heads, armed with rows of
great sharp teeth. Woe to the unlucky mariners
who had steered too close to shore! Drawn in
as by a drag-net by her twelve long arms, they
were crunched in the great jaws, and only the
bones were left to tell the tale. And if men escaped this horror, on the other side lay Char-
yb'dis, sucking down the water into her black
whirlpool and belching it forth again, three times
each day. Against these monsters even Poseidon's help was of no avail.

Fresh water as well as salt had each its own River-gods
and nymphs
deity. From the river at any moment its god
might rise up, the water streaming from his hair
and beard. So Alpheus rose to pursue Arethusa (see p. 84); so the god of the Xanthus
near Troy rose and fought with Achilles. (See
p. 296.) Sometimes the river-god took the form
of a bull. (See p. 225.) Each little brook and

spring had its own nymph, a lovely maiden with tossing hair, with laughing voice and lightly dancing feet. These are the Naiads. (See p. 184.)

CHAPTER IX

THE GODS OF THE EARTH

THE skies that rule over all, and the great seas, are male beings; Zeus and Poseidon rule there. The earth, that gives life to plants and animals and men, that cares for and generously nourishes her children, is the great mother goddess, Gæa.

Fig. 42. Cybele in her Car.

Rhea, the mother of the gods, was also an earth-goddess. The people of Asia Minor knew her as Cy'be le or the Great Mother, and represented her crowned with a turreted crown like the wall of a city; for she was the bringer of

Rhea or Cybele the Great Mother.

153

civilization, the protectress of cities. Lions drew her chariot, and about her were the Cor y-ban'tes, who acclaimed her with shouts and the clashing of cymbals, and led her worship with wild dances. This worship never took firm root in Greece, but it was introduced into Rome and was there one of the most influential of the foreign religious cults.

Demeter (Ceres).
More characteristic of the Greek people was the worship of De me'ter, the bountiful goddess of the grain. She was the sister of Zeus and had her place in the Olympic Council. We see her, of generous and kindly aspect, draped from head to foot, holding a torch, or ears of wheat and corn mingled with poppies. Per seph'o ne (or Pro ser'pi na), the fresh young corn of the new year, was her only daughter, looking to Zeus, the giver of rain and sun, as her father. The worship of these two is a beautiful, natural harvesters' worship, but trouble and loss enter in.

The Rape of Persephone (Proserpina).
When Persephone was still a young girl she was playing with the ocean nymphs one day, in the sunny land of Sicily. She had wandered a little way from her friends and stooped to pick a narcissus. As she uprooted the fragrant flower, out of the earth sprang the black horses and golden chariot of Hades, or Pluto, the king of the lower world. In spite of her cries for help, the black god carried the maiden off with him; as

Fig. 43.   Demeter.

she passed, the flowers fell from her hands. Then
the earth opened at the word of the god, and
Pluto descended with his prize into the gloomy
regions over which he ruled. Here he made her
his queen.

Demeter, who had gone to Asia Minor to visit
Cybele, heard of her loss, but did not know who
the robber was nor where she should begin her
search for her daughter. Disconsolately she
wandered over all the earth, her serene and kindly
face befouled by tears, her clothes torn and soiled,
her corn and flowers abandoned. Without her
ministry the fields yielded no crops, men and
beasts starved, and though they called on her, she
would not hear nor answer. At last, in her wanderings she came to the fountain of Cy'a ne, in
Sicily. Now the nymph Cyane had seen Pluto
with the stolen girl and had vainly tried to bar
his passage. In grief at her failure she had wept
herself into a fountain and so had lost the power
of speech. All that she could do was to wash
up at the mother's feet the girdle that the girl
had dropped in her passage. Then Demeter, in
her anger and despair, cursed the ground, and
above all the lovely land of Sicily that had betrayed its trust. Not far from Cyane is another fountain, once a nymph, Arethusa, who,
as was told above (see p. 84), in her flight from
the river Alpheus rushed down into the earth in
Greece and rose again in Sicily. On her way

through the lower world she had seen Persephone sharing Pluto's throne. From her, Demeter learned at last the truth and at once went to Zeus to demand redress. Induced, not alone by Demeter's tears and prayers, but by the agonized cries of all the suffering earth, Zeus decreed that Pluto should give up his stolen bride — on one condition, that no food had passed her lips during her stay beneath the earth. By ill fortune she had been persuaded by Pluto to taste the seeds of a pomegranate. A compromise was made: Persephone should return to her mother, but each year she should descend again into the lower world to stay as many months as she had eaten seeds of the pomegranate. And so each winter when the seeds of grain are sowed, the daughter of the grain-mother goes down into the dark ground, and the fields are bare and unlovely while the mother mourns. But when the time agreed upon is over, and Persephone comes again to the light, then Demeter is glad and looks to her fields. The fresh young spears of grain come out of the dark earth, and when the time comes and the crops begin to ripen, Demeter makes the fields beautiful with poppies, and then, when the ears are full, men gather them joyfully and bring them into their barns and praise the bountiful Demeter and her lovely daughter.

The Eleusinian Mysteries. El eu'sis is a small town a few miles distant from Athens. Here were celebrated the Mys-

Fig. 44. Demeter, Triptolemus and Persephone.

teries in honor of Demeter. All Athens took part in the procession and the purification, but to the Mysteries themselves only those who had been initiated were admitted. The ceremonies were kept very secret, but it seems that the rape of Persephone and her return were dramatically represented, and that the initiate gained some deeper trust in a happy immortality than was known to others. The story of the institution of these El eu sin'i an Mysteries is connected with Demeter's search for her daughter.

Exhausted by nine days of fasting and useless wandering, Demeter had come to Eleusis and had sat down beside a well. Here came the four daughters of the king of that land to fill their water-jars. Seeing the tired old woman, they spoke to her kindly and brought her with them to their father's house. The king's wife had lately borne a son, and the disguised goddess took the baby to nurse. She anointed him with ambrosia, and each night as he slept she placed him in the embers on the hearth, for so she intended to burn away the mortal part and make him as one of the gods. But the anxious queen watched through the door one night, and rushed in with terrified cries to rescue her baby from the fire. Then the goddess rose in all her divine majesty and said to the mother: "O foolish woman! now have you brought incurable evil upon your son; I would have made him immortal

Demeter and
Triptolemus.

and given him everlasting youth, but now must he suffer the common lot of men. Yet I will give him imperishable honor since he has lain on my breast. But come now, build me here a temple, and the rites in it I will myself prescribe." So they built to Demeter a great temple, and when the child Trip tol'e mus had grown

Fig. 45. Triptolemus in the dragon-drawn Chariot.

up, the goddess taught him to raise grain and corn and sent him in a dragon-drawn chariot through every land to teach men how to sow and reap. Through him, too, she gave the Greeks her Mysteries and a better hope for the future life. As the Greek poet Pindar says: "Happy is he that hath seen those things ere he go beneath the earth; he knoweth life's end, he knoweth its beginning given of God."

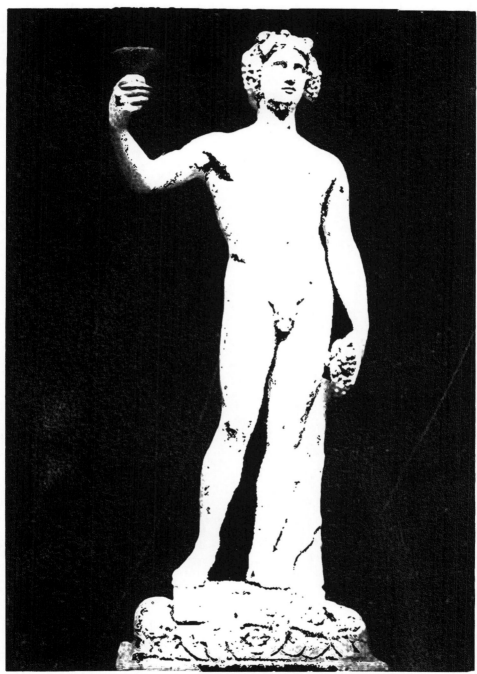

Fig. 46. Dionysus or Bacchus.

It was soon after the expulsion of the kings, Ceres. at the time of a failure of crops, that the Romans, in obedience to a command of the Sibylline books [22] introduced the worship of Demeter. Even then she was not worshiped under her Greek name, but was indentified with an old Latin goddess named Ceres, and Persephone was given the Latinized form Proserpina. Ceres was always the special protectress of the plebeians.

Di on y′sus or Bacchus is familiarly known as Dionysus or Bacchus. the convivial wine-god; but while the vine is most closely associated with him, he is, in truth, the vital strength of everything that grows, the power of fertility and of joyful, springing life.

His mother was Sem′e le, daughter of Cadmus His birth and travels. (see p. 256), the founder of Thebes, and his father was Zeus. Though Semele was of divine descent on both sides of her family, she was herself a mortal, and to make love to her Zeus put on the form of a mortal. At first she rejected his attentions, but when he told her who he was, she yielded and gladly received him. Hera knew of this and was filled with angry jealousy. Disguising herself as Semele's old nurse Ber′o ë, she led the girl on to talk of her love. When she had heard all the story, she pretended not to believe that the lover was Zeus. " If he were, why should he not come to you in all his glory,

---

[22] Books of prophecy said to have been received by Tar quin, the legendary king of Rome, from the Sibyl.

as he does to Hera?　He is treating you with very little respect." Semele's pride was touched. The next time her lover came she induced him to swear that he would grant whatever she should demand.　Then she asked that he should show himself to her in all his Olympian majesty.　The fatal oath by the Styx had been given; even to save one he loved Zeus could not recall it.　He came to her as God of Heaven, armed with the thunder-bolts.　No mortal could endure his glory or the flame of the lightning; poor Semele was reduced to ashes.　So the earth is scorched by the full blaze of the Greek sun at midsummer, or seared by the lightning; only the seeds within it remain alive.　Just so Semele's baby, Dionysus or Bacchus, came to birth from his mother's ashes, and ivy sprang up miraculously to shade him from the hot sky.　His grieving father took him and gave him to the mountain nymphs of Nysa to nurse.　As he grew older Si le'nus, one of the lesser divinities of earth, was given to him as a tutor, and with his help he discovered all the secrets of nature, especially the culture of the vine.　He taught his followers, the rustic deities, to make from the grapes wine, the mysterious source at once of womanish weakness, and invincible power and joyous freedom from care.　Intoxicated by the new drink, they thronged together in Bacchic revels.　Wherever he went, he was joined by crowds of women,

called Bac chan'tes, who celebrated his worship
by wild dances, the clashing of cymbals, the beating of drums, shrill flutings, and unrestrained
shouts. Always so accompanied, Bacchus traveled over the world, teaching the cultivation of

Fig. 47. Silenus with Dionysus.

the grape and the power of wine. He penetrated
to India, where even the panthers and lions fell
under his charm and obediently drew his triumphal chariot. As a conquering hero he returned to Greece and demanded worship every-

where. And everywhere the women flocked to his revels. Dressed in the skins of beasts, with streaming hair, brandishing snakes or the ivy-twined wand or thyrsus, they joined in the wild dances. With shrill outcries they tore in pieces the sacrificial animals and devoured the raw flesh.

The Bacchic rites. At Thebes Pen'theus, the king, forbade the revels, and when the women of his city, in de-

Fig. 48. Bacchic Procession.

fiance of his commands, went out to join the Bacchantes, he followed to spy on the secret rites. Enraged at this opposition, Bacchus made the women mad. They mistook the king for a wild beast and tore him to pieces, his own mother leading in the murderous assault. There is probably some historical basis for this story, for these extravagant wild rites, introduced from Thrace

or Asia Minor, met with bitter opposition in some
parts of Greece. But the promise they offered
of raising the worshiper above the bounds of
the natural, plodding human life and giving a
high and divine power through mystic union with
the god, overrode all opposition, and the Bacchic
mysteries were received and practised with immense enthusiasm.

Many stories are told of Bacchus and his trav- *The good helmsman.*
els, and of how he punished his enemies and re-
warded his friends. On one occasion, as he was
lying asleep on the shore of an island, some pirates
came upon him, and thinking that the beautiful
youth might be held for a large ransom, they
carried him off to their ship. The helmsman,
recognizing the god in his divine grace and beauty,
implored his companions to set him free, but they
were deaf to his words. When the god awoke
he tearfully besought his captors to take him to
the island of Naxos. Pretending to consent they
steered the other way. Suddenly the ship stood
rooted in the sea; ivy trailed up the mast, and
vines wreathed the sails; a sweet odor filled the
air, and wine flowed about the deck. The captive's bonds dropped from him, and in his place
crouched a lion. In their terror the sailors leaped
overboard and were instantly transformed into
dolphins — all but the god-fearing helmsman,
whom Bacchus saved and made his follower.

Midas.[23] Midas was a king in Phrygia. One day Silenus in a dazed and drunken condition was brought before him. Recognizing Bacchus' tutor in the muddled old man, Midas entertained him well ånd sent him back to his pupil. In return for this good office, Bacchus offered to fulfil whatever wish the king should make. When Midas, being excessively fond of riches, asked that whatever he touched might become gold, Dionysus was sorry for the foolish wish, but could not withdraw his offer. Midas returned home in delight. To try his new power he touched an oak branch; it became golden. He lifted a stone from the ground: it was a mass of gold. The very earth became hard and yellow at his touch. He picked some ears of grain; golden was the harvest. He pulled an apple from the tree; one would have thought it one of the golden apples of the Hesperides. If he touched the door-posts with his fingers, the posts shone as gold. When he washed his hands in fresh water, the drops that fell were like the golden shower that deceived Danaë. (See p. 200.) The servants placed a banquet before him; when he touched the bread it hardened under his fingers; when he raised a dainty morsel to his lips, his teeth closed on a lump of gold. He mingled wine with his water; molten gold flowed down his throat. And now he hated and loathed the wealth that he had loved; he was

[23] Following Ovid. *Metamorphoses*. XI. 85 ff.

starving in the midst of plenty. Raising his hands and gleaming arms to heaven he cried: "Have pity on me, kindly Bacchus, I have sinned! Oh, pity me, and take away the cursed boon!" Bacchus heard him. He bade him go to the river Pac to'lus and wash in the spring from which it rises. There the golden touch left him and was transferred to the river, whose sands are mixed with gold to this day.

Dionysus married A ri ad'ne, a beautiful princess of Crete, whom the hero Theseus (see p. 250) had carried away from her home and had then deserted on the island of Naxos. Her divine lover Dionysus came to her while she slept and wakened her by a kiss. The wedding of the pair was celebrated with great magnificence and joy, and as a wedding gift the god gave his bride a crown studded with brilliant stars. When she died, her grieving husband threw the crown up into the heavens. There it can still be seen as Corona, or Ariadne's Crown. *Ariadne.*

Although the Di on y'si a, or Bac cha-na'li a, were always celebrated with wild orgies and extravagant enthusiasm, Dionysus also received worship of a different character. Praise was given to him as the hospitable and genial deity who brings joy to the feast, frees men from care, and makes them of friendly and kindly feelings towards one another. He brought to men civilization and law; he was a lover of peace. By his *The Dionysia.*

exhilarating power he inspired poets and musicians and thus is associated with Apollo and the Muses.   The Attic drama originated at the festivals of Dionysus.   The rough dances and music were reduced to form; the choral dances became pantomimic, and the songs took on dramatic character.   From this was developed tragedy and comedy.   The great theater of Athens is in the precinct of Dionysus.

Dionysus: appearance and emblems.   There is much variation in the representations of the god; two distinct types are especially familiar.   In the one he appears as a mature man,

Fig. 49.   Youthful Dionysus.

bearded and heavily draped; this was the regular type in early times.   In the other he appears as a smooth-faced young man, of grace and charm that is almost feminine.   His hair is long, sometimes hanging in curls and sometimes caught up on his head like that of a woman.   He usually is either nude or wears a panther's or lion's skin over his shoulder.   His head is crowned with ivy or grape-leaves, and he holds in his hand grapes or a shallow cup of wine.   Sometimes he is represented as the eastern conqueror in his triumphal car, drawn by lions or panthers, while about him throng his followers, Satyrs, Sileni, Mænads (see p. 179), mingling with his votaries, the Bacchantes, who brandish snakes or ivy-twined staves.

Fig. 50. Bacchic Procession.

Tell me, Muse, concerning the dear son of Hermes, the goat-footed, the two-horned, the lover of the din of revel, who haunts the wooded dells with dancing nymphs that tread the crests of the steep cliffs, calling upon Pan the pastoral god of the long wild hair. Lord is he of every snowy crest and mountain peak and rocky path. (*Homeric Hymn to Pan.*)

This is that mysterious pastoral god, Pan, the spirit of the mountains and woods of Greece. The daughter of a mortal bore him to Hermes as he tended her father's sheep in the hills of Arcadia. A strange child he was, as the poet sings, goat-legged, with horns and a goat's beard, laughing and jumping even from his birth. His mother was frightened when she saw him, but Hermes was glad and wrapped him in the skins of hares and carried him off to Olympus to show him to the gods. They were all delighted with him, especially Dionysus, and they called him Pan.

Hither and thither he goes through the thick copses, sometimes being drawn to the still waters, and sometimes faring through the lofty crags he climbs the highest peak whence the flocks are seen below; ever he ranges over the high white hills, and ever among the knolls he chases and slays the wild beasts, the god with keen eye, and at evening returns piping from the chase, breathing sweet strains on the reeds. . . . With him then the mountain nymphs, the shrill singers, go wandering with light feet, and sing at the side of the dark water of the well, while the echo moans along the mountain crest, and the god leaps hither and thither, and goes into the midst, with many a step of the dance. On his back he wears the tawny hide of a lynx, and his heart rejoices with shrill songs in the soft meadow, where crocus and fragrant hyacinth bloom all mingled amidst the grass. (*Homeric Hymn to Pan.*)

So one can almost see him to-day as one listens in the hills to the Greek shepherds piping to their sheep, just as they did in the old days before Pan died. But it is not safe to see him, for he is a shy god and a mischievous, and if one spies upon him when he is sleeping or at play, one may have good cause to repent. Indeed it is best to avoid certain shady spots by springs at noon-day, for there Pan chooses to sleep while the big flies buzz in the sun-light and all else is still, and he does

Fig. 51. Pan and a Nymph.

not like to be disturbed. At night he lives in caves in the hills, and those places are sacred to him. There is one of these sacred caves in the cliff that forms the Acropolis, right in the city of Athens, but Pan deserted it long ago, and altars to Christian saints were set up near by. He had no worship in Athens until the time of the Persian Wars, and then the story goes that just before the battle of Marathon a runner sent to Sparta to ask for help against the Persians was met on the road by Pan, who told him that he wished well to the Athenians and would help them in the battle, although they had hitherto paid him no honor. And after the battle they remembered the unreasoning fear that had fallen upon the Persians and how they had fled before the Greeks, though so much fewer in number, and they set apart this cave as his shrine. Such fear as this is known as Panic terror. Sometimes it mysteriously comes upon men in the woods; often it seizes a flock of sheep and without cause they rush upon their own destruction.

But Pan is not always dangerous or ill-natured; The syrinx. to those he favors he sends increase of their flocks and keeps their herds safe from harm. Some shepherds whom he loved he taught to play on the pipes, and they taught others, and so the shepherds in the lonely hills can pipe to their ladyloves as Pan pipes to the nymphs. For Pan loves the nymphs, although they are a little afraid of his goat's legs and his queer goat-like face, and sometimes run away from him. So, they say, he wished to press his love on the nymph Syrinx, but she fled from him, and when he had followed her to the bank of a stream and thought he was just seizing her, his hand closed on a bunch of reeds. From his windy sighs a sweet, plaintive sound rose among the hollow reeds, so he broke off a few of unequal length, fastened them together with wax, and so made the syrinx, a musical instrument of that form.

The worship of Pan. As he is the mysterious soul of nature, Pan is very wise and knows even what the future holds, and so throughout Greece his oracles were consulted, and to Pan and the nymphs people prayed and brought offerings of milk and cheese and honey, or a kid from their flocks.

"Great Pan is dead." But "Great Pan is dead." The story is told by Plutarch. In the time of the emperor Tiberius a ship was sailing from Greece to Italy. As it passed by a certain island, all on board heard a voice calling, "Thamus." Three times the call was repeated and at the last an Egyptian of that name, who was of the ship's company, answered. He was told that when they came to a certain place off the coast of Epirus, he was to announce, "Great Pan is dead." When the ship reached this place, a calm fell, and Thamus did as he had been told. Immediately a sound of lamentation answered from the shore, as if an unseen multitude were mourning. The Christian tradition told, that this was about the time of Christ's death, and, that the mysterious voice announced the end of the gods of Greece, who withdrew lamenting before the cross of Christ.

Fig. 52.   Votive Offering to Pan and the Nymphs.

Pan is not always represented with the goat's legs and beard; sometimes his form is entirely human except for the slightest indication of horns to mark his animal nature. In this he is almost indistinguishable from the Satyrs.

Not only in appearance but in nature and origin

His appearance.

Satyrs.

Pan's companions, the Satyrs, bear a close resemblance to him. They, too, are wild spirits of the woods and hills, half timid, playful animals, and half human. They have short, flat

noses, pointed ears, and little tails, sometimes, too, goats' legs. They follow Dionysus, or they dance and play with Pan and the nymphs, and are always hankering after wine and women. The country people feared them, for they sometimes stole away the herds and killed the goats and sheep, but they imitated their rough, lively dances and their noisy songs, and so developed a

Fig. 53. Dancing Satyr.

popular kind of drama, called satyric drama, in which the chorus was composed of men dressed as Satyrs. These dramas were given in honor of Dionysus. In later times Satyrs appear in art as younger, gentler, and more innocent, just as one may see in the graceful young Satyr or Faun of Praxiteles, who leans pensively against a tree, holding a flute in his hand.

Faunus. Faunus was an old Roman god of flocks and herds, who through his power of prophecy and his pastoral character became identified with Pan.

Finally many Fauns were conceived of and confounded with the Satyrs.

Another of the company of Dionysus was his tutor Silenus, he who was brought in an intoxicated condition to King Midas. There were many Sileni, and they were first heard of in Asia Minor, where they were represented with horses' ears and tails and were connected with fountains and running water and were credited with the gift of prophecy. That same King Midas by mixing wine in a fountain is said to have caught a Silenus and forced him to tell him the future. The Sileni, like other rural deities, were musicians. To Athena is attributed the discovery of the flute, but when she saw what distortion of face its use required, she threw it aside in disgust. It was picked up by the Silenus, Mar'syas, who became so skilful in its use that he impudently challenged Apollo to a musical contest When the prize of victory, as was right, had been adjudged to Apollo and his lyre, Marsyas paid a terrible penalty, for Apollo had him flayed and

Fig. 54. Faun of Praxiteles.

Silent: Marsyas Midas.

his empty skin hung on a tree as a warning to
all.   Some say that Midas was present at this
contest and that in punishment for his foolish
judgment in favor of the Silenus he was given

Fig. 55. Athena and Marsyas.

ass's ears.   Ovid, however, tells that this indig-
nity came upon him for his decision in favor of
Pan in a musical contest with Apollo.   The king
tried to hide his deformity by wearing a large
turban, but his barber, unable to contain the se-

cret, dug a hole in the ground and whispered it to the earth. On that place reeds grew up and, as they rustled in the wind, ever repeated, " Midas has ass's ears." [24]

The Sileni usually appear as the most repulsive and ludicrous of Dionysus' company. They have short, bloated bodies, and ugly, drunken faces;

Fig. 56.   Apollo and Marsyas.

they are rarely separated from their cherished wine-skins. The original and higher type is retained when Silenus appears as the nurse of Dionysus; in Greece he was sometimes regarded simply as the eldest of the Satyrs and was represented accordingly.

[24] *Ovid, Metamorphoses,* XI. 146 ff.

nymphs.

The name *nymph* in Greek simply means *young woman;* it is used of all those nature-spirits of trees and brooks, woods and hills, that were conceived under maiden form.   In their groves and brooks they lived, spinning and weaving, singing and dancing in the meadows, or, when no one was by to see them, bathing in the clear springs. They accompanied Artemis in the chase, followed Dionysus' noisy throng, or played and quarreled with the mischievous Satyrs.   Sometimes, too, they loved mortal men, and many of the heroes had nymphs for mothers or for brides; but it was an uncertain relationship, for often the mortal, longing for his own people, deserted his nymph, or she grew tired of human restraints and returned to her wilds.

There were different kinds of nymphs.   The Naiads were the bright elusive spirits of the springs and brooks, the Oreads were the mountain spirits, the Dryads and Hamadryads lived in the trees.   Unlike a god, a nymph was not immortal, and when the hour came and the tree died, the Dryad died too.   When some woodsman felled a great tree in the forest. he turned aside with a murmured prayer as it fell, for then the nymph sighing passed out of her body and vanished.   The Greek writer Hesiod says that a crow lives nine times as long as a man, a deer four times as long as a crow, a raven three times as long as a deer, a phœnix nine times as long as a raven, and a nymph ten times as long as a phœnix.

Echo was a nymph whom Pan loved and pursued, but she loved a Satyr, or, as others say, she loved the beautiful youth Nar cis'sus. He did not return her love, but seeing his own reflexion in a stream, loved that, and ever gazing into his own eyes, withered away with vain passion. Then Echo, too. pined from disappointed love until she was nothing but a disembodied voice that lives on among the rocks and hills.

The nymphs were worshiped throughout Greece, and offerings of lambs, milk, oil, and wine were brought to their groves and grottoes.

CHAPTER X

THE WORLD OF THE DEAD

The Greek view of death. THE Greeks, who found in this world so much that was interesting, beautiful, and heroic, utterly dreaded the coming of death to take them from this very real present life and plunge them into an unknown future. They believed, indeed, in a life after death, but it was a shadowy and unreal one, not to be compared to the most humdrum existence on the sun-lit earth. The great hero Achilles, when his shade appeared before Odysseus on his visit to the world of the dead, earnestly declared:

Nay, speak not comfortably to me of death, O great Odysseus! Rather would I live upon the earth as the hireling of another, with a landless man that hath no great livelihood, than bear sway among all the dead that be departed. (*Odyssey*, XI. 488 ff.)

The realm of the dead. Just where the realm of the dead was is uncertain. In the *Odyssey* Homer tells of a land far to the west, by the river Ocean, beyond the setting of the sun, where in eternal darkness and mist lived the souls of the departed; but generally people thought of this gloomy land as being far beneath the earth, in the darkness of the lower world. Near Cumæ, in the vicinity of Naples, where volcanic vapors, hot springs, and strange upheavals of the ground suggest the nearness of mysterious powers below the earth, a cave with unexplored depths offered entrance to the land of the dead, and A ver'nus, a lake whence rose deadly vapors, was thought to' be but the overflow of the rivers of Hades. Other localities in Greece and the islands afforded passage for the departing soul to its long home, and permitted occasional intercourse between the dead and the living.

To this gloomy land, wherever it was, the soul, when it left the body, journeyed under the guidance of the god Hermes. Though the body of the dead might lie upon his bed in his own home, or upon the battle-field, the soul, thought of as a tiny winged creature in form like the living man, but insubstantial and shadowy, joined the great throng of pale shades that were always unhappily waiting on the shores of the river Ach'e ron. Here he must wait in uneasy expectation until the friends he had left behind him should give his body due burial with sacrifice and provide him with a small coin, an obol, for his passage money. Only then would old Charon, the terrible ferryman of the dead, receive him into his leaky skiff and set him across the hated stream. For all Hades was cut off from approach by its rivers,

The journey of the soul after death.

Acheron, River of Woe, and its branches, Cocy'tus, River of Wailing, and Phleg'e thon, River of Fire. The fourth river of Hades was the Styx, by which the gods swore their unbreakable oaths. Once across the Acheron the soul

Fig. 57. Charon in his Skiff.

must pass by the three-headed watch-dog, Cer'ber us, to appease whom he was provided with a little cake made of seed and honey. Then he entered through the wide gates of Hades into that immense home of the dead, open in hospitality to all men, as the Greeks grimly said.

Here Hades, or Pluto reigned, the dark and hateful brother of Zeus, and beside him the stolen Persephone (Proserpina), no longer young and happy as when she played with the nymphs in the bright fields of Sicily, but stern and cruel on the throne beside her black lord.   When the Cyclopes gave to Zeus the thunderbolts and to Poseidon the trident as the symbols of their power, they gave to Pluto the helmet of darkness that made its wearer invisible.   Only twice do we hear of the infernal king leaving his kingdom to appear in the light of the sun; once when he came to carry off Persephone, and again when the hero Heracles had wounded him, he was forced to visit Olympus to get the help of the divine physician.   Pluto had deputed judges to weigh each dead man's good and evil deeds and assign each to his proper place — Minos (see p. 230) the former just king of Crete, his brother Rhad a-man'thus, and Æ'a cus (see p. 283), the righteous grandfather of the hero Achilles.   If the soul was condemned, the Furies, or Eu men'i des, avengers of crime, terrible with their snaky locks, drove the criminal before them to a place of punishment yet lower than Hades and buried in threefold night, while the righteous were led to the place of the Blessed.[25]

---

[25] This conception of a judgment with its consequent punishment and reward was not developed until long after the time of Homer.

Tartarus.

In the place of torment, Tar'tar us, were those Titans whom Zeus had overthrown, the rebellious giants, and wicked men who here paid the penalty for their crimes against the gods. Impious Ix-i'on for his inhuman cruelties was bound to a fiery wheel and racked and torn by its swift revolutions. Sis'y phus (see p. 236), who tried to cheat even Death, must forever roll up-hill a heavy stone, which ever rolled down. Tantalus (see p. 281), who abused the hospitality of the gods, ever tortured by hunger and consuming thirst, tried vainly to reach fruits hung just above his head, or stooped to drink the water which always eluded his parched lips. From this comes our word *tantalize*. The forty-nine daughters of Dan'a us, who had murdered their husbands, hopelessly fetched water in leaky vessels. (See p. 199.) All the air sounded with groans and shrieks, and the Furies drove the victims who would escape back to their endless torture.

The Elysian Fields.

The Elysian Fields were originally regarded as the last home only of a few favored heroes, sons of the gods, but afterwards men thought of them as peopled by others too, those who, through their noble lives or perhaps through participation in the Mysteries of Demeter, were admitted to this glorious companionship. These fortunate ones lived in calm happiness in the Elysian Fields or Island of the Blest.

Far from gods and men, at the farthest end of the earth, in the deep-flowing ocean, where the earth bears thrice in a year.— Hesiod, *Works and Days*, 197 ff.

No snow is there, nor yet great storm, nor any rain; but always ocean sendeth forth the breeze of the shrill west to blow cool on men.— *Odyssey*, IV. 566 ff.

Here the heroes feasted or wandered together through the flowery fields, contended in games

Fig. 58. Heracles carrying off Cerberus.

and enjoyed a repetition of the pleasures of the upper world.[26]

Though the lower world was generally closed to the living, yet some few heroes visited it in life. Heracles came to carry off the watch-dog Cerberus. The hero Odysseus (Ulysses) came

Visits of heroes to the lower world.

[26] It is not possible to give a simple and consistent account of the life after death that will accord with the various descriptions in the Greek poetry of different periods.

by the advice of the sorceress Circe, to ask about his future course. Æneas, the Trojan ancestor of the Romans, came for the same purpose. These stories will be told in detail later on. (See pp. 223, 311, 343.)

Orpheus and Enrydice. One man won his entrance and safe departure through his divine gift of music. This was Or'pheus, son of Apollo and the Muse Calliope, who had learned from his father to play the lyre so marvelously that at his song wild beasts became tame, serpents came out of the earth to listen, the very stones obeyed his will. When his wife Eu ryd'i ce died from the sting of a snake, he followed her to Hades, by his music persuading even grim Charon and the dog Cerberus to let him pass in. Pluto, too, yielded to his song and allowed him to carry away Eurydice, on condition that he would not look back at her until he should reach the upper world. But just as they were about to come to the light of earth, the desire to see his beloved wife overpowered Orpheus, and he turned and looked at her. Then Hermes gently took Eurydice by the hand and led her back to the home of the dead. Orpheus refused to be comforted and rejected the advances of all other women. In the end, he met his death by the violence of some frenzied Bacchantes. Charmed by his music, the stones they threw fell harmless at his feet, until the mad shouts of the women drowned the strains of his lyre. Then

Fig. 59. Parting of Orpheus and Eurydice.

they killed him and tore him limb from limb. His head and lyre, floating down the river, still gave forth melodious sounds. The Muses buried the fragments of his body, and above his grave the song of the nightingale is sweeter than anywhere else in the world.

PART II
THE HEROES

CHAPTER XI

STORIES OF ARGOS

THE family of Dan'a us and his famous de- Danaüs and his fifty daughters. scendant Perseus sprang from that Io, the daughter of the river-god In'a chus, whom Zeus had loved. (See p. 24.) Still in the form of a heifer, she came to Egypt, where she was restored to her human form and gave birth to a son. Some of her descendants remained in Egypt and ruled there as kings.

One of these Egyptian kings had two sons, Æ gyp'tus and Danaüs, of whom the former was the father of fifty sons and the latter of as many daughters. Danaüs had cause to fear his nephews, and when they wished to marry his daughters, he fled to Argolis; but Ægyptus and his sons followed them and pressed the marriage. While pretending to yield, Danaüs ordered his daughters to carry concealed daggers and each to murder her husband on the wedding night. Forty-nine of the fifty obeyed, but the fiftieth, Hy perm nes'tra, spared her husband, Lynceus. About the fate of the forty-nine there is some difference of opinion. Some say that Danaüs found suitors so scarce after this that he was compelled

to give them to the contestants in a race. Others
say that Lynceus killed them all to avenge his
brothers, and that they were punished in Hades
by being compelled eternally to carry water in
leaky vessels. Perhaps these Da na'i des represent the springs of Argolis, whose waters quickly
run away and are absorbed by the dry and porous
soil of that country.

Danaë and Perseus. Hypermnestra and Lynceus had a grandson
named A cris'i us, to whom was born one daugh-
ter, Danaë, and no son. When he sent to the
oracle at Delphi to know whether he might hope
for a male child, he received the answer that he
was fated to have no son and that he should meet
death at the hands of a son of Danaë. Hoping
to avoid this danger, he had a great bronze chamber constructed in the earth, and here he imprisoned his daughter with her nurse. After some
years, when he was one day passing near the
opening of this strong prison, he was astonished
to hear the voice of a little child at play. Summoning his daughter before him he inquired who
was the father of her child. She answered him
that through the opening in the roof of her prison
Zeus had come to her in the form of a golden
shower, and that it was he who was the father
of her child, Perseus. Acrisius, by no means believing this story and determined to be rid of
his dangerous grandson, had the mother and child
shut up in a great chest and set adrift on the

Fig. 60. Carpenter making the chest for Danaë and
Perseus.

sea.   The Greek poet Simonides tells of the love
and despair of the young mother:

When, in the carven chest,
The winds that blew and waves in wild unrest
Smote her with fear, she, not with cheeks unwet,
Her arms of love round Perseus set,
    And said: O child, what grief is mine!

But thou dost slumber, and thy baby breast
Is sunk in rest,
Here in the cheerless brass-bound bark,
Tossed amid starless night and pitchy dark.
  Nor dost thou heed the scudding brine
Of waves that wash above thy curls so deep,
Nor the shrill winds that sweep,—
Lapped in thy purple robe's embrace,
Fair little face!
But if this dread were dreadful too to thee,
Then wouldst thou lend thy listening ear to me;
Therefore I cry,— Sleep, babe, and sea be still,
And slumber our unmeasured ill.
  Oh! may some change of fate, sire Zeus, from thee
Descend, our woes to end!
But if this prayer, too overbold, offend
  Thy justice, yet be merciful to me! [27]

Zeus did not fail to hear her cry, but guided
the chest to the island of Se ri'phus, where a
fisherman, Dictys by name, drew it ashore in his
net. Unlike the other inhabitants of the island,
he was a kindly man and he cared for the unfortunate castaways in his own home.

The quest of the gorgon's head.

It happened · that a brother of the fisherman,
Pol y dec'tes, who was king of the island, fell in
love with Danaë and, as he was an unjust and
cruel man, wished to make her accept his love
even against her will. But by this time Perseus
had grown into a particularly strong and brave
young man, and Polydectes was afraid of him.
He therefore formed a plan to get him out of his

[27] Translation by John Addington Symonds.

way. Inviting a number of young men to a feast, he asked them each to bring him some valuable gift. Perseus impulsively declared that he was ready to attempt anything, even to getting the head of the gorgon Me du'sa, the most impossible feat imaginable. Now Medusa had once been a beautiful maiden, who was over-proud of her beauty, and especially of her glorious hair.

Fig. 61. Head of Medusa.

When she dared to compare herself to Athena, the goddess avenged the insult by turning her hair into snakes and her face into so terrible a sight, with its great glaring eyes, and its huge mouth with protruding tongue, that any one who looked upon it was turned to stone. Polydectes caught at Perseus' offer, and while he demanded only a horse as a gift from each of the other young men, he insisted that nothing but this horrible head would be acceptable from him. One cannot wonder that Perseus was thrown into the depths of despair at the thought of this hopeless adventure.

As he wandered along the shore, however, Hermes met him, urged him not to lose hope, and instructed him how he should accomplish the task. · For his success three things were necessary, the helmet of Hades, which made its wearer invisible, the winged sandals, and the magic wallet. These were in the care of the nymphs, and no one could tell him where these nymphs were except the Græ′æ, three extraordinary old women who had among them just one tooth and one great bright eye. Hermes, therefore, sent Perseus off under the guidance of Athena, to find these old women.

The Grææ. But when Perseus came to them, the Græ æ refused to tell him where the nymphs lived, and it was only when he adroitly seized the eye, as the old women passed it from one to another, that he compelled them to tell him what he wanted upon pain of being forever deprived of sight. Having thus found the nymphs and having received from them the helmet of Hades, the winged sandals, and the magic wallet, still under the guidance of Hermes and Athena the young hero flew far away to the west, where the stream of Ocean encircles the world. Here, by the shore, were sleeping the gorgons, Medusa and her two terrible and immortal sisters.

Fig. 62. Perseus killing Medusa.

Now the wise Athena had warned Perseus that he must not look directly at the gorgons, but must fly down from above, guiding himself by

The gorgon Medusa slain.

the reflection in his brightly polished shield. Perseus did exactly as he was told, and with one blow of his sharp sword severed Medusa's head from her body, and thrust it into the magic wallet. But the two sisters were awakened by the hissing of the snakes, and as the hero flew away on the winged sandals, they pursued him and would certainly have caught him had not the helmet of Hades made him invisible.

Atlas turned to stone. On his return journey, Perseus came to the entrance of the Mediterranean Sea, where the giant Atlas ruled, rich in flocks and herds and proud of his Garden of the Hes per'i des, where grew trees of golden apples. Now Atlas had learned from an oracle that one day a son of Zeus would come who would rob him of the cherished golden fruit. When, therefore, Perseus came, announcing himself as the son of Zeus and demanding rest and a hospitable welcome, Atlas not only refused him but tried violently to drive him from his land. Perseus was no match for the giant in strength, but he drew from the wallet the terrible gorgon's head. Atlas was changed into a mountain; his beard and hair became trees, and his bones, rocks; his head towered high among the clouds, and the sky with all its stars rested upon his shoulders. This is the Mt. Atlas in Africa that still guards the entrance to the Mediterranean Sea, rising opposite Gibraltar.

Next the hero came to the land of Ethiopia, Perseus and Andromeda. where Cepheus and his wife Cas si o pe'a ruled. Because the queen had boasted that she was more beautiful than the ocean nymphs, Poseidon in

Fig. 63. Atlas supporting the Heavens.

anger had sent a terrible sea-monster to devastate the coast, and the oracle had pronounced that only by the sacrifice of the princess An drom'e da could the land be freed from this terror. So, when Perseus came flying by on his winged sandals, he saw a lovely maiden chained to a rock and raising tearful eyes to heaven. He stopped, learned of the cruel sacrifice, and secured from Cepheus the promise that if he should kill the monster and free the maiden, he should have her as his wife. The sword that had severed Medusa's head from her body now put an end to Poseidon's monster, and the grateful parents received the conqueror as a worthy son-in-law. But while they were celebrating the wedding-feast, Phineus, to whom Andromeda's hand had been promised, but who had held back while the terrible sea-serpent threatened, rushed in with a strong band of followers and attempted to claim his bride and slay his courageous rival. Again Medusa's head was drawn out, and Phineus and his company were turned to stone.

Polydectes turned to stone. During Perseus' absence Polydectes had become more violent and tyrannical than ever, and Dictys and Danaë had been compelled to take refuge at a shrine. Here they were when the hero returned in triumph to Seriphus. Polydectes was seated in the midst of his wicked court, assembled to witness the discomfiture of the foolish young man who had gone out on such an impossible adventure. Even when Perseus came before them and showed the wallet, the king refused to believe that it contained the dreadful head. As the company looked scornfully on him, the hero drew forth the head, and instantly Polydectes and his whole court became stone images. Dictys was made king of Seriphus, the gorgon's head was presented to Athena, on whose breast-plate, or ægis, it ever after appeared, and Perseus, accompanied by his mother and his bride, returned to his native land of Argos.

The hero's grandfather, Acrisius, had heard that his grandson was coming and had fled to another town to avoid his fate, but Perseus, innocent of any evil intention, followed him, wishing to persuade him to return. In an athletic contest Perseus threw a discus, which, bounding aside, hit Acrisius on the foot, thus causing his death and bringing the fulfilment of the old prophecy. After this Perseus felt unwilling to succeed to the throne of his grandfather; he therefore effected an exchange with his cousin and became king of Mycenæ and Tiryns.

CHAPTER XII

HERACLES (HERCULES)

Of all the heroes, Her'a cles, better known by
his Roman name, Her'cu les, was by far the most
widely honored and the greatest, and the stories
of his deeds of prowess are many. His mother
was Alc me'na, a grandchild of Perseus, and a
daughter of E lec'try on, king of Mycenæ. Her
father married her to a famous warrior, Am-
phi'try on by name, who by accident killed his
father-in-law and was forced with his wife to
flee to Thebes. On one occasion when Amphitryon was away fighting, Zeus visited Alcmena
in the form of her husband, and later, when twin
sons were born to her, the one, Heracles, was
declared to be Zeus's son, while the other was the
son of Amphitryon.

Now just before Heracles' birth Zeus had declared in the assembly of the gods that a descend-
ant of Perseus would soon be born who should
rule mightily over Mycenæ. Hera, always jealous of Zeus's children by other wives, plotted to
foil his purpose. She extracted from him a
promise that the child first born on a certain day

Fig. 64. Heracles.

should be the ruler in that land.   Having secured
this, she retarded the birth of Heracles and
brought his cousin Eu rys'theus first to the light.
Nor did her jealous hatred end there, for throughout his life Heracles suffered labors and great
unhappiness at her hands.

His troubles and dangers began in his babyhood.   For one night when Heracles and his twin
brother were ten months old, their mother had
laid them side by side in their father's great
curved shield, and rocking the shining cradle had
hushed them to sleep: " Sleep, my babes, sleep
sweetly and light; sleep, brothers twain, goodly
children.   Heaven prosper your slumbering now
and your awakening to-morrow."   At midnight
Hera sent two terrible serpents with evil gleaming eyes and poisonous fangs to kill Heracles.
Then the babies awoke, and the mortal's son cried
aloud and tried to slip from the cradle, but Heracles gripped the poisonous serpents by the
throats and strangled them with his baby hands.
Alcmena heard the cry and called upon her husband to make haste and see what was wrong.
Calling on his slaves to follow, Amphitryon
sprang from his bed and rushed to the cradle.
There was Heracles capering with joy and holding out the strangled serpents for his father to
see.   His parents, appalled at the evil omen, consulted a seer as to what it might mean, and were
told that their son was to be a mighty hero, who,

Heracles
strangles the
serpents.

after many labors, should go to share the life of the immortals.[28]

Heracles' education. So Heracles, commonly known as Amphitry-on's son, grew strong and active; from his father

Fig. 65.   Heracles strangling the Serpents.

he learned to drive a chariot, from a son of Hermes all kinds of athletic games, and from a son of Apollo he learned music. This unfortunate tutor was the first to feel his pupil's power, for in a moment of rage the boy killed him with a blow of his lyre. Then Amphitryon sent him

[28] Theocritus, *Idyl* XXIV.

to be brought up among the shepherds. It is told that once at cross-roads Heracles met two women, Duty and Pleasure, and that each asked him to take her as his guide. Notwithstanding the enticing offers Pleasure made him, the hero chose Duty and followed her through life.

When he was grown, Heracles married the daughter of the king of Thebes. But Hera, who

The Twelve Labors.

Fig. 66. Five of Heracles' Labors.

still hated Alcmena's son, sent a cursed madness upon him so that he threw his own children into the fire. Seeking purification from his crime, he left his country and his wife and journeyed to Delphi. The god commanded that he should serve his cousin Eurystheus and so make atonement. Thus, as Hera had planned, Zeus's son became the servant of Eurystheus, at whose bidding he performed twelve great labors. The number was twelve because Heracles is a sun-god, and the labors follow the course of the sun through the months, beginning near at hand in Argolis and ending in the lower world.

(1) The Nemean Lion. A ferocious lion, whose lair was a cave in the mountains of Argolis, was ravaging the country round. Eurystheus ordered Heracles to rid him of this terror. Finding that his arrows did not even pierce the beast's hide, Heracles finally caught him in his cave and strangled him; then he bore him back to Mycenæ. But Eurystheus was so terrified by the sight of the dead lion that he ordered the hero never thereafter to enter the city, but to display his spoils outside the walls. The skin of the lion, impervious to all weapons, Heracles always afterwards wore.

(2) The Lernean Hydra. In the marsh of Lerna, also in Argolis, lived the Hydra, a serpent with nine heads, and so poisonous that its touch or its foul breath caused death. This beast Heracles attacked with his sword, but finding that as he cut off one head two grew in its place, he ordered his nephew and faithful companion Io la'us, to burn each neck the instant he had severed the head. One head was immortal; this he buried under a stone. The Hydra seems to represent the malaria coming from a marsh, until it is dried up by the sun.

(3) The Erymanthian Boar. The scene of the next three labors was Arcadia. First, Heracles caught a fierce wild boar in a net and brought it alive to Eurystheus, who was so fearful of it that he jumped into a large jar and only peeped out at it over the rim.

Next, a golden-horned doe, unlike most does (4) The Cerynian Doe. very dangerous, had to be caught. Its brazen hoofs never knew fatigue, and it led Heracles a chase for a whole year before it was caught and brought to Mycenæ.

Near the Stym pha'li an Lake lived huge birds (5) The Stymphalian Birds. with arrow-like feathers and mighty talons, who

Fig. 67. Heracles killing the Hydra.

used to snatch men and beasts and carry them away. At Athena's suggestion, Heracles aroused these birds with cymbals and then shot them with arrows which he had dipped in the Hydra's poison.

His next task carried the hero to Elis, where (6) The Stables of Augeas. he was sent to clean the stables of Au ge'as, which had not been cleaned in thirty years. This he ac-

complished by turning the course of the river
Alphe'us so that it flowed through the stables.
King Augeas cheated him of the reward he had
promised, and later, when he was free, Heracles
took vengeance upon him and, at the same time,

Fig. 68.   Heracles carrying the Boar.

established in Elis the Olympic Games in honor
of his father Zeus.

(7) The Cretan Bull.   King Minos of Crete had been presented with
a beautiful bull by Poseidon, but, as he refused
to offer it in sacrifice, it had been driven mad
and was a menace to the whole island.   Heracles
tamed the brute and rode it across the sea back
to Greece.   Later the bull escaped and went to

Marathon, where the hero Theseus finally killed it.

Di o me'des was a son of Ares and ruled as (8) The Horses of Diomedes. king in the savage land of Thrace. He had marvelous horses whom he fed on the flesh of men. When Heracles attempted to capture these fierce beasts, the Thracians in great numbers attacked him, but he and Iolaüs drove them off and bore the horses back to Eurystheus.

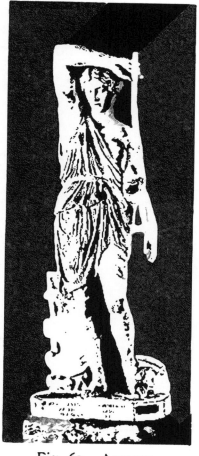

Fig. 69. Amazon.

Hip pol'y ta was at this time the queen of the Amazons, a warlike tribe of women that lived near the Euxine Sea. Ares had given her a girdle, and Eurystheus' daughter coveted it. When Heracles arrived at her court and asked for the gir- (9) The Girdle of Hippolyta. dle, Hippolyta was so struck by his strength and beauty that she would have given it him, had not Hera, unwilling that he should get off so easily, roused the other Amazons to attack him. Then Heracles, thinking that the queen had played him false, killed her. On his way home from this adventure, when he had come to Troy, he found the king La om'e don in great trouble. For when Poseidon and Apollo had built for him the walls of his city, he had failed to give them the reward he had promised. Poseidon had, therefore, sent a dreadful sea-monster to ravage the coast, and nothing would free the city from this terror but that He si'o ne, Laomedon's daughter, should be offered to the monster. The maiden was waiting to be devoured when Heracles came and agreed to kill the serpent in return for the gift of some wonderful horses that Laomedon had received from Zeus in payment for his stolen son, Gan'y mede. The incorrigible king cheated Heracles, too, and later paid for his dishonesty with his life.

(10) The Cattle of Geryon. His tenth labor called Heracles to the far west, where the sun sinks into the stream of Ocean. Here lived Ge'ry on, an extraordinary being with three bodies, six legs and six arms, and a pair of monstrous wings. He was very rich, and thousands of glorious red cattle fed on his land under the guard of an ever watchful dog and a strong herdsman. Heracles sailed thither in a golden bowl, which the sun had given him, using his lion's skin as a sail. As he passed through the straits that separate Europe from Africa, he landed and set up the Pillars of Hercules as a monument of his feat. On arriving at the country of Geryon he was attacked first by the dog and then by the herdsman, but he killed them both, and finally, after a terrific struggle, crushed Geryon himself and drove off the cattle. Just

Fig. 70. Heracles in the bowl of the Sun.

what route he took on his homeward way it is difficult to say, but he seems to have visited all the lands of western Europe and to have had many adventures and done many marvelous deeds. On the Aventine Hill, later a part of Rome, he met and killed the giant Cacus, who had stolen some of his cattle, dragging them off to his cave by the tails so that their tracks might mislead Heracles. But the other cattle lowed as they passed the cave, and the captives answered them, thus betraying the hiding-place. Approaching Greece from the north, at last he brought the cattle to Eurystheus, who sacrificed them to Hera.

(11) The Apples of the Hesperides.

When Zeus had married Hera, she had presented him with some golden apples, which were kept up in the north near the land of the Hyperboreans and were guarded by a dragon. To learn just where to find them Heracles must catch and hold Nereus, the Old Man of the Sea, who, like Proteus, had the power of changing his form. But whether he became a raging lion or a flame of fire or flowing water, Heracles held him fast and at length had his question answered. On his way he had various adventures, for in Libya he met the giant Antæus, a son of Earth, who was accustomed to challenge all comers to wrestle with him. As every time he fell to earth he rose with redoubled strength, he had always been the victor, and a temple near by was adorned with the skulls of his victims. Heracles conquered him by holding him up in his arms, away from his mother Earth, until he crushed in his ribs. While the hero was sleeping after this combat, the Pygmies swarmed about him and tried to bury him alive in the sand, but he awoke and amused himself by picking them up and bundling them into his lion's skin to carry home with him. In Egypt the king tried to sacrifice him, as he did all strangers, to Zeus, but Heracles burst his bonds and dashed out the brains of his captors. In the Caucasus Mountains he found and freed Prometheus, who for ages had been bound there for having disobeyed Zeus and given fire to men. (See p. 10.) At last he came to the garden where the apples grew and there found Atlas holding up the heavens. (This would make it seem that the garden was in the west, but mythological geography is sometimes hard to follow.) He persuaded Atlas to get the apples for him, taking the giant's burden while he was gone. Atlas returned with the apples but refused to take up his burden again, preferring to be the bearer of the apples to Eurystheus. Heracles, pretending to agree, asked him to take the heavens only for one moment while he put a cushion on his shoulder. The stupid giant was taken in, and, of course, once the transfer had been made, Heracles went on his way leaving Atlas to his old burden.[29]

His twelfth and last labor took Heracles to the lower world. Here he was guided and assisted by Athena and Hermes, and with their help safely passed by the dangers of the way and

(12) Cerberus.

[29] Cf. the story of Perseus turning Atlas to stone, p. 207; such inconsistencies are due to the independent development of the separate stories.

came to the presence of King Pluto. The king agreed to let him take the three-headed watch-dog, Cerberus, if he could get him without using a weapon. This his great strength enabled him to do, and he took the dog to Mycenæ. Cerberus was afterwards returned to the lower world.

The Service of Omphale. Although his twelve labors were now ended, Heracles had no rest; Hera's hate still pursued him. While he was staying with a certain king, he killed his host's son, out of resentment for an imagined injury, and because of this violation of hospitality he suffered from a painful illness. When he went to Delphi to ask how he might escape this trouble, Apollo refused to answer, whereupon Heracles stole the tripod and was about to set up an oracle of his own. Apollo hastened to defend his sacred shrine, and the combatants were parted only by a thunderbolt from Zeus. They thereupon swore loyal friend-ship with one another, and Apollo gave the hero an answer to his question. He might expiate his crime by having himself sold as a slave at public auction and giving the price to the family of the slain man. Om'pha le, Queen of Libya, having bought him, he served her faithfully for the allotted term. Part of the time he was fighting his mistress' enemies and keeping her country from harm, but most of the time he sat at her feet in womanish clothes, employed in spinning and weaving and other feminine tasks.

At the end of his term of service he turned his attention to avenging himself on the faithless Laomedon. Assembling a force of men and ships he attacked Troy and took it, putting to the sword the king and all his sons except Priam. Him he made king in his father's place.

The destruction of Troy.

On his return to Greece he married De jan i'ra, after fighting and conquering her former unwelcome lover, the river-god Ach e lo'us. Ancheloüs in the struggle took the form of a bull, and the horn which Heracles broke off was afterwards used as the horn of plenty or cornucopia.[30] After this victory again he was attacked by his madness and killed a boy at his father-in-law's court. Self-exiled, with his wife, he left the country, and starting again on his wanderings, came to a river where the centaur Nessus acted as ferryman. When Nessus, after carrying Dejanira over on his back, attempted to run away with her, Heracles drew one of his poisoned arrows and shot him. Before he died he gave Dejanira a vial filled with his own blood, telling her that if her husband's love ever seemed to fail she should dip a robe in the blood and his love would be restored.

Dejanira and Nessus.

Not long after this the hero undertook to punish a king who had once refused to give him his daughter in marriage. He took the city and car-

The death of Heracles.

[30] Some say that the horn of plenty was the horn of the goat Amalthea; see p. 7.

ried off the princess I'o le as his captive.   Stop-
ping on his way home to sacrifice to Zeus, he sent
a messenger to get him a suitable garment to wear

Fig. 71. Nessus running off with Dejanira.

at the sacrifice.   Then Dejanira, fearing that his
love had turned from her to the captive Iole,
remembered the centaur's advice and sent him a
robe that she had dipped in the blood.   When

Heracles put it on, it clung to his body and ate into his flesh like fire. In his agony he threw the messenger that had brought the garment into the sea, and then, preferring death to such torture, having ordered a great funeral-pyre to be raised on a mountain-top, he laid himself upon it and begged his friends to set fire to it. All refused to be responsible for the hero's death, until at length Phil oc te'tes, partly from pity and partly because of Heracles' offer of his famous bow and arrows, applied the torch. Amid columns of smoke, and thunder and lightning sent by Zeus to glorify the end of his son, the hero's spirit left the earth. Thereafter he was taken into Olympus and made a god, and Hera, relenting, gave him to wife her own daughter Hebe. His earthly wife Dejanira, in grief and remorse, killed herself.

Heracles was worshiped both as a hero and as a god, and was called upon especially in the palestra and in all athletic contests. Young men regarded him as their special friend and helper. In Athens a temple was built in honor of Heracles, the Warder off of Evil, in memory of his many good deeds to men, and in Rome, as Hercules, he was worshiped as the Unconquered and the Defender. He is represented as a gigantic man of remarkable muscular development. His lion's skin hangs over his shoulder and his club is in his hand.

The worship of Heracles.

CHAPTER XIII

STORIES OF CRETE, SPARTA, CORINTH, AND ÆTOLIA

I. STORIES OF CRETE

Europa.[31] EU RO′PA, the daughter of the Phœnician king, with her friends and companions was one day

Fig. 72. Europa on the Bull.

gathering flowers in the meadows by the seashore; merrily they were filling their baskets with

[31] Following Moschus, *Idyl* II.

daffodils and lilies, violets and roses, contending who could gather the most. Looking down from his high heaven on the pretty group, Zeus marked the princess Europa in the midst, preëminent among her companions, just as Aphrodite is preëminent among the Graces. To see her was to desire her for his own, so he laid aside his scepter and his thunderbolt and put on the form of a white bull, a beautiful bull that had never felt the yoke nor drawn the plow. So he came into the flowery meadow, and the maidens did not fear him but gathered around him and began to stroke his snowy sides. At Europa's touch he lowed gently and beseechingly and kneeling down looked back at her with gentle, loving eyes as if to invite her to his broad white back. She spoke to her playmates and said: "Come, dear companions, let us ride on this bull's back, for he looks kind and mild, not at all like other bulls, and so like a man's is his understanding that he lacks only the power of speech." So she sat down smiling upon his back, and the others would have followed her, but suddenly the bull, having gained what he wanted, stood up and in all haste made for the sea.

Then Europa stretched out her hands to her companions, crying aloud for help. But already they had reached the shore, and still the bull rushed on, right over the waves with hoofs unwet. The Nereids rose from the waters and frolicked about them, riding on the dolphins; Poseidon, calming the waves, guided them on their watery path, and the Tritons, trumpeting on their long shells, sounded the marriage-hymn. Europa, holding with one hand to the horn of the bull and with the other holding up her long robe that it might not be wet with the waves, spoke to the bull: "Whither are you bearing me, O godlike bull? It is clear that you are a god, for none but a god could do this thing. Alas! why did I ever leave my father's house to follow you and to journey alone on such a strange sea-voyage!" And the bull answered: "Take heart, dear maiden, and fear not the salt sea-waves, for I am Zeus himself, and it is love of you that has driven me to journey over the sea in the form of a bull. Soon Crete shall receive you, and the island that nourished me as an infant shall be your wedding-place, and there you shall bear me famous sons that shall rule as kings."

Minos I, and Minos II.   In Crete, then, Europa bore to Zeus three sons, of whom one, Minos, became king of the island, and by his just and enlightened rule brought civilization and prosperity to his country and extended its power over neighboring lands. After his death, in consideration of his righteousness and wisdom, he and his brother Rhadamanthus were made judges of the dead in the lower world. (See p. 189.) Minos II, the grandson of this Minos,

Fig. 73. Dædalus and Icarus.

seems to have been of very different character;
for when, in answer to prayer, Poseidon had sent
him from the sea a splendid white bull for sacrifice, he offered to the gods an inferior animal and
put the bull among his own herds. In punishment, Poseidon inspired in his wife an unholy
passion for the bull, so that she left her home and
followed the beast all over the island. From
their union sprang the Minotaur, half bull and
half man.

During the reign of Minos there had arrived Dædalus.
on his shores an exile from Athens, Dæ'da lus,
who was the most skilful artist and engineer of
his time. When a safe place in which to confine
the Minotaur was needed, Dædalus built the Labyrinth, so winding and complicated a structure
that no man or beast once shut inside could ever
find the exit. Notwithstanding this and other
services the artist fell under the king's displeasure
and was himself, with his son, imprisoned in the
Labyrinth he had designed. Knowing no way
of escape to be possible, he constructed for himself and his son Ic'a rus wings and fastened them
on with wax. Unfortunately, however, though
Dædalus had warned his son not to fly too near
the sun, Icarus forgot the injunction, and before
he could be recalled the wax had melted, and the
boy fell into the sea that from him was called
the Icarian Sea, the part of the Ægean between
the Cyclades and Asia Minor. Dædalus himself

made good his escape to Italy and there dedicated his wings in a temple of Apollo.

II. STORIES OF SPARTA

Castor and Polydences. The Di os cu'ri, Castor and his brother Pol y-deu'ces, the latter better known by his Roman name, Pollux, were the local heroes of Sparta.

Fig. 74. The Dioscuri (Ancient statues now set up before the king's palace in Rome).

Their mother Leda, whose mortal husband was the king Tyn da're us, had by him two children, Cly tem nes'tra, who became the wife of King Ag a mem'non of Mycenæ, and Castor. But Zeus made love to Leda, taking upon himself when he visited her the form of a swan, and to him she bore two other children, Helen, whose divine beauty brought about the Trojan War, and Polydeuces. Castor was famous as a trainer of horses, while Polydeuces was the greatest of all boxers. Between the two brothers there was so great a love that when the mortal's son, Castor, was killed, Polydeuces, immortal by virtue of his divine father, obtained permission to divide his immortality with his brother. Therefore on alternate days after their death the two were among the dead in Hades, and among the gods in heaven, where they are still visible as the bright stars, Castor and Pollux, in the constellation Gemini, or the Twins. They were patrons of sailors, to whom they appear as balls of fire upon the masts, giving promise of clear weather after a storm.[32] Among the Romans they received worship, and after the battle of Lake Regillus, fought between the Romans and the exiled Tarquins, they appeared in the Forum as two glorious youths on white horses and announced to the Romans the victory of their armies. In their honor a temple was built on the spot where they had appeared.[33]

[32] This may perhaps be identified with the phenomenon known as St. Elmo's Fire.

[33] Some say that it was Castor alone who appeared.

III. STORIES OF CORINTH

Sisyphus. Corinth, through its situation on the isthmus holding command of two seas, was from the beginning an important commercial city, and its people were known as clever business men able to outwit all comers. This reputation began with the founder of the city, Sis'yphus, who began his career by bargaining with the river-god A so'pus for the never-failing spring Pi rc'ne, on the citadel of Corinth, in return for which he was to give the river-god information about his daughter, stolen by Zeus. In punishment for this interference with his plans, Zeus sent Death to take Sisyphus. Death himself, outwitted by the shrewd Corinthian, was caught, and while he was kept in chains, no one on earth could die. This state of things could not be allowed, and Ares succeeded in freeing Death and even in giving Sisyphus over to him. Before he was haled off to the lower world, however, the king exacted in secret a promise from his wife that she would offer no funeral sacrifices. When Pluto complained bitterly of this neglect, Sisyphus, feigning righteous indignation, offered to see that his wife did the proper thing. if for the purpose he was allowed to return to the upper air. Permission was given, and once outside the gates of Hades the wily king refused to return, lived to a ripe old age and at last died a natural death. But no one may cheat the gods and escape punishment, however clever he may be. In Hades Sisyphus was condemned eternally to roll a weighty stone up a hill, which ever, as it reached the top, rolled down again.

Sisyphus' grandson Bel ler'o phon was of very different mold. In his youth he was forced into exile because he had unintentionally killed a man. Hoping to be purified he went to Tiryns, and here the wife of King Prœ'tus fell in love with him, and when he would not respond to her love,

Bellero-
phon.

Fig. 75. Chimæra.

falsely accused him to her husband. Fearing divine anger if he himself killed a guest, Prœtus sent him to the king of Lycia, and with him a secret message asking to have him slain. The king of Lycia at first treated Bellerophon with generous hospitality, but when he had read the message he sent him off on the dangerous adventure of killing the Chi mæ'ra. This beast had the fore part of a lion, the hinder part of a dragon, and in the middle the head of a goat, and breathed out fire from her nostrils. A seer consulted by Bellerophon told him that his success depended upon his catching and taming the winged horse Peg'a sus, and advised him to pass a night beside Athena's altar that he might secure the goddess' help. Pegasus was the offspring of Poseidon by Medusa, from whose neck he had sprung when Perseus cut off her head. Athena had given him to the Muses, and he had opened for them by a blow of his hoof the sacred spring of Hip po cre'ne on Mt. Hel'i con. While Bellerophon slept by her altar, Athena appeared to him and put into his hand a golden bridle, with which he easily caught Pegasus while he was drinking at the spring of Pirene. Mounted on the winged horse he flew down from above and killed the terrible Chimæra. The Lycian king sent him on other dangerous adventures and at last set an ambush to kill him. But when Bellerophon came out safe and victorious from all, the king, seeing that he was favored by the gods, gave him his daughter in marriage and half his kingdom as dowry. In time Bellerophon became so elated by his achievements that he challenged the immortal gods themselves, for he attempted to fly to Zeus's very dwelling on the winged horse. Zeus hurled a thunderbolt, and Bellero-

Fig. 76. Bellerophon and Pegasus.

phon fell to earth maimed and blinded — an example to the proud not to attempt flying too high. Pegasus came to the dwelling of Zeus and was given the honor of drawing the thunder-chariot.

IV. THE CALYDONIAN BOAR HUNT

During the time when the god-descended heroes lived in Greece, several joint expeditions were undertaken by them. One of these was the Calydonian boar hunt. Calydon was a town of Ætolia ruled over by Œneus, who was the first man of that part of Greece to learn of Dionysus the culture of the vine. He was married to Al the'a, who bore to him a son Mel e a'ger. When the boy was seven days old, the Fates told Althea that he would die when the log that was then burning on the hearth should be consumed. Hearing this Althea quenched the brand and put it away in a box.

When Meleager had grown to be a young man, one harvest time his father Œneus, offering sacrifice of the first-fruits to all the other gods, passed over Artemis alone. In anger at this neglect the goddess sent into his country a great and ferocious boar, which laid waste all the country around. Meleager summoned the heroes from all parts of Greece, promising to him who killed the boar its hide as a gift of honor. It was a very distinguished company that assembled for the hunt: Castor and Polydeuces, from Lacedæ-

mon, Theseus, from Athens, and his friend
Pi rith'o us, Jason, later the leader of the Argonauts, Am phi a ra'us of Argos, and many other
famous heroes. When the huntress At a lan'ta,

Fig. 77. Meleager.

daughter of the king of Arcadia, joined their
number, many were indignant that they should
be expected to share the danger and glory of the
enterprise with any woman, however strong, but

Meleager loved Atalanta and insisted upon her being received.

Œneus entertained the company for nine days, and on the tenth they started the hunt. Three of the number lost their lives before any one had even wounded the beast, and Atalanta was the first to strike him, shooting an arrow into his back. Then Amphiaraüs shot him in the eye, but it was Meleager who finally despatched him, piercing between his ribs. The hide, which belonged to him by right, he gave to Atalanta. This mightily enraged some of the hunters, for they thought it unworthy that a woman should 'go off with the prize of honor for which so many men had striven; therefore the two uncles of Meleager lay in wait for the maiden and took away 'the hide, declaring that it belonged to them if Meleager did not choose to keep it. Meleager killed his uncles and restored the hide to Atalanta. When the news of her brothers' murder at the hands of her son came to Althea's ears, she seized the brand from its box and threw it on the fire. As it consumed the vital strength left Meleager's body, and as it fell in ashes the spark of his life went out. Althea too late repented of her act of vengeance and took her own life. The weeping women about her were changed into birds.

CHAPTER XIV

STORIES OF ATTICA

Cecrops. THE Athenians were proud in their belief that their early kings were not, as were those of other Greek states, foreigners who had come to their shores, but true sons of Attica, born of its soil. The first king, Cecrops, who had been witness to Athena's victory in her contest with Poseidon for the city, was born, half man, half serpent, from the earth.

Erectheus. Another earthborn king was E rec'theus,[34] whose form was wholly that of a serpent. At his birth Athena took him under her protection, and gave him in a basket into the care of the three daughters of Cecrops, enjoining them, under pain of her displeasure, not to seek to know what the basket contained. Curiosity was too strong for them, and when they saw the serpent lying in the basket, they were driven mad and leaped to death off the rock of the Acropolis. Athena then brought Erectheus up in her own temple and made him king of Athens. It was he that set up the sacred wooden image of the

[34] The earthborn serpent was called by some Erecthonius, and his grandson, Erectheus.

goddess in her temple and instituted the Panathenaic Festival in her honor. At his death he was buried in the temple precinct and was afterwards worshiped with Athena in the Erectheum.

O ri thy'ia, one of the daughters of Erectheus, was wooed by Bo're as, the northeast wind, but rejected his advances. One day he came upon her as she was carrying sacrifices for Athena on the Acropolis and bore her off to his wild northern kingdom of Thrace. Boreas still conscious of his kinship to the Athenians, served the Greeks well at the time of the battle of Thermopylæ, when the Persian fleet was threatening the whole coast. The Delphic oracle ordered the Athenians to call upon their son-in-law for help, whereupon they prayed to Boreas, who answered by shattering the Persian ships at Artemisium.

Orithyia and Boreas.

Another daughter of Erectheus was Procris, who was married to a young hunter named Ceph'a lus. Aurora, goddess of the dawn, loved Cephalus and stole him away, leaving Procris inconsolable. In her loneliness she took to hunting with Artemis, from whom she received a dog that never grew tired and a javelin that never missed its mark. As Aurora could not make Cephalus forget his love for his wife, she finally sent him back, and he joyfully returned to his life as a hunter, receiving from his wife the wonderful dog and javelin. Unfortunately Procris, being of a jealous disposition and suspecting her

Cephalus and Procris.

husband of a love affair with Aura, the morning breeze, one day concealed herself in the bushes to spy on them.   Cephalus, hearing a rustling in the underbrush, thought it some wild beast, hurled his unerring javelin, and killed his wife.

Fig. 78. Cephalus and the Dawn-Goddess.

Procne and Philomela.   Procne and Phil o me'la were the daughters of another early king of Athens.   The Thracian king Tereus had married Procne, but afterwards he fell in love with the sister, Philomela, and persuaded her to marry him by telling her that Procne was dead.   To conceal this deed from his wife he cut out Philomela's tongue and imprisoned her in a hut in the woods. But she wove her story into the web of a robe and contrived to send it to her sister. At an opportunity offered by the celebration of the festival of Dionysus, Procne visited the lonely hut and brought Philomela in disguise to her palace. The two sisters then wreaked on the faithless Tereus a horrible vengeance, for Procne killed her son It'ylus and served him up to his father at a feast. When Tereus pursued the murderesses and was about to kill them, the gods transformed the three into birds, Tereus into a tufted hoo-poe, Procne into a swallow, and Philomela into the nightingale who still pours out her mournful notes, grieving over the slaying of the boy Itylus.[35]

As Heracles was the great hero of the Peloponnesus, who freed all the country around from danger, so Theseus was the hero of Attica, who cleared the roads of giants and robbers and gave liberty and unity to the city of Athens. There was a question about his birth; some said that his father was Poseidon, and alleged as a proof of this that once when King Minos, to try the hero's divine birth, threw a ring into the sea, Theseus, diving in after it, returned with the ring and a golden crown given him by Amphi-

Theseus.

[35] Some identify Procne with the nightingale and Philomela with the swallow.

trite. It was more generally supposed, however, that his father was Ægeus, the king of Athens, and his mother Æthra, daughter of the king of Trœzen. Before his son was born, Ægeus left Æthra at Trœzen, after placing his sword and sandals under a great rock with the instructions that the boy, so soon as he was strong enough to lift the stone and get them from under it, should be sent to Athens.

Theseus frees the roads of giants.

Theseus grew up clever and courageous, and tall and strong as well, so that at sixteen he easily lifted the stone and joyfully set out for Athens. His mother and grandfather urged him to go by sea, for it was a short and comparatively safe voyage, but, wishing to emulate Heracles, he preferred the perilous journey by land. On his way he met with six great adventures. First he came upon the giant Per i pha′tes, a son of Hephæstus, who brained all travelers with his iron club. Theseus overcame him and took his club. Next he met Sinis, who compelled every passer-by to help him bend down a tall pine tree and then, fastening the unfortunate by the head to the top of the tree, let it go suddenly. This fate Theseus inflicted on the giant himself. He killed a great sow that ravaged the country; some say this sow was really a woman whose foul manners earned her this name. His fourth adventure was with Sciron, a giant who kept watch on a narrow pass where the cliff falls abruptly into the sea. This giant forced all travelers to wash his feet, and when they knelt down to do so he gave them a kick that sent them into the waters below, where an enormous turtle swallowed them. Theseus gave the turtle a final feast on the giant himself. The next giant he met he overthrew in a wrestling match. Last of all he overcame Pro crus'tes, who pressed upon strangers the hospitality of his iron bed; but if they were too long, he cut them off, and if they were too short, he stretched them out to fit the bed.

When he had reached Athens and had purified himself in the river of all this slaughter, he entered the city. His long hair and his foreign appearance exciting the laughter of some builders, he took a cart that contained huge building blocks and tossed it lightly over the roof of a house. At the palace, although he did not disclose his identity, his father's new wife, the sorceress Me de'a (see p. 279), recognized him and plotted his death. She persuaded Ægeus to invite him to a feast and offer him a cup of poisoned wine. As they feasted, however, Theseus drew his sword to cut a piece of meat, and his father, instantly recognizing the weapon, dashed the poisoned cup to the floor and sprang to embrace his son. In a rage of disappointed hate, Medea called her dragon-drawn chariot and flew away. Ægeus now proclaimed Theseus as his heir.

Theseus meets his father.

Theseus kills
the Minotaur.
But the hero, thirsting for glory and adventure, first went to Marathon, where he captured the bull that Heracles had brought from Crete, and then, when the time came around for seven young men and seven maidens to be sent as a tribute from Athens to King Minos of Crete (see p. 233), he offered himself as one of their number, hoping to win their return. The tribute had come about in this way. King Minos' son had been killed by the Athenians, and Minos had besieged the city. The Athenians might have stood out against him and his army, but the gods sent a famine and pestilence upon them, and the oracle declared that the divine displeasure would not be appeased until they should accept whatever terms Minos offered. He demanded that every year seven boys and seven girls should be sent to Crete to be given to the Minotaur. When the ship bearing Theseus and the thirteen other victims started out, it was equipped with a black sail, but Theseus promised his father that should he succeed in his adventure and kill the Minotaur, on the return voyage he would change the black sail for a white one. On their arrival in Crete King Minos' daughter A ri ad'ne fell in love with the hero at first sight and secretly gave him a ball of string to enable him to thread the mazes of the Labyrinth, and a sword to kill the Minotaur. Having succeeded by this means in his difficult adventure, Theseus set sail for home,

carrying with him on his ship his benefactress Ariadne. On the island of Naxos, however, he deserted his bride while she slept,— some say because he loved some one else and wanted to get rid of her, others, because he was warned to leave her there to become the wife of Dionysus. Perhaps it was in requital of his faithlessness to

Fig. 79. Theseus killing the Minotaur.

Ariadne that the gods made him forget his promise to raise a white sail if he returned successful. For Ægeus, having watched long from a high rock for the returning ship, thinking, when he saw the black sail, that his son was dead, threw himself from the rock and was killed.

Theseus was recognized as king, and immediately set about instituting reforms. He gave

Theseus as king of Athens.

up his absolute royal power, and after uniting in one state all the divisions of Attica, he made of it a free self-governing commonwealth. After this he started out again on a career of adven-

Fig. 80. Theseus and the rescued Athenians.

ture. Like Heracles he went to the Amazons' country and from there carried off their queen Anti'ope. To recover her the Amazons besieged Athens, though Antiope herself had fallen so in love with Theseus that she fought by his side against her own people. The Amazons were driven off, but the queen was killed.

Pi rith'o us, king of the Lapiths, having heard the fame of Theseus and, wishing to make trial of him, drove off some of his cattle. Theseus pursued him, but when they had come near to one another, each was so filled with admiration of the other's noble bearing and courage that by mutual consent they gave up all thought of fight-

The battle of the Lapiths and Centaurs.

Fig. 81. Centaur and Lapith.

ing and swore an oath of friendship. Soon after this Pirithoüs celebrated his wedding and invited Theseus to attend. The Centaurs, who were also guests, becoming inflamed with wine, attempted to steal the bride. In the battle that followed Theseus fought bravely by the side of his friend Pirithoüs and the Centaurs were driven off.

The theft of Helen and Persephone.

The two friends were now fired by the ambition each to have a divine wife; Theseus, therefore, carried off Helen, the beautiful daughter of Zeus and Leda. As she was not yet of marriageable age, he left her under the care of his mother, and before he returned to claim her, her two brothers, Castor and Polydeuces, rescued her and took her back to Sparta. Pirithoüs' attempt was yet more daring, for he induced Theseus to help him carry off Pluto's wife, Persephone. Not even Theseus was strong enough for this adventure, and the two heroes were caught and chained in the lower world. Theseus' adventures might have ended here had not the mighty Heracles, in his quest for Cerberus, found and freed him. On his return to Athens he found that his people had turned against him and accepted another as king. He therefore retired to the island of Scyros, and there met his death by being thrown from a cliff.

The Theseum.

The Athenians said that at the battle of Marathon a glorious hero, whom they recognized as Theseus, appeared amongst them in full armor and led them on to victory, and after the war the oracle commanded that Theseus' bones should be brought from Scyros and given honorable burial at Athens. The Athenian leader Cimon carried out this command, and having brought the hero's remains home amid great rejoicings, interred them in the middle of the city and erected a temple in his honor. The wonderfully preserved temple in Athens called the Theseum is, unfortunately, probably misnamed, and the true shrine of Theseus has disappeared.

CHAPTER XV

STORIES OF THEBES

Cadmus'
search for
Europa. WHEN Europa had been carried off to Crete
by Zeus in the form of a beautiful white bull,
her father A ge'nor had ordered his sons to go
out in search of their sister and not to return
unless they found her. Cadmus, one of the sons,
therefore, set out from Phœnicia and wandered
for many years through the islands and coasts
of the sea, until at last, despairing of success,
he came to Delphi to consult the oracle. Apollo
told him that the search was quite vain and commanded him to follow a cow who would lead
him to the spot where he was destined to found
a new city. Hardly had Cadmus left the oracle
when the cow appeared and going before him
into Bœotia lay down near the place where later
stood the citadel of Thebes.

The founding
of Thebes. Wishing to make a sacrifice to his patron goddess Athena, Cadmus sent his men to the spring
of Ares, close at hand, to fetch water for the
purification. The spring was guarded by a terrible dragon, himself a son of Ares, and no one
of Cadmus' men returned to tell the tale. Puz-
zled at the long delay, Cadmus went himself to

the spring. There lay the bloody and mangled bodies of his companions, and over them threatened the huge triple jaws and three-forked

Fig. 82. Cadmus and the Dragon.

tongues of the dragon. At the bidding of Athena Cadmus killed the beast with a stone and sowed in the ground its huge teeth, from which sprang up a crop of armed men of more than human size and strength. Still at Athena's bidding, Cadmus threw a stone into their midst, whereupon they turned their weapons upon one another and fought on fiercely until only five were left. These five made peace with one another and with Cadmus and became under him the founders of the five great Theban families.

Harmonia's necklace. To atone for the blood of Ares' sacred dragon slain by his hand, Cadmus had to serve the god for eight years. At the end of this time Athena made him king of the new city he had founded, and Zeus gave him as wife Har mo'ni a, the daughter of Ares and Aphrodite. All the gods came down from Olympus to honor the wedding, and the Muses, led by Apollo, sang the marriage hymn. Cadmus gave to his bride a marvelous necklace; some say it was made for him by Hephæstus, and others that he received it from Europa, to whom it had been given by Zeus. Whatever was its origin, Harmonia's necklace always brought disaster to its owner; indeed, notwithstanding the splendor of his marriage, an ill fate pursued Cadmus. Hoping to avoid his destiny, he left his city and settled in Illyria, but even there the resentment of Ares pursued him. At last, quite discouraged, he declared in bitterness that, since a serpent was so cherished and so faithfully avenged by the gods, he wished that he might be one. Immediately his wish was granted and Harmonia shared his fate. The tombs of the hero and his wife were set up in the land of their exile and were guarded by their geniuses in the forms of serpents. Cadmus is credited with having introduced the alphabet into Greece from Phœnicia.

The evil fate of Cadmus pursued his descendants. One of his four daughters was Sem'e le, the mother of Bacchus, who, as was told in the account of that god (see p. 165), was burned to ashes by the brightness of her lover Zeus. Another was the mother of that unfortunate Actæon who was torn to pieces by his own dogs. (See p. 85.) A third became a votary of Bacchus and in her madness tore to pieces her own son Pentheus. (See p. 168.) The fourth inflicted and suffered terrible woes through Hera's anger at her for taking care of Semele's child Bacchus. *The descendants of Cadmus.*

The curse laid upon the family of Cadmus *Œdipus.* passed over his one son and that son's son, but fell with redoubled force in the next generation upon the family of La'i us. It was in defiance of the warning of the gods that Laius married his cousin Jo cas'ta, for an oracle had pronounced that he was destined to meet his death at the hands of a son born of that union. In order to avoid this danger he commanded that the baby born to his wife should at once be put to death. The duty was entrusted to a shepherd, who, however, being tender-hearted, could not bear to take the infant's life, but after piercing his feet and binding them with thongs, intended to leave him to his fate on Mt. Cithæron. It happened that a shepherd of the king of Corinth, who was pasturing his flocks on the mountains, received the poor maimed infant and took him to his king and queen. As they were childless, the royal couple gladly adopted him and brought him up as their own son.

The prophecy. The boy, called Œdipus or Swollen-Foot, grew up in the belief that he was the real son and rightful heir of the king of Corinth, but a certain insulting hint that he once received with regard to his birth troubled him enough to send him to Apollo's oracle at Delphi to ask the truth. He received no direct answer to his question, but was told that he was destined to kill his father and marry his mother. Horrified by this prophecy, he turned his back on Corinth, resolved never to return while his supposed parents lived.

Fulfilment of the prophecy. As he hurried along the steep mountain path leading away from Delphi, he met a chariot coming from the direction of Thebes. The charioteer somewhat arrogantly ordered him out of the way, and Œdipus, accustomed to being treated as a prince and being, besides, deeply troubled over the tragic prophecy, violently resented the order and provoked a blow from the master of the chariot. In a passion of rage Œdipus drew his sword and killed both master and charioteer. The old man was King Laïus. On his arrival at Thebes Œdipus found the city in great tribulation over the destruction caused by a mysterious being with the body of a lion, the head of a woman, and the wings of a bird. This creature, the Sphinx, had seated herself above the road and asked all passers-by the following riddle:

Fig. 83. Œdipus and the Sphinx.

"What is it that, though it has one voice, is four-footed, and two-footed, and three-footed?" Those who could not answer the riddle the Sphinx killed, and a great pile of whitening bones lay about her. But Œdipus was not daunted by the fate of those others who had gone before, and when the question was put to him he answered:

"It is man, since in his babyhood he goes on hands and knees, in his manhood he walks upright, and when old supports himself with a cane." In chagrin at being answered the Sphinx threw herself over the cliff, and thus the city was freed. The Thebans honored the stranger who had come to their relief in every way, and even made him their king and gave him as wife the widowed queen. Jocasta bore to him four children, two sons and two daughters, and for a long time he lived in peace and prosperity, loved and honored by all his grateful people.

The prophecy made clear. But at last the day of retribution came, and a blight and pestilence fell upon the city, so that the fields yielded no grain, and men and beasts died. To the ambassadors sent to Delphi to learn the cause the answer was returned that not until the city was purged of the murderer of King Laïus would the curse be removed. Œdipus had never suspected that the old man he had killed on the road from Delphi was the Theban king, and the truth was the less likely to come to him since the sole attendant of the murdered king who had escaped had told a big story of a robber band that had attacked them on the road. Œdipus, therefore, proclaimed that whosoever knew anything of the men who had done this deed should declare it, and that the guilty ones should be put to death or driven into banishment. A blind seer who was brought to testify before the king at first refused to speak, and when, goaded by a charge of treachery, he declared, "Thou art the man who has brought pollution upon this land!" Œdipus turned upon him in furious disbelief. Only when he learned the time and place of the murder and the age and appearance of the murdered man, was he convinced of his own guilt, and with this conviction came a yet more bitter discovery. For through the testimony of the Theban and Corinthian shepherds who had been concerned in his exposure and his adoption as an infant he learned that he was the son of Laïus whom he had killed and the husband of his own mother. The terrible truth had already broken upon Jocasta, and she had gone into the private chambers of the palace and hung herself. With the pin of her brooch her wretched husband put out both his eyes, that he might never look upon the holy sun again.

Jocasta's brother Creon took the throne, and blind Œdipus, led by his heroic and faithful daughter An tig'o ne, went into exile. His end was mysterious. At Athens, under the noble king Theseus, he found refuge and protection, but with prophetic knowledge of what his fate was to be, he sought the sacred grove of the Furies at Co lo'nus, close to Athens, and there amid thunder and strange portents he disappeared from the sight of men.

Œdipus death.

The curse that rested on the family was not lifted by Œdipus' death. His two sons, E te'o-cles and Pol y ni'ces, who had deserted their father in his old age and blindness and by him had been cursed for this faithlessness, quarreled about the throne, and Eteocles drove his brother from the kingdom. Polynices, therefore, went to Argos and persuaded the king A dras'tus, to champion his cause. An army was gathered, and seven great chiefs were found to undertake the expedition against seven-gated Thebes. The seer Am phi a ra'us went unwillingly, for he knew that the war was contrary to the will of the gods, and that from it he should never return alive. But when he married it had been agreed that if any difference should arise between him and his brother-in-law Adrastus, his wife E ri'phy le should be the judge. Polynices, therefore, bribed her with Harmonia's necklace, and she treacherously sent her husband to the war. Of the seven heroes Adrastus alone returned alive. The brothers, Eteocles and Polynices, meeting in single combat, died at one another's hands, thus fulfilling the curse with which Œdipus had cursed them when they had deserted him in his day of trouble and exile.

Eteocles was buried by Creon and the Thebans with all due honor, but it was decreed that the body of Polynices, as that of a traitor, should be left for the dogs and vultures to devour. Antigone, loyal to her brother as she had been to her father, at the risk of her life and in spite of the dissuasion of her weaker sister Is me'ne, gave the body the last rites of burial, without which the shade must wander hopeless on the banks of Acheron. In punishment she was buried alive, and her lover, Creon's son, killed himself upon her tomb. With Antigone's act of self-sacrifice and dreadful death the long tragedy of the family of Cadmus came to an end.

In the next generation the city of Thebes finally fell before the seven sons of the original Seven, and the son of Polynices was established on the throne. This war is known as the war of the Ep ig'o ni or descendants.

The Epigoni.

CHAPTER XVI

THE ARGONAUTIC EXPEDITION [36]

The Golden Fleece. ALTHOUGH Ath'a mas, a king in northern Greece, had two children, Phrixus and Helle, he left his first wife and married again. This second wife, like the traditional step-mother wish-

Fig. 84. Phrixus and the Ram.

ing to get rid of the children, persuaded Athamas to sacrifice Phrixus to Zeus, and the sacrifice was about to be accomplished when Hermes sent a ram with golden fleece which carried off the

[36] Apollonius Rhodius, *Argonautica*

two children on his back. As they passed over
the strait now known as the Dardanelles, Helle
lost her hold and fell off into the water. That
is how this strait in ancient times came to be
called the Hellespont. Phrixus kept on to Colchis, on the Euxine (now the Black) Sea, where
he offered up the ram to Zeus and gave the golden
fleece to Æ e'tes, the king, who hung it on a tree
in the sacred grove of Ares, under the guardian-
ship of a sleepless dragon.

The nephew of Athamus, Pe'li as, king of I ol'-
cus, a violent and unjust man, seized the power
and possessions that belonged to his half-brother
Æson. Fearing for the life of his son Jason,
Æson sent him as a baby to be brought up by
the centaur Chiron, who, unlike most of the centaurs, was wonderfully wise and just and was
famous both as a physician and as the tutor of
many of the heroes. Jason had taken part in
the Calydonian boar-hunt when he was hardly
more than a boy. He had learned from Chiron
kindness and courtesy as well as courage; once
when he found a feeble old woman waiting for
some one to help her across a raging mountain
torrent, he cheerfully took her on his back and
set her over. As the old woman happened to
be Hera in disguise, he was rewarded for his
courtesy by securing a powerful friend. Soon
after this, when Pelias was holding a great sacrifice in honor of Poseidon, Jason determined to

attend. In crossing a river he lost one sandal in the mud and went on without it. Now Pelias had been warned by an oracle to beware of a

Fig. 85. Centaur.

man who should come to him wearing one sandal; when, therefore, Jason appeared before him, he determined to put him out of his way. So when the young man quite simply and frankly demanded of him the kingdom that of right belonged to him, Pelias answered cautiously that he would willingly give it up but it seemed only right that Jason should first prove his courage by bringing back from Colchis the famous golden fleece. Thus he thought he should make sure of his death.

Without delay Jason sent messengers all over Greece to gather comrades for this dangerous enterprise. When assembled they were fifty in all — each one a famous hero, the son or grandson of a god. Chief of all was Heracles, who had just returned from his adventure with the Erymanthian boar. Orpheus was there, the divine musician; Castor and Polydeuces, the twin-brothers of Helen; Meleager of Calydon; Peleus and Telamon, whose sons, Achilles and Ajax, were to be great heroes of the Trojan War; the two sons of Orithyia and Boreas, the north wind, came from Thrace on their dark, cloudy wings scaled with gold, their black hair streaming behind them as they flew. Theseus would surely have been among the company, but at that time he was still a prisoner in Hades. A ship was built by a son of Phrixus, Argus, with the help of Athena herself, and was named from its builder, Argo. In its prow Athena had set a beam from the sacred oak of Dodona, possessed of a voice and prophetic power like that of the trunk from which it was cut. All the city came

The Argonauts.

out to see the heroes depart.[37] From the wooded shore across the bay Chiron waved farewell to his pupil and held out for his father to see Peleus' son, the baby Achilles, who had been given into his charge. The young men dipped their long oars to the music of Orpheus' lyre, the fishes frolicked about the ship, and the gods looked down from high heaven in admiration at the glorious band of heroes.

The voyage. Many were the adventures on this famous voyage. Sometimes the sea threatened to sink the ship; sometimes the strangers among whom they landed were hostile and they were compelled to fight for their lives. At the island of Lemnos the women, who had recently murdered their husbands and fathers, tried to keep the Argonauts with them, offering them a share of their island. Once they were pursued by a tribe of six-handed giants. Finally when they had landed on the shore of an island to rest, they lost the strongest of their company, Heracles, and two others with him. Heracles had gone into the woods to cut a new oar in place of one that he had broken, and his young friend and follower Hylas had gone to get water from the spring.

[37] This assembling of hardy and adventurous men from all quarters for a hazardous enterprise suggests the enlistment for a polar expedition. The same courage and resourcefulness are required, and the appeal of the dangerous and unknown is the same.

The nymphs, thinking that this charming young stranger would be a delightful playfellow and partner in the dance, put out their long white arms and drew the boy down into their fountain.   One of the company heard his last despairing cry and started to the rescue, calling to Heracles as he ran.   Supposing that robbers had stolen him the two scoured the country and were gone so long that the other heroes sailed away leaving them behind.

When at last Jason and his companions had passed through the Bosphorus they came to the home of Phineus.   This Phineus, because by his gift of prophecy he told men all the future, Zeus had cursed with blindness and had sent the Harpies (see p. 150) to torment him.   These dreadful deities of storm and death snatched away or defiled whatever food was set before their victim. The coming of the Argonauts brought relief to the starving, blind old man, for when the Harpies swooped down upon the banquet set for the hero the two sons of Boreas drew their swords with a great shout and pursued them.   Far over the sea they flew, and they would in the end have caught and killed the Harpies, but Iris came between them and forbade it.   In return for this good deed Phineus told the voyagers of all that lay before them and especially of the perilous Sympleg'a des, or Clashing Rocks.   So when they had set sail again and saw the waves breaking and

Adventures with the Harpies and with the Clashing Rocks.

the foam tossed high from these terrible rocks, they loosed a dove as the seer had bidden them, and when she had passed safely through with only the loss of her tail feathers, they dashed in as the rocks rebounded and forced the ship through, rowing with all their might, before the rocks could close a second time. Yet even so the ship might not have escaped, but Athena pushed it on and held back the rocks with her hand. From that time those rocks have remained rooted fast together, no longer affording that dangerous passage.

Further adventures. The next day, just before dawn, they landed on a small island, and there Apollo met them as he passed on his way to the Hyperboreans. About his head his hair fell in golden curls, in his hand was his silver bow, and under his feet the island quaked. The heroes were amazed when they saw him, and feared to look into the shining eyes of the god. So when he passed on they made sacrifice to him and sang the pæan and called that island sacred to Apollo of the Dawn. Then they sailed on by many strange lands and peoples, the coast of the Amazons and the island of Ares. Here there flew out a flock of birds who rained down upon the rowers' heads a rain of feathers, sharp as arrows; but the heroes raised over the ship a covering of their shields, set close together, and so passed by in safety. Further on they saw the Caucasus Mountains rising before them, and a great vulture, with wide-spread wings, flew over the ship, and from the cliff above sounded cries of agony as Prometheus suffered once more his age-long torture; for Heracles had not yet come to free that much-enduring friend of man. (See pp. 10, 223.)

Now as the ship neared Colchis, Hera and Athena in heaven held a council together to plan how they might aid Jason in his adventure. They called Aphrodite and persuaded her to send her son Eros, or Cupid, to Æëtes' daughter Me de'a to cause her to take Jason's part. The goddess of love found her little son playing dice with Zeus's young cup-bearer, the boy Ganymede, and by the promise of a golden ball she won him to do what she asked. Meanwhile the heroes had landed and had gone up to the great palace of Æëtes, adorned with the work of Hephæstus, four fountains always flowing, one with oil, one with wine, one with milk, and one with water. There King Æëtes entertained the travelers royally, while Medea sat by, her heart filled with love and pain as she looked at Jason, for Eros' sharp arrow had pierced deep. Then Jason told the king that he had come to get the golden fleece, and Æëtes answered craftily, saying that he would freely give it when he had tried Jason and found that he was worthy to receive it. But first, as proof of his skill and courage, let him

Jason and Medea.

harness to a plow the bronze-hoofed bulls that breathed out fire from their nostrils and plow with them the field of Ares. When this was done, let him plant the dragon's teeth that Athena had given. Then, if all this was accomplished between dawn and sunset, he should receive the golden fleece. Though he looked upon it as an impossible task, Jason could do no better than accept the king's conditions, but he returned to his ship and his comrades in utter discouragement. As for Medea, she was in an agony of doubt as to whether to drive this love from her heart and allow Jason to perish or to be disloyal to her father and help with her magic arts. Love got the upper hand, and she took powerful herbs and ointments and went to meet Jason at the shrine of Hecate beyond the walls. As Jason came to meet her the gods made him of nobler bearing and more glorious than before, and he talked to the maiden Medea with winning words. So she gave him a charm made of a flower that grew from the blood drawn from Prometheus by the vulture, and gathered and treated in magic ways. She told him, too, how to propitiate Hecate by mysterious sacrifice performed at midnight, and how afterwards, when he had smeared his body and his weapons with the magic ointment, he could safely sow the dragon's teeth. Jason promised her in return his undying love and gratitude and that he would carry her home with him and make her his wife.

When it was time for the trial, all the people assembled, and the Argonauts looked on with dread as the fire-breathing bulls rushed upon their leader.   But the ointment made him invulnerable to fire, and he grappled with them and forced them to their knees and put the yoke upon their necks.   So he plowed the field of Ares and then he sowed the dragon's teeth.   Thereupon a crop of armed men sprang up, as they had from the dragon's teeth sowed by Cadmus at the founding of Thebes.   Jason remembered Medea's warning and threw into their midst a great stone, and immediately they fell upon one another, and others Jason himself slew with his sword until none were left.

Jason harnesses the bulls.

But Æētes had no intention of fulfilling his agreement and giving up the golden fleece, and he plotted to burn the ship *Argo* while the heroes slept.   Once more Medea saved Jason, for she told him where to find the tree on which the fleece was hung, and she gave him a sleeping potion to pour over the dragon's eyes, and herself lulled him by a magic song.   So in that night they secured the fleece and secretly boarding the ship set sail.   When the king knew of their flight and that they had taken not only the famous fleece but his undutiful daughter as well, he started out in hot pursuit.   Then Medea did

Jason secures the golden fleece.

a horrible thing, for she slaughtered her own brother, whom she had taken with her, and cut up his limbs and cast them behind her on the waters, so that her father, in gathering them up for burial, might be delayed in his pursuit.

The return from Colchis. About the course followed by the Argonauts on their return voyage there is much uncertainty, but they seem to have met with many of the monsters and strange beings that Odysseus (or Ulysses) afterwards encountered. At last, however, they landed on their native shores and were

Fig. 86.   Medea preparing the magic brew.

received with joy by Æson and with feigned satisfaction by Pelias. Years and anxiety had greatly enfeebled Æson, and his son longed to see him young and strong again. Medea undertook to satisfy his wish. Nine nights under the full moon she scoured the earth in her dragon-drawn chariot in search of rare herbs and other things of use in the sorcerer's art. Then she built altars to Hecate and the goddess of youth, and sacrificing to the gods of the under world she called upon them by name. The old man she purified three times, with fire, with water, and with sulphur. Then she concocted a brew of magic herbs, of frost got by moonlight, of the wings and flesh of bats, of the vitals of a wolf, the liver of a stag, and the beak and head of a long-lived crow. She stirred it all together with a stick of dry olive-wood; the stick grew green and put forth leaves, and where the liquid spattered on the earth fresh grass sprang up. Then the sorceress opened the veins of her patient, and as the blood flowed out, she poured into his mouth and veins her magic liquid. And his white hairs grew dark again, the color came into his sunken cheeks, and his feeble form grew strong and straight. When Pelias' daughters saw this marvel, they begged to have the same treatment given to their father as well. Medea pretended to consent, and having made a powerless brew of herbs and water, gave the signal for the credulous daughters to slaughter their father.

Because of this murder of Pelias, Jason and Medea were obliged to leave Iolcus and take refuge in Corinth. In time Jason grew tired of his passionate and mysterious wife and announced his intention of marrying a princess of

The tragedy of Medea.

Corinth. Medea, covering up her bitter resentment with a show of submission, sent the bride as a wedding gift a beautiful robe, but when she put it on it consumed her flesh like fire, and her

Fig. 87. Medea preparing to kill her Children.

father in trying to help her perished with her. This was not enough to satisfy Medea's hatred. That the perfidious Jason might not have sons to care for his old age and to perpetuate his race, she conquered her maternal feelings and killed her two children. Then in her dragon-drawn chariot she flew away. In Athens she married Theseus' father Ægeus and almost brought about the hero's death by persuading his father to offer him a poisoned cup. When Ægeus' sudden recognition of his son thwarted this plot, the sorceress flew away and disappeared from story. (See p. 249.)

Jason passed thereafter a forlorn and useless life. His only comfort was to go and sit in the shade of the old ship *Argo*, the outward symbol of his only great achievement. One day its rotting timbers fell on him and crushed him.

Jason's

CHAPTER XVII

THE TROJAN WAR

The legend of Troy. THE story of the Trojan War was the subject of a great cycle of legends, and the deeds of the heroes engaged in it inspired the imagination of the Greeks in all ages. Homer's *Iliad* is but the greatest of many epics written about the siege of Troy, and the *Odyssey* is concerned with the adventures of one of the heroes of that war on his return voyage. All the great writers of tragedy turned to some phase of the struggle or to the history of one or other of the families engaged in it. Alexander the Great set Achilles before him as his ideal hero and turned aside from his march of conquest to visit his reputed tomb. The fame and influence of the story descended upon Rome, and the poet Vergil took as the subject of his national epic the wanderings of Trojan Æneas from burning Troy until he settled in Italy and became the ancestor of the Roman race. For more than two thousand years scholars have discussed the historical basis for the legend, and not fifty years ago a German business man, having acquired a sufficient fortune, determined to devote the rest of his life and a large part of his money to excavating beneath a little Turkish village on the legendary site of Troy. There, buried beneath three other ruined cities, were unearthed the remains of a walled town of the time of which Homer tells. Whether history, legend, or myth, the Trojan War has left its mark deep on the thought and poetry of our world, and the actors in that drama are pictured on the walls of our libraries and public buildings along with Columbus and the Pilgrim Fathers, as part of our heritage from the past.

The siege took place in the generation succeeding that of the Calydonian Boar Hunt, the Seven against Thebes, and the voyage of the Argonauts, and many of the warriors engaged before Troy were the sons of the earlier heroes. Three families are of especial importance in this connection.

Ag a mem'non and Men e la'us, the leaders of the Greek hosts, were descended from Tan'ta lus, who was the son of Zeus. This Tantalus was remarkably favored by the gods, for he was invited to their banquets, partook of their nectar and ambrosia, and shared their secrets. For what crime he lost his exalted position and in what way he was punished is a matter of dispute. Some say that he stole nectar and ambrosia and shared it with his friends; some, that he divulged the secrets of Zeus; some, that he

The family of Tantalus.

became so presumptuous that to test the gods he
served up to them at a feast the flesh of his own
son Pelops. There are also differing accounts
of the punishment he received: that he stood in
Hades below a rock that seemed ever about to fall
and crush him, or that, as was told in an earlier
chapter (see p. 190), in the presence of food and
drink he was always unable to reach it and appease his torturing hunger and thirst. Though
Pelops had been served up in this cannibal fashion, he had been restored to life by Hermes and
came out of the ordeal whole and strong except
for one shoulder, which Demeter, in the absent-
mindedness induced by her grief for her daughter, had unfortunately eaten. For it she sub-
stituted a shoulder of ivory. It was Pelops who
won his wife Hippodamia by contending with her
father in a chariot race (see p. 147), and some say
that it was his violence to the charioteer Myrtilus
that brought on his family the curse that pursued it through three generations. Because of
their murder of their brother, Pelops drove his
sons A'treus and Thy es'tes, from his kingdom,
and they came to Mycenæ where they succeeded
to the power after Eurystheus' death. Atreus
caught Thyestes in an attempt to deprive him of
his power and, while appearing to forgive him,
avenged himself by serving up his son to him at
dinner. The sons of Atreus were Agamemnon
and Menelaüs, the former, king of Mycenæ and

overlord of a large part of the Peloponnesus and surrounding islands, the latter, ruler of Sparta and husband of Zeus's beautiful daughter Helen.

Achilles was descended from Æ′a cus, who was noted for his uprightness and justice. He was the son of Zeus by Æ gi′na, whom Zeus in the form of an eagle had stolen from her father, a river-god, and had carried off to the island near Athens that still bears her name. Hera, in anger at the island for affording hospitality to a rival, sent upon it a plague that destroyed all the inhabitants except Æacus, who in his loneliness called upon his father to give him a people. Zeus answered his prayer by turning a tribe of ants into men, called from the Greek word Myr′-mi dons. Because of his righteousness, Æacus after death was made a judge in the lower world. (See p. 189.) Æacus' son Peleus, with the Myrmidons, migrated to a part of Thessaly called Phthia. As a young man he took part in the Calydonian boar hunt and the quest of the golden fleece. His wife was the Nereid Thetis, whom Zeus himself had been deterred from marrying only by the prophecy that she would bear a son greater than his father. The issue of this marriage was Achilles. Because of a prophecy that her son would die in war, Thetis had tried to make him invulnerable by dipping him as a baby in the potent waters of the Styx. The heel by which she held him had been unwet by the waters and

The family of Æacus.

hence was the one vulnerable spot.[38] After this Thetis left her husband and child and returned to her father Nereus in the depths of the sea, and Achilles was given to the centaur Chiron to be educated. He grew up strong and beautiful, and so swift of foot that he needed no dog nor spear in hunting but overtook his game and caught it alive.

The royal family of Troy. The earliest mortal ancestor of the Trojan royal family was Dar'da nus, a son of Zeus, who founded a city on the slopes of Mt. Ida, in the northwestern corner of Asia Minor. From his grandson Tros the Trojans took their name. One of Tros's sons was the beautiful boy Ganymede, whom Zeus took to be his cup-bearer, and another was Ilus, who transferred the seat of his power to Ilium or Troy, a new city built between Mt. Ida and the Hellespont. The walls of the new city were built by Poseidon and Apollo for Ilus's son, the faithless Laomedon. After the destruction of the city and the death of Laomedon at Heracles' hands (see p. 225), the rule fell to Laomedon's only living son, Priam, a just and god-fearing man, by whom the city was splendidly restored. Priam became the father of fifty daughters and fifty sons, of whom the noblest was Hector. Another of his sons was the ill-omened Paris, the curse of Troy.

[38] Anatomists still call the tendon attached to the heel "Achilles' tendon."

The golden apple that the goddess had thrown The causes of the war. in among the gods assembled as guests at the wedding of Peleus and Thetis (see p. 111) had not only brought discord between Zeus's wife and his

Fig. 88. The persuasion of Helen.

daughters, Athena and Aphrodite, but it was the first cause of the war between Greeks and Trojans, which, after lasting for ten years, ended in the utter destruction of Troy and the death of hundreds of heroes. For the Trojan prince and shepherd Paris, whom Zeus had made judge in the matter, had given the prize of beauty to Aphrodite because she had promised him as wife the most beautiful woman in the world. Now the most beautiful woman in the world was Helen, the daughter of Leda and Zeus (see p. 235), who, after being sought in marriage by all the princes of Greece, had been given by her step-father to Menelaüs, king of Sparta. Fulfilling her promise, Aphrodite led Paris to the court of Menelaüs, who, in accordance with the gracious custom that required hospitable treatment of strangers as a law of Zeus, received him kindly and entertained him at his palace. Then Paris did a treacherous thing; for while Menelaüs was away from home, he induced Helen to desert her husband, and putting her and much treasure on board his ship, he sailed away to Troy. Greek poets seem not to have attached so much blame in the matter to Helen as we might expect, partly, no doubt, because she had yielded to Aphrodite's persuasions, but partly, it would seem, because such divine beauty as hers seemed to them to cover a multitude of sins. But Paris' action was unreservedly condemned.

The call to arms. When the Greek chiefs had been contending for the hand of Helen, they had agreed that if violence should be done to her or to the man whom she married, they would all unite in avenging it. And so when Menelaüs and his brother Agamemnon, king of Mycenæ, called·upon them to take arms against the Trojans, they hastened to fulfil their pledge. Agamemnon, as the most powerful prince of Greece, was chosen leader of the armies. His most trusted counselor was the aged Nestor, whose long reminiscences of the glories of his youth and the mighty deeds of the heroes of his generation met with unfailing respect from the courteous princes. Di o me´des, son of Tydeus, came from Argos; he was the bravest of Greeks, except only Achilles. Ajax, son of Telemon, led his forces from Salamis and earned for himself the title of "great bulwark of the Achæans." The catalogue of ships, as Homer gives it, amounted to more than twelve hundred; these were all rowed with great oars and carried fifty to one hundred and twenty men each. All the heroes were anxious to secure the help of Odysseus, prince of Ithaca, whose reputation for courage and endurance was equaled by his reputation for cunning devices and persuasive talk. But Odysseus was living happily with his wife Pe nel´o pe and his little son Te lem´a chus and wished to avoid going to the war. So when an embassy came to summon him, he feigned madness, and harnessing an ass and a bull to his plow, sowed his field with salt. But the clever ambassadors laid the baby Telemachus before the plow, and when Odysseus turned it aside, they proved his sanity and induced him to join the expedition. Once forced to throw in his fortune with theirs, Odysseus was more than ready to help in securing the company of young Achilles. For Achilles' mother, the sea-goddess Thetis, having prophetic knowledge that her son was not destined to return alive from the war, had sent him, disguised as a girl, to serve among the attendants of the princess of Scyros. Odysseus came to the court in the disguise of a peddler, bringing among the feminine silks and trinkets a sword. While the princess and her maids eagerly tried on the ear-rings and veils, Achilles with sparkling eyes seized upon the sword and brandished it above his head. Then Odysseus threw off his disguise and easily persuaded Achilles to join the army. He was the strongest and bravest of all the princes, in beauty, strength and noble nature the ideal hero of the Greeks. With Achilles came his friend Pat ro'clus, and so close was the affection between the two that their friendship takes its place beside that between David and Jonathan.

The sacrifice of Iphigenia at Aulis. The armies of the Greek leaders assembled at Aulis,. on the eastern coast of Central Greece. There Artemis, in punishment for the killing of a sacred hind, refused them favorable winds and would not allow them to sail, until Agamemnon, summoning his young daughter Iph i ge ni'a on the plea of giving her in marriage to Achilles,

offered her as a sacrifice. At the moment when
the knife was about to descend upon her, Artemis snatched her away to serve as priestess in
her temple at Taurus, putting in her place a hind.
Then favorable winds brought the fleet to Troy.

Fig. 89. Sacrifice of Iphigenia.

There is nothing more moving in all tragedy than
Iphigenia's appeal to her father, as Euripides tells
it, and nothing more noble than her final willing
submission when she knew that without it her
people could never be victorious.

The early
years of
the war.

A second act of self-sacrifice marked the landing of the Greeks. Pro tes i la'us, knowing the prophecy that the man who first touched Trojan soil should meet his death, leaped from the ship, offering his life for the cause. His devoted wife La od a mi'a prayed to the gods that he might return to her for one day. The prayer was granted, and when he died the second time she threw herself upon his funeral pyre and so accompanied him to Hades. The siege of the city now began. The gods took an active part in the struggle, protecting and inspiring their sons and favorites among the heroes and in some cases even entering the battle in person. On the Trojan side were Aphrodite (Venus), Ares (Mars), and Apollo; on the Greek side, Hera (June), Athena (Minerva), and Poseidon (Neptune). Zeus (Jupiter) held victory in the balance, yielding to the persuasion now of this god, now of that, for Greeks or Trojans, but keeping his eyes fixed on the fate that required the ultimate overthrow of Troy. For nine years the siege continued with varying fortune, yet, on the whole, advantage lay with the Greeks, since they had driven the Trojans within their walled city and had ravaged the neighboring country.

The quarrel
between Aga-
memnon and
Achilles.

After one of these raids Agamemnon had received as his share of the booty a maiden named Chry se'is, whose father was a priest of Apollo. The priest, coming to ransom his daughter, was driven off with insults, and called upon the god for vengeance.

And Phœbus Apollo heard him and came down from the peaks of Olympus wroth at heart, bearing on his shoulders his bow and covered quiver. And the arrows clanged upon his shoulders in his wrath, as the god moved; and he descended like to night. Then he sate him aloof from the ships, and let an arrow fly; and there was heard a great clanging of the silver bow. First did he assail the mules and fleet dogs, but afterward, aiming at the men his swift dart, he smote; and the pyres of the dead burnt continually in multitude. (*Iliad*, I. 42 ff.)

On the tenth day of the plague brought by Apollo's arrows Achilles, inspired by Hera, called the Greeks to an assembly and urged the prophet Calchas to tell what had aroused the anger of the god. When the prophet made known the truth, Agamemnon was furiously angry against him and against Achilles for protecting him, and declared that if Chryseïs was taken from him he would take in return Achilles' slave maiden Bri se'is. So began the quarrel between Agamemnon and Achilles, which, as Homer says, "hurled down into Hades many strong souls of heroes." For Achilles, in wrath at the loss of Briseïs and in indignation at the insolent invasion of his rights, retired to his tent and refused to lead his Myrmidons to battle. Moreover he complained of his ungrateful treatment to his mother Thetis, calling her up from her home in the depths of ocean to listen to his angry complaints. And she "rose from the gray sea like a mist," and caressed her son and promised to go to Father Zeus and demand Agamemnon's punishment. So when Thetis came to Olympus and clasped his knees, Zeus bowed his ambrosial head in assent, promising that the Greeks should flee before the Trojans until Agamemnon should bitterly repent of his insolence. It is the story of this quarrel between the heroes and its results which Homer tells in the *Iliad*.

The Trojans set fire to the ships. Though he delayed in its accomplishment, Zeus did not forget his promise, and he laid his stern command upon all the gods to refrain from further interference in the battle. Then Hector rallied the Trojans and drove the Greeks back to their ships, and the battle swayed now this way, now that, and all the plain was strewn with dead and wounded. For a time Agamemnon took the lead and seemed invincible, but at the last he was disabled by a wound, and Menelaüs was wounded, and Odysseus, and many others of the chiefs. So Hector led his people against the wall that the Greeks had built about their camp, and Apollo, disobeying Zeus's command, put himself at their head and cast down the wall "as a boy scatters the sand beside the sea." Fire was thrown on one of the Greek ships and the whole fleet might have been destroyed and the Greeks cut off from return home if great Ajax had not stubbornly held the Trojans at bay.

At this desperate crisis Patroclus, grieving for the sufferings of his friends, went to Achilles and begged that if he was unwilling himself to forget his resentment and return to the conflict, he would permit him, clad in his armor, to lead the Myrmidons to the rescue. For he hoped that the Trojans seeing Achilles' well known arms would think that the hero himself had come against them and so would lose confidence. Half unwillingly Achilles gave his consent, at the same time earnestly warning Patroclus that when he had driven the Trojans back and saved the ships he should refrain from pursuing to the walls of the city. On the appearance of Patroclus in Achilles' armor the tide of the battle was turned, and the Greeks drove back the Trojans. Then Patroclus, in the fury of the fight, forgot his chief's orders and pursued even to the city and would have scaled the wall at the head of his victorious Myrmidons if Apollo had not appeared on the ramparts and forced them back. Although the Trojans rallied, Patroclus held his ground beneath the walls of the city, until Apollo, coming behind him, struck him and cast off his helmet and broke his spear. So, unarmed by the god, Patroclus was overthrown and killed by Hector, prophesying as the breath left his body the approaching death of his victorious foe at the hands of the vengeful Achilles. Menelaüs and Ajax, standing over the body of their fallen comrade, with grim determination beat back the fierce attacks of the Trojans. But Achilles' armor fell into Hector's hands, though the horses and chariot were saved and driven out of the field. Homer says of those immortal horses:

As a pillar abideth firm that standeth on the tomb of a man or woman dead, so abode they immovably with the beautiful chariot, abasing their heads unto the earth. And hot tears flowed from their eyes to the ground as they mourned in sorrow for their charioteer. (*Iliad*, XVII. 434.)

Achilles returns to the war. A messenger from the battle came to Achilles as he sat beside the ships, waiting anxiously for the return of his friend. When he heard the news "a black cloud of grief enwrapped Achilles, and with both hands he took dark dust and poured it over his head and defiled his comely face, and on his fragrant doublet black ashes fell." Thetis heard her son's moans and rose from the sea and came and, sitting beside him, tried to comfort him. She promised to go to Hephæstus and persuade him to make for the hero arms greater and more glorious than those he had lost, so that he might return to the battle and avenge his dead friend. After Thetis had left him, Hera sent Iris, bidding him show himself to the Trojans, even unarmed as he was.

Around his strong shoulders Athena cast her tasseled
ægis, and around his head the bright goddess set a
crown of a golden cloud, and kindled therefrom a blazing flame.

So when Achilles shouted aloud, the Trojans were
dismayed and drew back, and the Greeks drew the
body of Patroclus from under the heap of slain
that had fallen on him and carried him to Achilles' tent. Meanwhile Thetis, fulfilling her promise, found Hephæstus working at his forge and
made her request. And the lame god made for
Achilles marvelous armor, worthy of a god. The
shield was wrought in wonderful designs, the
earth and heavens, the sun, moon, and stars, were
in the middle of it, and there were two cities,
one at peace, where people were being married
and dancing and holding their law-courts, the
other under siege, and the gods mingling in the
fight. On other circles of the shield he pictured
fields plowed and harvested, and a vineyard, and
herds of cattle attacked by lions, and flocks of
sheep; besides these, a dancing-place where boys
and girls were dancing to music. All around the
edge of the shield he wrought the river of Ocean.
When Achilles had received the glorious armor
from his mother, he was filled with a furious
eagerness to join battle with the Trojans and
avenge himself on Hector; but first he went to
the assembly of the Greeks and became reconciled with Agamemnon. The other heroes were

glad of his return, but most of all, Agamemnon, who acknowledged the wrong he had done and offered all the reparation in his power. So Zeus's promise to Thetis had been fulfilled, and now, calling the gods to assembly, he bade them go and enter the conflict, helping whatever heroes they would.

The deeds of Achilles. The most terrible battle of the war now began, and Achilles raged across the plain like a god, seemingly invincible. All that met him fell before him, among them two sons of Priam. At last the river Xanthus, choked with the bodies of the sons of Troy, rose in his might against the hero and pursued him across the plain, threatening to overwhelm him in his great waves. Achilles might well have died there, with his vengeance unaccomplished, if Hera had not roused her son Hephæstus to meet and check the oncoming flood of the river with a flood of fire. Freed from the pursuit of the river-god, Achilles returned to the pursuit of his enemies and drove them before him to the city. From his post on the walls Priam saw the danger of his people and ordered the gates to be thrown open to afford them a refuge. This might have been the signal for the destruction of Troy, for Achilles was so close on their heels that he had almost entered the gates behind them, when Apollo inspired one of the fugitives to stand and meet him. Then, when Achilles would have killed the rash mortal, the god snatched him away, and assuming his form, drew Achilles in pursuit away from the open gates.

But brave Hector still stood outside the gates of the city and would not hear the prayers of his father and mother that he should follow his comrades into safety; for he dreaded the reproach of his people that he had led them on to battle and had brought many to death and had then feared himself to stand against Achilles. So when Achilles returned from his vain pursuit of the god, Hector boldly stood to meet him,— only for a moment, for when he saw him near, in his blazing armor and brandishing his great spear, a panic seized Hector and he turned and fled. Three times around the walls of Troy Hector fled and Achilles pursued.

The death of Hector.

But when the fourth time they had reached the springs, then the Father hung his golden balances, and set therein two lots of dreary death, one of Achilles, one of horse-taming Hector, and held them by the midst and poised. Then Hector's fated day sank down, and fell to the house of Hades, and Phœbus Apollo left him. (*Iliad*, XXII. 208.)

Then Athena, the enemy of Troy, came in the form of his brother and urged Hector to stand and wait for Achilles' onset, and he was deceived and obeyed. But when, having thrown his spear against Achilles and missed him, he turned to receive a second spear from his brother and saw no one near, he knew that the gods had deceived him and drew his sword for the last desperate chance.   The end had been determined by fate, and noble Hector fell before Achilles, as Patroclus had fallen before him, "and his soul flew forth of his limbs and was gone to the house of Hades, wailing her fate, leaving her vigor and youth."   Then Achilles took a savage vengeance for his friend's death, for he bound his fallen enemy to his chariot by the feet and dragged him in the dust about the walls of Troy. · This last insult to the noblest of their sons Priam and Hecuba saw from the walls, and his people could scarcely prevent the old man from rushing out to his own death.   And Hector's noble wife An drom'a che, as she waited at home for her lord's return, hearing the moans and laments rushed in terror to the walls, and seeing that terrible sight joined her despairing grief with theirs.

The redemption of Hector's body.

So Achilles returned victorious from the battle with all his purpose accomplished, and he held a splendid funeral for Patroclus, with a feast and a great sacrifice and a triumphal procession about his funeral pyre.   And when the body had been burned, he gathered the ashes and put them in a golden urn and buried them and raised over them a mound.   Then followed the funeral games — chariot-racing, boxing, wrestling, spear-throwing, and other contests, and Achilles offered splendid prizes, and all the heroes entered the lists. When this was over, Zeus sent Iris to Priam to bid him go to Achilles' tent to ransom the body of his son. As Priam went in his chariot, Hermes met him and guided him safely through the sleeping guards and brought him to Achilles' tent. And Achilles, who had been warned by Thetis that this was Zeus's will, re-

Fig. 90. Priam ransoming Hector's Body.

ceived the old man courteously, and thinking of his own father, far away in Greece, whom he should never see again, spoke kindly to him and granted his request. He had the body washed and anointed and laid over it a rich robe and set it on the wagon. Then he had a feast spread and he and his enemy's father ate and drank together, and Priam gave a great ransom. So Priam brought Hector's body back to the city, and all Troy came out to meet him with weeping and laments, and Achilles granted a truce of eleven days that the Trojans might perform their funeral rites.

The death of Achilles. With the funeral of Hector the *Iliad* ends, but from other sources we learn of the later events of the war. Twice the hopes of the Trojans were raised by the coming of powerful allies. The first of these was Pen thes i le'a, queen of the Amazons, who came with her band of warrior women and brought momentary success to the sinking cause of Troy. After many great deeds, she fell in a fierce encounter with Achilles, though it was said that when her helmet fell off and disclosed her noble beauty, the hero repented of his success. Memnon, son of the goddess of dawn, came from Ethiopia with a great following, and he too fell before Achilles. But the hero's great career was run, and he met his death, as the Fates decreed, by the arrow of Paris, guided by Apollo, to pierce him in the only vulnerable spot, his heel. When the Greeks had rescued his body, they burned it, and putting his ashes in a golden urn with the ashes of his friend Patroclus, raised over it a great mound. Near the shore of the Dardanelles at this day there is a hill that bears the name of the "Tomb of Achilles." His spirit joined the other great heroes in the Elysian Fields.

The last incidents of the war. After this a contest arose between Ajax and Odysseus as to which of them should receive the arms of Achilles, and when the decision was given in Odysseus' favor, Ajax, crazed with anger, made an onslaught on an innocent flock of sheep, imagining them to be Odysseus and his followers. When he came to his senses, he killed himself. Then the gods made it known to the Greeks that they could never take Troy until Phil oc te'tes, who was the possessor of Heracles' bow and poisoned arrows (see p. 227) should be brought from the island of Lesbos, where his comrades had most cruelly left him suffering from a horrible wound. With some difficulty Philoctetes was induced to forego his resentment and come to the Greek camp. Being cured of his wound he met Paris in battle and killed him with one of his poisoned arrows. Even then two things were still necessary before the gods would give Troy over to her enemies. Achilles' son Ne op tol'e mus had to be summoned from Greece to take his father's place, and the Pal la'di um, or sacred image of Athena, which had fallen from heaven long ago, and on the possession of which the safety of the city depended, must be taken. This extraordinary feat was performed by Odysseus and Diomedes, who, entering the city by night, abstracted the image from the shrine and carried it to the Greek camp.

The final device by which Troy fell into the hands of its besiegers was planned with the help of Athena. A huge hollow structure in the form

The wooden horse.

of a horse was set up near the walls, and in the belly armed men, the bravest of the Greeks, were placed in ambush. Then the hosts sailed off,

Fig. 91. Laocoon and his Sons.

pretending to be returning to Greece, while, in reality, they concealed themselves behind the island of Tenedos, ready to return at a given signal. The Trojans poured out of the city, rejoicing in the unexpected freedom and wondering at the wooden horse. The question as to what it meant and what should be done with it was decided by the testimony of a clever Greek named Sinon, who, having gained the confidence of the Trojans, explained the horse as a final tribute to Athena, which, if taken within the city by the people of Troy, would certainly protect them from harm. La oc'o on, the priest of Apollo, suspecting the wiles of the Greeks, urged that it be thrown into the sea and raised his weapon to strike the wood a blow. Immediately two horrible serpents appeared on the sea, and glided with their slimy lengths over the water, caught Laocoön and his two sons and strangled them with their coils. Then all believed that the gods had sent retribution upon the priest for his impious doubts, and resolved to draw the horse within the walls As it was too high to go under the gates, a piece of the wall was thrown down and the horse brought in amid great rejoicing.

That night while all Troy slept, the Greek spy Sinon unloosed the bolts and let out the heroes concealed in the horse. At the signal given by fire, the fleet returned from Tenedos, the gates were opened from within, and the Greeks fell upon the sleeping city. The brave resistance offered by the Trojans, taken unawares in the blackness of night, was useless. The prophetic

The destruction of Troy.

daughter of Priam, Cas san'dra, was dragged
from the sanctuary of Athena and carried into
slavery; the same fate overtook Hector's wife

Fig. 92.　Priam slain on the Altar.

Andromache, after she had seen her infant son
dashed from the wall that his father had so long
defended. Priam was cut down before the altar
in his own palace, and all the city sank in ashes.

CHAPTER XVIII

THE WANDERINGS OF ODYSSEUS

AFTER the fall of Troy the chiefs with their The return of the heroes. followers sailed for home. But in those days even the comparatively short voyage from Asia Minor to Greece was filled with danger; moreover, some of the heroes in the course of that long war had incurred the enmity of one or another of the gods, who, therefore, cut off altogether or delayed their return home. Certain of the Trojans after long wanderings founded new cities on strange shores; many of both nations met their death by drowning or by the violence of savage men and monsters; one returned only to be foully murdered. "The much enduring Odysseus" (more familiarly known by his Latin name, Ulysses) added ten years of wanderings and of marvelous adventures to the ten years of the war, and returned home to his faithful wife Penelope after an absence of twenty years. Homer tells his story in the *Odyssey*.

When he had set sail from Troy with his men Odysseus comes to the Lotus-eaters. and ships, Odysseus made a fairly prosperous voyage as far as the southern point of Greece and was within a few days' sail of Ithaca, his

305

home, when a great wind arose and drove him from his course. After nine days the ships came to land in the Lotus-eaters' country, and the men were kindly entertained and given to eat of the lotus. This plant had the strange power of taking from him who ate of it all remembrance of the past and all ambition for the future and making him desire only to live on in a dreamy and effortless present. Those of Odysseus' men, therefore, who had tasted the lotus could be forced to continue on their voyage only by being bound in the ships until the effect of the food had worn off.

The Cyclops. The next land reached by the voyagers was very different, a rough and rocky island inhabited by a tribe of savage giants, called Cy clo'pes, whose peculiarity it was that each had but one great eye, set in the middle of his forehead. Leaving the rest of his companions on another island, Odysseus beached his own ship on the shore of the Cyclopes, and as none of the terrible inhabitants was about at the time, he and his men disembarked and trustfully wandered about the island until they chanced upon a great cave where a plentiful supply of milk and cheese tempted their appetites. While they were eating, the Cyclops Pol y phe'mus returned, driving his sheep before him, and coming into the cave closed its entrance with a huge rock. Though his natural craftiness and caution led Odysseus to conceal his true name and give, when asked, the name Noman, with apparent confidence he requested of his monstrous host hospitality and the gifts that Greek courtesy usually gave a guest as his due. But Zeus and his law of hospitality were not recognized by this savage giant, and his only answer was to seize two of his guests and devour them raw. Then he lay down to sleep. In the morning, after breakfasting on two more of the men, he drove his sheep out of the cave, and rolling the stone against the opening, left Odysseus and those of his company who remained uneaten to sit and wait for their fiendish host to return for his next meal. But Odysseus was not the man to sit and expect his fate at the hands of a stupid and barbarous Cyclops. He planned escape and vengeance. At the fall of evening, when Polyphemus returned with his flocks, the wily hero talked pleasantly with him and offered him some particularly fine and strong wine that he happened to have with him. In high good humor Polyphemus washed down his dinner of two Greeks with this drink — a pleasant change to one accustomed only to sheep's milk — and stretched himself out to sleep. Then Odysseus and his men seized a great long pole which, during the day, they had sharpened to a point and hardened in the fire, and using all their strength, drove it deep into the Cyclops' one eye. Polyphemus sprang up, bellowing with

pain, and madly called on his brother Cyclopes
for help. But when, hurrying to the mouth of
the cave, they asked him who was troubling him,
he could only answer: "Noman is slaying me
by guile, nor at all by force." So they went
away, telling him to pray to his father Poseidon,
since, if no man was killing him, it must be by
the will of the gods, whom no one can resist.
It was now morning and time to let the sheep
out, so the Cyclops, still groaning with pain,
rolled away the stone from the door and sat down
by it, stretching out his hands to feel if any man
passed out. Odysseus took the sheep and fastened them three together; he ordered one of his
men to stretch himself flat on the middle one of
each group, and so all but he passed out safely.
Then he himself clung firmly to the under side of.
the great thick-fleeced ram, and the blind Cyclops, though he felt over the ram's back and
wondered that he should be behind his flock, failed
to detect the hero. So the men escaped to their
boat. Although they had been saved by their
leader's wits, they were a second time endan-
gered by his rashness, for when they were once
afloat Odysseus could not resist calling back
tauntingly to his enemy, and the Cyclops, dashing
down to the shore, hurled immense rocks after
the departing ship. If his aim had not been poor
because of his blindness, the ship would surely
have been sunk. Failing in this, Polyphemus

called aloud upon Poseidon for vengeance, and from that time on the sea-god turned against the heroes and relentlessly kept them wandering over the waters.

Some time after this adventure the heroes came to the floating island of Æ′o lus, the king of the winds. Here Odysseus was kindly received and entertained, and on his departure was presented by Æolus with a huge bag in which were imprisoned all the winds except the favorable west wind. So after nine days' fair sailing they had actually come so near to Ithaca that they could see men moving on the rocks, and Odysseus, for the first time feeling free from his anxieties, lay down in the boat to rest. Then the men conspired to rob him, and supposing that the bag contained precious treasure they eagerly opened it. In an instant all the contrary winds rushed out together and drove the ships far off their course straight back to the island of Æolus. But Æolus, thinking that one so unfortunate as Odysseus must for his sins be under the disfavor of the gods, sent him angrily away, refusing to give him any more help.

Next they came to the land of a people named Læs try go′ni ans, who fell upon the strangers and destroyed eleven of the ships with their companies. Only the twelfth, with Odysseus on board, got off in safety. In great grief over the loss of their companions, the remnant of

The island of Æolus.

Circe.

Odysseus' company sailed on until they came to the island of the sorceress Circe. Having learned discretion from his previous misfortunes, Odysseus did not risk all his men at once, but sent half, under a trustworthy leader, to explore the country while the other half remained by the shore. The scouting party, as they went through the woods, were alarmed by meeting great numbers of lions and wolves, but as these beasts instead of attacking them came and fawned upon them appealingly, they took heart and continued on their way until they came to a palace. The peacefulness of the place and the reassuring sound of a woman singing emboldened the adventurers to enter. Circe turned from her weaving to greet the strangers and hastened to set before them food and drink. The thirsty men did not see the magic drops their hostess mingled with their wine. At a touch of her wand the lordly Greeks dropped down and trotted, grunting reproachfully, to the sties. But one man, their leader, had not gone into the house with them. At their prolonged absence he became uneasy and returned in haste to the ship to tell what he feared. So Odysseus set out alone to rescue his men. As he went, Hermes met him and warned him of the danger that lay before him and gave him an herb to protect him against Circe's spells. When, therefore, Circe received him as she had his followers, and after giving him the potion, raised

her wand and ordered him to the sties, the hero
grappled with her and threatened to kill her unless she at once restored his men to their proper
forms. Recognizing in this successful resistance
to her magic the hand of a god, and charmed by
her new guest's cleverness and strength, the sorceress yielded to all his demands and sending
for the rest of the company from the ship entertained them all royally for a whole year. But
at the end of that time, when they all began to
long for the return home, Circe told Odysseus
of a terrible ordeal that lay before him before
he could reach Ithaca. He, a living man, must
go to the realm of the dead to consult the seer
Ti re'si as.

With dread at his heart Odysseus followed out The visit to
the sorceress' directions and sailed on to the very Hades.
edge of the world, where the stream of Ocean
rolls by the land of the Cim mer'i ans, a land always shrouded in mist and darkness, for the
sun never rises upon it. From there he proceeded along the shore of the Ocean until he
came to the grove of Persephone, where was the
entrance to Hades. By the place where the
rivers of the lower world, fiery Phleg'e thon, and
Co cy'tus, the river of wailing, flow into gloomy
Ach'e ron, he dug a trench, as Circe had directed
him, and poured a libation to the dead. Then
he sacrificed black sheep and let their blood run
into the trench. And the shades of the dead

crowded around with ghostly cries, eager to drink of the blood,— boys and maidens, and warriors that had fallen in battle. But Odysseus kept them off with his sword that the shade of the seer Tiresias might first drink and tell him what he wished to know. So Tiresias came and drank, and prophesied to the hero his safe home-coming and how he should find violent men wasting his substance and should kill them all and so live to an old age in peace and plenty among a happy people. But then he told him, too, of Poseidon's anger at the mutilation of his son Polyphemus, and that yet for many years he would keep Odysseus away from Ithaca, and he warned him especially that destruction would overtake them all if they should injure the cattle of the sun when they came to the island of Trinacria. When the seer had finished, Odysseus' mother came, and when she had drunk of the blood she knew her son and told him of her own death, caused by grief at his long absence, and of his old father, and of his wife Pe nel'o pe, and his little son Te-lem'a chus. But when he tried to embrace her, like a shadow or a dream she faded away. Then there came about him many of the women famous in story — Leda, the mother of Helen and of Castor and Polydeuces; Alcmena, Heracles' mother; Ariadne, whom Theseus had deserted on Naxos, and many others. He saw and talked with the heroes who had fought with him at

Troy — Agamemnon, who told him of his treacherous murder, and Achilles, preëminent here as
in the world above. There were the heroes of
ancient times, even the shade of great Heracles
— the shade only, for he himself was now a god
in Olympus. There he saw Minos sitting as
judge, and those who had sinned against the gods
suffering eternal punishment, Tantalus, Sisyphus,
and others.

Returning safely from that land that so few The Sirens.
living men have ever visited, the company stopped

Fig. 93. Odysseus and the Sirens.

once more at Circe's island. There they were entertained for a day while Circe told Odysseus of
the dangers that next confronted him and how he

might win safely through them. From there they sailed on until they saw on the shore at a distance the meadow of the Sirens, who bewitch men by their songs. But Odysseus stuffed his companions' ears with wax and had himself bound hand and foot to the mast, as Circe had told him. And when the ship came near, the Sirens called to him to leap from the deck and come to them, for they had knowledge of past and future and could give him happiness. So he tried to break away and go to them, and he made signs to the others to loose him, but they pulled steadily on and so escaped that danger.

Scylla and Charybdis. Soon two cliffs appeared, rising one on either side of the course between Italy and Sicily; in the one crouched Scylla, her twelve feet dangling down from the cave, and her six heads turning in every direction in search of ships. On the other side was a lower cliff with a fig tree at the top, and below it Char yb'dis, who three times a day sucked in the water and cast it out again. As the ship passed through, keeping, as Circe had told them, well away from Charybdis, Scylla stretched her long necks forward and seized a man in each of her terrible jaws. As they were drawn up, squirming like fishes caught on a hook, they cried out in anguish to Odysseus, and all that were left of that company shuddered as they passed on.

Towards nightfall Odysseus saw before them the island of the Sun, Trinacria, and he ordered his men to row on, remembering the warnings of Tiresias and Circe. But they were exhausted with hard rowing and the strain of the terrible meeting with Scylla and insisted upon landing for the night. The next morning unfavorable winds were blowing, and continued for a whole month, until all the food and wine was exhausted. Then while Odysseus was sleeping, his companions preferring any other form of death to starvation, killed some of the sacred cattle that grazed on that island and made a feast. When Odysseus awoke and saw it, he knew that destruction had come upon them, for the empty hides crept mysteriously, and the flesh on the spits bellowed. At last favorable winds blew, and they put out to sea. But the sun-god had complained to Zeus of the loss of his cattle, threatening that if his wrong were not avenged he would leave the world in darkness and go to shine among the dead. So Zeus sent a storm to overtake the ship, and all the men were swept into the sea and drowned, and only Odysseus clung to the boat. He was carried straight back to Charybdis, who, as she threw out the water, shattered and then swallowed down the ship; Odysseus escaped only by grasping hold of the fig tree when the water cast him up. There he hung suspended until Charybdis heaved up the wreckage of the ship again. Then he dropped upon one of its timbers and rowed with his hands until he was out of reach of the whirlpool.

Calypso's island. After this hairbreadth escape the hero, now quite without companions, was washed ashore on the island of Ca l yp′so, the daughter of Atlas. There he lived for eight years in the company of the charming nymph, eating and drinking of the best and living the most peaceful and luxurious of lives on that beautiful island. Yet he did not forget his home and his wife, but sat day after day by the sea eating out his heart with home-sickness. For, as he himself said:

Surely there is naught sweeter than a man's own country and his parents, even though he dwell far off in a rich house, in a strange land, far from them that begat him. (*Odyssey*, IX. 34 ff.)

At last, at the complaint of Athena that her favorite was kept too long away from home, Zeus sent Hermes to command Calypso to let him go. Yielding unwillingly, she gave him the tools and material to construct a raft and a sail, and when it was ready, she stocked it with food and wine and gave him clothes and rich gifts and so sent him away. For eighteen days he had sailed prosperously along on his raft before Poseidon caught sight of him, and still brooding over the injury to Polyphemus, sent a furious storm against him. The sail was carried away and the raft itself was swept and torn by the waves. To the solitary adventurer out on those wide waters it seemed that his own gods had deserted him and that death was close upon him. But a sea-goddess saw and pitied him, and rising in the foam beside him held out to him her filmy scarf and spoke wisely and reassuringly. Borne up by the new courage she inspired and by the mysterious power of the scarf, Odysseus struck bravely out when the raft finally parted, and swimming continuously for two days and two nights, came at last in sight of land. But the waves were breaking high on the rocky coast, and the exhausted swimmer was beaten against the rocks and again sucked back by the undertow until it seemed he must go under. At one point a back current offered possible landing; there he managed to come to land and drew his bruised and soaked limbs up on the shore. Among the bushes on the bank he lay down and fell into the sleep of exhaustion.

The shore on which Odysseus had landed was Nausicaa. that of the Phæ a'ci ans, a good and prosperous people at peace with all the world and in great favor with the gods. On the night of the hero's perilous landing the king's daughter Nau sic'a a had been bidden by Athena in a dream to go down to the shore to wash her clothes in preparation for her coming wedding day. As her father had not yet even decided upon any one of her suitors as her husband, the princess felt shy about suggesting wedding preparations, but not wishing to displease the goddess, she modestly asked for the ox-cart that she and her maidens might carry down her brothers' clothes to wash them in the sea. The cart was brought around, the queen packed a basket with bread and honey and wine, and the young girls drove off for the shore. When the clothes had all been washed and spread out in the sun to bleach, they sat down on the

Fig. 94. Odysseus appearing before Nausicaa.

grass to eat the food the queen had provided, and then, tucking up their skirts, they joined in a game of ball. It happened that the spot they had chosen for their noisy fun was close to the place where Odysseus had all this time been lying asleep. What was the astonishment and terror of the girls when suddenly a strange and wild-looking man appeared in their midst! Only Nausicaa stood her ground with dignity, and when the hero approached and begged for help and hospitable treatment, she showed him every

kindness. She gave him oil to anoint his lame
and battered limbs and some of her brothers'
newly washed clothes to put on, and bade him
follow her to the city, where her father would
entertain him. Being a prudent girl and fearing
gossip if she appeared in company with a hand-
some stranger (for the oil and the fresh clothes
had restored Odysseus' fine appearance), she
thought it best not to take him with her in the
ox-cart.

As Odysseus, so long an exile from civilized
human life, approached the king's palace, he wondered at the great wharves thronged with ships
and at the beautiful city with its fine streets and
houses and its busy and prosperous people, and
more than ever a longing came over him for his
own well-ordered land. The considerate and
gentle treatment he received when he presented
himself as a stranger before the king and queen
proved that the reputation of the Phæacians was
not undeserved. For they provided him with
warm baths and entertained him royally with a
feast and music, dancing and athletic sports, nor
did they so forget the courtesy of hosts as ever
to show curiosity about who the stranger was
or on what business he was bent. When, however, the proper time had come, Odysseus told
them all his story since the day that Troy fell,
and he ended with earnest entreaties that his hosts
would provide him with a ship and oarsmen to

The Phæa-
cian court.

set him across the sea to Ithaca. So they gave him all that he asked and added splendid gifts, more valuable than all the booty he had gathered at Troy and then lost in his wanderings. While he slept, for he was still overcome with weariness, he was set ashore on the island of Ithaca. Then those generous Phæacians received a poor reward for their hospitality, for as the ship returned, Poseidon rooted it fast in the sea and turned it to stone, to a little rocky island that still lies there off the island of Corfu and by its name, "The Island of Ulysses," witnesses to the truth of the story.

Penelope's web.

The twenty long years of the hero's absence had brought anxiety and distress to his people and to his wife and son. For after the news of the fall of Troy had reached Ithaca, and the other Greek princes who were still alive had returned to Greece, and still no word came of Odysseus, it came to be commonly believed that he was dead, and a great number of suitors from Ithaca and elsewhere began to demand Penelope in marriage. Telemachus was still too young successfully to defend his mother from their insolent insistence or his house from their greedy violence, and year after year saw them living riotously and extravagantly on their absent host's hospitality. The faithful Penelope, still hoping against hope for her noble husband's return, put them all off from day to day with a device that was worthy of her crafty husband. Promising that she would make a decision so soon as she had completed a shroud she was weaving for her old father against his death, she spent her days in the chambers among her maidens, weaving her great web, and at night when no one was by to see, she unraveled all that she had done the day before. For three years the suitors had been deceived, but at last they had learned of the trick and were now pressing more insistently than ever for a decision.

Meanwhile, as Telemachus grew to be a young man, more and more he chafed at the wasting of his inheritance and the arrogant behavior of the suitors, yet he was unable either to turn them out of his house or to protect his mother from their persistency. Shortly before Odysseus' landing at Ithaca, however, the goddess Athena, extending to his son the favor she had always shown to Odysseus, roused him to brave the anger of the suitors and go in search of his father. With the goddess as guide he came first to the court of Nestor and afterwards to that of Menelaüs. Both heroes received the son of their old comrade with cordial kindness, but the aged Nestor could tell him nothing of his father. Menelaüs, however, had heard from Proteus, the prophetic old man of the sea, that Odysseus was held captive on an island by the nymph Calypso. Strengthened in his resistance to the suitors by

Telemachus in search of his father.

the knowledge that his father was still living, Telemachus started on his return voyage. But the suitors, made anxious by the increased courage and determination the young man had displayed in equipping a ship and venturing across the seas, planned to catch him on his return and take his life.

Odysseus in the swineherd's hut. When Odysseus awoke on the shore of his own island, Athena appeared to him and warned him of the dangers that still awaited him. To secure him further she changed his appearance to that of an old and ragged beggar. It was in this disguise that he presented himself at the hut of the faithful old swineherd Eu mæ'us and asked for

Fig. 95.   Odysseus makes himself known to Telemachus.

food and shelter. True to the hospitable custom of his absent master, the swineherd received the old stranger with kindness, and while he set before him the best he could provide, entertained him with an account of the sorry state of affairs on the island, speaking always of his lord Odys-

seus with loyal and affectionate regret. As they
talked, Telemachus, just landed and happily escaped from the ambush set for him, appeared
at the hut. His father's heart rejoiced to see the
boy grown so strong and confident, and to receive at his hands the fine courtesy and respect
for age that distinguished noble Greeks. But he
restrained his feelings, and not until Eumæus was
called away, leaving father and son alone together, did he reveal himself to Telemachus. So
the two planned together the destruction of the
troublesome suitors, and before the swineherd returned Odysseus had resumed his disguise.

Not as an honored hero returning from the war
did Odysseus reënter his home after his twenty
years of absence, but as an old and wretched beggar asking for charity. Yet even so two faithful friends knew him. His old hunting-dog, lying neglected in the dirt outside the door, knew
his master as he passed by means of that strange
dog's sense that humans cannot understand, and
with one last pricking of the ears and feeble wag-
ging of his tail, died happy. The second friend
who knew him was not his wife, who, though
she had him brought to her to ask him for any
news of her husband he might have learned on
his travels, gave him only that attention she gave
to every stranger. It was his old nurse Eu ry-
cle'a who, as at Penelope's command she washed
the old stranger's feet, saw a scar he had had

Odysseus among the suitors.

since he was a boy and at once knew him. In the great hall where the arrogant suitors sat all day and feasted none knew that despised old man, and all with one accord joined in scornful and ungenerous treatment of him. For how could Zeus's law of hospitality bind men who so dishonored an absent hero's house and so persecuted the unprotected? It was only by the spirited interference of Telemachus, supported by the less shameless of the princes, that Odysseus was saved from violence. At last Athena put it into Penelope's mind to appear among the suitors with the great bow her lord had left behind him, and announce that she would keep them waiting no longer, but that to him who was man enough to bend that bow and shoot through the holes in nine ax-heads set up before them she would give herself as wife. All tried. boastfully and hopefully, and all failed even to bend the bow. Then the old beggar rose and demanded that he be allowed to make the trial. Amid the jeers and disgusted protests of the princes he received the bow from Penelope's hand. The tough wood bent, the arrow whizzing from the string pierced through the nine axes. Then his disguise fell from him, and standing revealed the hero turned his arrows now this way, now that, upon those wretched suitors. By order of Telemachus all the weapons had been removed from the hall the night before, and the faithful swineherd and an equally faithful keeper of cattle had been posted at the exits. So the men were slaughtered like sheep, and Odysseus and his son would have met with no resistance had not a disloyal slave smuggled in some swords and shields for those who had not yet fallen. Even against these odds

Fig. 96. Odysseus avenging himself upon the Suitors.

the father and son, aided by their protectress Athena, were victorious, and not one of the suitors or their followers lived to leave that hall of death. At the end of this bloody act Odysseus made himself known to his wife; the house was cleansed of its murderous stains, and a period of peace and prosperity followed the hardships of those twenty years.

CHAPTER XIX

THE TRAGEDY OF AGAMEMNON

Clytemnestra and Ægisthus. WHEN Agamemnon went to lead the armies of Greece against Troy in vengeance for the wrong done to his brother Menelaüs, he left both the care of his children and the rule of his wide kingdom to his wife Cly tem nes'tra. Though no protracted wanderings doubled for him, as for Ulysses, the time of his absence, the avenging fates had prepared for his home-coming a tragedy so black as to be the fitting culmination to the course of crime and horror that marked the history of his race. Æ gis'thus, Agamemnon's cousin, who was at once the guilty lover and the associate in power of Clytemnestra, was a son of that Thyestes who, ignorant of what he did, had been forced by his brother Atreus to eat of the flesh of his own son, served to him at a feast. (See p. 282.) The hatred engendered by this horrible crime had been handed down from father to son, and Ægisthus only waited an opportunity to avenge his father's wrong on Atreus' son Agamemnon. Clytemnestra, too, in addition to her secret passion for Ægisthus, had other causes to wish her husband's death. Ever since that day when, under pretense of giving his daughter in marriage to Achilles, Agamemnon had summoned his wife to bring Iphigenia to Aulis and had then offered the maiden in sacrifice to Artemis, Clytemnestra had nourished fierce resentment towards her lord and with Ægisthus secretly planned his ruin.

At last the watchman, who from his high tower had watched and waited for nine long years for the beacon light that was to tell the fall of Troy and the return of his conquering lord, announced that the fiery signal had been passed along and Agamemnon was at hand. Preparations were made for his honorable reception, and the citizens joyfully gathered to greet him. He came accompanied by those of his followers who still survived, and bringing with him as a slave, Priam's daughter Cassandra, to whom Apollo, because he loved her, had given the gift of prophecy, and because she rejected his love, had added the curse that her prophecies should never be believed. As the king in his chariot drew up before the palace, the great doors opened, and Clytemnestra in festal robes came out to greet her lord and with feigned honor and affection led him within. The palace doors closed behind them. Then Cassandra, who had refused to leave the chariot, raised her prophetic voice in lamentation and unintelligible warning of coming tragedy. All the bloody and unnatural crimes of

The murder of Agamemnon.

that house rose before her, and she saw them about to be crowned by another yet more terrible. But none could understand her warnings; only when a great cry of agony rose from within those closed doors and was repeated again and again did her meaning become plain. Insolent in her vengeance, Clytemnestra threw wide the doors and displayed the body of her husband bleeding from the wounds she had inflicted as he stepped into the bath prepared to make him ready for the feast of his home-coming. Cassandra too met death at the hand of jealous Clytemnestra.

Orestes avenges his father. The terrible law of retribution in those days required of a son to avenge his father, and Clytemnestra and Ægisthus, knowing this, would have slaughtered Agamemnon's little son O res'tes had not his older sister E lec'tra sent him out of the country for safe-keeping. That Electra herself might never be in a position of influence to arouse a revolt against the murderers, she was compelled to become the wife of a humble servant. She could only pray that the distant brother would return when the time came to fulfil his duty of vengeance. And when the time came and Orestes with his faithful friend Py'la des arrived, the brother and sister, meeting before their father's tomb were in full agreement about the duty before them. Ægisthus and Clytemnestra were celebrating a religious feast when Ores-

!es came upon them, and taking them unawares, killed them both.

This revolting murder of a mother by her son, though done in accordance with the law of vengeance, brought defilement and the anger of the gods. The Eu men'i des, or Furies, the divine avengers of crime, pursued Orestes and drove him mad. He wandered from land to land, always accompanied by his faithful friend Pylades, until at the god's command he came to the land of the Taurians to obtain the sacred image of the goddess Artemis. It was to this land that Iphigenia had been carried by Artemis when she was saved by her at Aulis, and here she had lived ever since, serving as Artemis' priestess in her temple. In accordance with the barbarous custom of this country all strangers who landed on their shores were offered in sacrifice to the goddess, and it was to Iphigenia that the duty of this sacrifice fell. When Orestes and Pylades were about to be offered up, however, they became known to the priestess, and through her extraordinary power and influence they were enabled to secure the sacred image of Artemis and escape unharmed, carrying Iphigenia with them. Even then, before Orestes could be purified of his crime, he was compelled to appear before the A re o'pa gus, the great Athenian court of justice. Here the Eumenides acted as his accusers, and though he pleaded in defense Apollo's ap-

Orestes' madness and purification.

proval of his act, the court was equally divided on the question.   Athena cast the deciding vote for acquittal, the Eumenides left him, and the curse on the family of Pelops had run its course.

CHAPTER XX

THE LEGENDARY ORIGIN OF ROME

THE Romans, tracing the history of their race back beyond the times when events were recorded in history into the realm of tradition and myth, honored Æ ne'as, the son of An chi'ses, by the goddess Venus, as the founder of their race. Throughout the Trojan War Æneas had proved himself one of the bravest and ablest leaders of the Trojan forces, standing next, perhaps, to Hector in general esteem. On the occasion of his single combat with Diomedes his goddess-mother had intervened to save his life; he had joined in the contest over Patroclus' body and had even stood to meet the invincible Achilles. So much we learn from Homer, but it is the Latin poet Vergil who narrates the full story of Æneas' deeds and wanderings, making him the central fig-ure in his great Roman national epic, the *Æneid*.

On the night when, neglecting the wise coun-sels of Laocoön, the Trojans had drawn the wooden horse within their walls, the weary citi-zens, relieved of immediate anxiety by the ap-parent departure of the Greeks, had given them-selves up to much needed rest and sleep. Æneas'

rest was disturbed by the vision of nis dead cousin
Hector appearing before him, all bloody from the
wounds he had received at Achilles' hands, and

Fig. 97. Æneas Wounded.

bidding him arouse himself and see the destruction that had at last come upon Troy. Springing up, the hero rushed to the roof of his house
and from that point could see that the city was

already in the hands of its foes. Reckless of personal danger and caring little for his own life if he might yet bring some support to his falling city, he led a band of Trojans in one last desperate struggle. Driven from one point to another he came at last to Priam's palace and saw the old king lying slain before his household altar, his last son lying near him and his women huddled together in despair. But the fates decreed that Æneas should not perish in burning Troy, but should live to found a new and greater city on the banks of Tiber. Venus appeared to her son, and "drawing aside the veil that dims mortal sight," showed him the gods directing the destruction of the city. Then Æneas yielded and hurried at once to his home to save his own family. Bidding his father Anchises take up the images of the Penates or family gods, he took the old man upon his back, seized his little son As ca'ni us, or I u'lus, by the hand, and bidding his wife Cre- u'sa follow close behind, he made his way through the flames and confusion to a place of safety outside the walls. Not until he had passed the city gate did he discover that his wife was not following. In his distracted and hopeless search for her he met only her shade which came to tell him that the gods detained her on those shores and that it was their will that he should go on his way without her. Other Trojans who had escaped in the course of a few days joined the little group in their place of hiding between the mountains and the sea, and here they built and fitted out twelve ships on which the next spring they set sail.

Æneas's wanderings. Then began a period of wandering almost as full of adventure as the nine years of Ulysses' seafaring. First the company landed in Thrace, where Æneas hoped to found a new city, but the strange portent of a bush which, when uprooted, dripped blood and spoke in the voice of Priam's murdered son Pol y dor′us.[39] drove them to seek a more propitious land. They sailed to Delos to consult Apollo, and understanding a reference of the oracle to an ancestral home as meaning Crete, whence, tradition held, their forefathers had gone to Troy, they made their way thither. While they were building the new city, a terrible pestilence fell upon them, blighting the grain and killing men and beasts. Then the Penates warned Æneas in a dream that the ancestral land Apollo prophesied was Hesperia, or Italy, whence, as legend told, Dardanus, the ancestor of the Trojans, had originally come. In pain and grief, but still hopeful, the diminished band started on their western voyage; but a terrible

[39] During the war Priam had sent Polydorus, only a boy at the time, to seek protection with the king of Thrace, but when the news of the fall of Troy came to him, the king murdered his charge and seized the treasure that Priam had sent with him.

storm drove the ships out of their course to the island of the Strophades, haunted by those dreadful Harpies which the Argonauts had met. While the exhausted sailors were feasting, these horrible bird-women swooped down and seized the food off the tables. Driven off by the men, they yet left despair behind them, for their leader prophesied a long and destructive voyage, and that finally the day should come when hunger would force the wanderers to eat their own tables. Leaving the Strophades the Trojans sailed northward along the coast of Epirus, passing Odysseus' rocky island of Ithaca and the coast of the Phæacians, and landing finally in a harbor further up the coast. Here they were overjoyed to find a new city modeled on Troy and ruled over by Priam's prophetic son Hel'e nus. Hector's wife Andromache, who at the fall of Troy had been given to Achilles' son Neoptolemus, was now living with Helenus as his wife. At the moment of the Trojans' landing she was occupied in offering a sacrifice at the empty tomb of her noble first husband. She and Helenus received their wandering countrymen with enthusiastic hospitality, and when Æneas felt that they must continue on their divinely guided way, they loaded him with gifts, and after Helenus had warned him of the dangers that lay before him, they unwillingly let him go. Sailing westward they sighted Italy, but knowing that the towns of this part of south Italy were Greek they gave the coast a wide berth. As they neared Sicily they saw the cave of dreadful Scylla and the waters thrown high from the whirlpool of Charybdis, but, more fortunate than Ulysses, had no need to pass between. Not knowing the risk they ran, the sailors beached their ships on the south coast of Sicily near the cave of the Cyclops Polyphemus and came on shore to spend the night. But Ætna belching forth flames and thundering in full eruption drove sleep away and kept the men in terrified suspense. At dawn a man, hairy, savage, and emaciated, came to them pitifully begging to be taken from this terrible island. He was a Greek, a companion of Ulysses, who had been left behind when those whom Ulysses' craft had saved from being devoured had made their hasty escape, but in the face of the savagery of the inhuman Cyclops race-enmity was forgotten and the wretched Greek found refuge on the Trojan ships. They did not get away from the island without seeing Polyphemus and his brothers, however, for Polyphemus, coming down to the water to bathe his bloody eye-socket, heard the sound of their oars and bellowed aloud. The other Cyclopes heard him, and hurrying to the shore, stood there towering up like great trees and threatening the ship with destruction. On the further shore of Sicily a grief of which Æneas had not been forewarned awaited him:

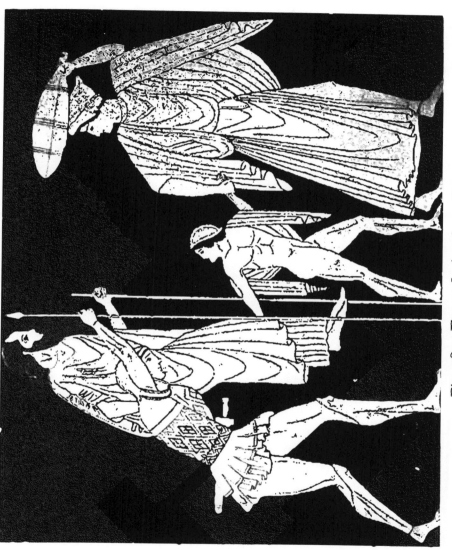

Fig. 98. Æneas fleeing from Troy.

his old father Anchises, who had nobly borne with him the hardships of these years of wandering, died and had to be given a grave in this foreign soil. From Sicily it was but a short voyage to the destined home in Italy, but when the ships had been launched and were well out at sea, Juno, still cherishing resentment against the hated Trojan race, persuaded Æolus, king of the winds, to let out conflicting blasts against the ships. Driven directly south, they finally sought shelter in an inlet on the coast of Africa where the new city of Carthage was building. Æneas, setting out with his faithful comrade Acha'tes to explore the neighborhood, was met by his mother Venus disguised as a huntress and by her was directed to the city.

Though on the coast of Africa, Carthage was a Phœnician city, founded by a Phœnician king's daughter, Dido, who with a large following had secretly departed from her native land after the murder of her husband by her wicked brother. She was well acquainted with the story of Troy, and the name of Æneas was familiar to her, so she welcomed the unfortunate strangers cordially and generously, and even urged them to share her new city and happy prospects. Venus had a hand in this extreme good-will shown her son, for she sent her powerful boy Cupid to take the form of little Ascanius and inspire in the widowed queen love for the noble stranger. Indeed

Æneas entertained by Dido.

Æneas, who, not unresponsive to the queen's advances, had united with her in a secret marriage, might have been tempted to remain in Carthage, had not Jupiter sent Mercury to warn him against such an alliance and to remind him of his great destiny as founder of that Roman race that was to hold the world under its rule. So, obedient to the gods' will, the righteous Æneas put behind him his personal feelings and also, from the human standpoint, all thought of gratitude and honor towards his generous hostess and wife, and fixing his eyes only on the command of the fates, hastened to launch his ships and sail away. Then the unfortunate Dido, thus betrayed by the goddess into a passionate and unwise love, and by the god-fearing Æneas deserted while her passion still burned at its hottest, had a great pyre erected in the court of her palace, and mounting to the top, killed herself with the sword her faithless lover had left behind him, on her lips curses against her betrayer. As the Trojans sailed away towards their unknown future home, the sea behind them was lighted by the red flames of that tragic pyre.

The burning of the ships. But the ships came safely to Sicily, where kind Aces'tes, the king of Trojan descent who ruled over that part of the island, received them hospitably. Here they stayed to offer sacrifices and hold the postponed funeral games in honor of Anchises. While the men were thus employed, unrelenting Juno sent her messenger Iris down to tempt the Trojan women to burn the ships and thus thwart the fates and secure for themselves an end of their wanderings and the settlement they longed for in Sicily. Some ships had been previously lost in the storm, now others were destroyed by fire, and too few were left to transport all the company to the land decreed by fate. Therefore the older and weaker men and the women, already regretting their rash act, were left behind with Acestes, and with his diminished following Æneas started on once more. For the final voyage Venus secured from Neptune favorable seas; yet one man was demanded as a sacrifice for his favor — Pal i nu'rus, the skilful pilot, overcome with sleep, fell backward into the sea and was lost. A point of land on the west coast of Italy, where his body came ashore, still retains his name.

The friendly seer Helenus had told Æneas that before he could reach his future home and found a city he must visit the Sibyl of Cumæ and through the help of the prophetess descend to the lower world and obtain his father's advice on his future course. Leaving his men on the shore a few miles from where Naples stands, Æneas sought the cave of the Sibyl. This cave with its hundred dark mouths, was near Avernus, a lake mysteriously formed from the waters of the lower world and not far from the cave that

The Sibyl of Cumæ.

opened into Hades. Within it sat the Sibyl and uttered her prophecies when the god Apollo inspired and took possession of her. After the sacrifice had been offered and Æneas had prayed for help, the Sibyl poured forth her prophetic warnings and promises:

The Trojans shall come to the kingdom of Lavinium (Italy); dismiss this anxious care from your heart; but they will wish that they had not come. Wars, horrid wars, and the Tiber flowing with blood, I see. . . . Yet yield not to misfortune, but go boldly forward.

Undaunted, Æneas only asked that the Sibyl should open to him the way to the lower world that he might go to see his father, penetrating, as those other sons of the gods, Hercules, Theseus, and Orpheus, had done, the fearful places of the dead. The Sibyl answered:

Easy is the descent to Avernus; day and night the gates of black Dis (Pluto) lie open, but to retrace your steps, and escape once more to the upper air, that is the toil, that is the difficult task. (*Æneid*, VI, 126 ff.)

Yet it might be done if the hero could first find and pluck the golden branch that Proserpina claimed as her due offering. In the thick wood where the strange tree grew that one golden bough could hardly have been found had not Venus sent two doves to lead the way for her son.

After Æneas had offered the proper sacrifice of black sheep to the infernal deities, the Sibyl led him through a black cavern upon the gloomy road that led to the kingdom of Pluto. Here before the gates sat Grief and avenging Cares, pale Disease and sad Old Age, Fear and evil Famine, and shameful Want, and Death's twin brother Sleep, and death-dealing War on the threshold. Here were the iron chambers of the Furies, and here was mad Discord, her snaky locks bound with bloody fillets. In the middle of the open space was a huge elm beneath whose leaves clung deceiving Dreams, and about were many other monstrous forms, Centaurs, Scyllas, flaming Chimæra, Gorgons, and Harpies. Yet these were only unbodied shades against which, the Sibyl warned the hero, his sword could have no effect. Below this place seethed black Acheron, where the foul ferryman Charon waited with his frail skiff. About the bank crowded the shades of the dead whose funeral rites had been left undone, " as many as the leaves that fall in the woods in autumn at the first touch of frost." But the ferryman refused them all and sent them away to wander vainly about the shore until a hundred years should pass; then they win a passage to the sunless shore beyond. Here Palinurus greeted Æneas and begged him, when he returned to the upper air, to seek his body on the

The lower world

shore and give him proper burial. Charon at
first refused to accept a living man in his little
boat, but the word of the Sibyl and the sight
of the golden bough overcame his unwillingness,
and he turned out his ghostly passengers to make
room for the hero, and so set him across the
stream. A honey-cake thrown by the Sibyl pacified three-headed Cerberus. Then his guide led
Æneas through the places of the dead. First
they passed those who had died in infancy and
those who had suffered death on false accusa-
tions; next were those who had taken their own
lives, and the Fields of Mourning inhabited by
unhappy lovers, and among these the hero recognized unfortunate Dido, fresh from the funeral
pyre she herself had built. He would have
stopped to talk with her and excuse to the shade
his desertion of the living woman, but she silently turned from him and glided away, to rejoin her first husband. Proceeding they came
to where thronged the great warriors. The
Greeks fled before the Trojan hero, but his friends
and countrymen stayed to speak with him and
ask of the world they had left. Then they came
to the fiery river Phlegethon, encircling the adamantine walls of Tartarus, guarded by the Furies.
From here arose groans and the sound of blows
and the clank of iron chains. In the pit below
writhed the Titans and the rebellious giants and
those who had sinned against the gods or had

been guilty of unnatural crimes. Into this deep hell Æneas could not look, but the Sibyl told him of it as they passed by. In contrast to the fiery tortures of Tartarus the Elysian Fields spread before them, lighted by their own sun and stars, and bathed in a generous air and rosy light. Here the great heroes, children of the gods, contended in games, or joined in the song and choral dance. Here were the great founders of the Trojan race, Ilus, Dardanus, and others. Afar off in a green secluded valley of this realm at last Æneas met Anchises, reviewing the long line of souls who, having stayed the allotted time in the lower world and having drunk forgetfulness from the stream of Lethe, were ready to return in other bodies to the upper air as the descendants of Æneas, the glorious Roman race, Romulus who was to found Rome; all the seven Roman kings, and the great governors and generals who should make of Rome a world empire, all up to Augustus, in whose time Vergil wrote his great poem. When Anchises had shown his son all the future glories of their race, and warned him of the hardships that yet lay before him, he brought him to the Gates of Dreams. Through the gate of horn pass dreams that are to be fulfilled; through that of ivory, those sent to deceive mortals. From hence Æneas proceeded to the world above.

Sailing up the west coast of Italy, the Trojans finally beached their ships near where the Tiber, yellow with the sand it washes down, empties into the sea. When they had landed and prepared a hasty meal, their hunger led them to devour not only the food intended for them but the flat cakes of bread on which the food had been laid out. Seeing this, young Ascanius cried: "See, we are eating our tables!" So Æneas, recognizing that the prophecy of the Harpy was thus harmlessly fulfilled and that the land granted them by fate had at last been reached, gave thanks and worshiped the divinities of the place. The king of this part of the country was La ti'nus, whose daughter La vin'i a was sought as wife by the king of a neighboring tribe, Turnus by name. Though the parents of the girl would have been glad to have this prince as a son-in-law, the gods had warned them against the marriage, since a hero from over the sea was to have her as wife and by her raise up a race that should rule the world. When, therefore, Æneas sent messengers to Latinus, the king recognized his destined son-in-law in the stranger, and readily formed an alliance and offered him his daughter in marriage. But Juno, still implacable towards Æneas, sent one of the Furies to rouse Turnus and Latinus' queen against the Trojans. Moreover she made trouble between the newcomers and some Latin herdsmen, and finally threw open the gates of Janus' temple and roused all the country in war.[40] By night Father Tiber, the river-god, rose from his stream, and speaking to the sleeping Æneas, bade him proceed up the river to where the good king E van'der had his palace. With willing obedience Æneas made his way up the stream until at noon he came to Evander's settlement, its humble roofs clustered among the seven hills that later bore the massive buildings of imperial Rome. Fitly entertained by Evander on the spot later to be made glorious by his descendants, Æneas formed a compact of mutual help with the king, and on his new ally's advice proceeded thence northward to Etruria to draw into his alliance an Etruscan king who was already a bitter enemy of Turnus. Thus reinforced, Æneas returned at last to his camp by the Tiber to find a fierce battle in progress. Notwithstanding the superior numbers of the enemy and the brave deeds of Turnus and his allies, the Trojans were victorious, and Turnus died at Æneas' hand. At this point Vergil's story closes, but we know that Lavinia became Æneas' wife and that in her honor he named the town that he founded Lavinium.

Æneas' son Ascanius, or Iulus, founded Alba

Romulus and Remu

---

[40] Janus was the Roman god of beginnings. In time of war the gates of his temple were opened; in time of peace, closed.

Longa on the slope of the Alban Mount, and here his descendants continued to rule after his death. The last of the line to hold · the throne was Nu'mi'tor, whose younger brother A mu'li us wickedly supplanted him, and to preserve his own power, put to death Numitor's only son, and consecrated his daughter Rhea Silvia to the service of the goddess Vesta as a Vestal Virgin. But the virgin was loved by the war-god Mars and by him became the mother of twin sons. When Amulius, persisting in his wicked designs, ordered the babies to be drowned in the river, the trough that held them was carried down the stream into the Tiber, and by the guidance of the gods was washed high up on the bank and left by the retreating waters under a fig tree on the Palatine Hill. A she-wolf, wandering that way, was attracted by the babies' cries, and adopting them as her own whelps, nourished them with her milk. It is said that a wood-pecker, a bird sacred to Mars, also brought the babies food in her beak. After some time a kindly shepherd came upon the little savages and took them home to his hut on the Palatine Hill. As they grew, the twins, called by their foster-parents Romulus and Remus, became the acknowledged leaders of all the young shepherds about and fought against many wild beasts and robbers. After a quarrel with some herdsmen of Numitor Remus was taken before his grandfather and was recognized by him as his daughter's child. Amulius met at the young men's hands the death he deserved, and Numitor was restored to his kingdom. But Romulus and Remus, having a particular affection for the hills where they had lived as boys, put themselves at the head of a band of young men and set out to found a new city on the banks of the Tiber. A dispute arising between the two

Fig. 99. The wolf with Romulus and Remus.

as to whether the Palatine or the Aventine Hill was the more favorable site, they agreed to leave the matter to be decided by the gods. To Remus, looking for the divine sanction on the Aventine, appeared six vultures, but when he would have claimed the decision in his favor, Romulus on the Palatine reported the flight of twelve vultures. Disappointed in his hopes and wishing to show his contempt for his successful brother's plans,

Remus mockingly leaped over the wall Romulus was building. Romulus in a rage killed him on the spot. The new settlement was soon enlarged by the people from the country around, who were gladly afforded refuge there from enemies and a hospitable reception. Only wives were lacking. To supply this deficiency, when he had vainly tried more peaceful methods, Romulus adopted a somewhat treacherous device. Under pretense of celebrating sacred games, he invited his neighbors, the Latins and Sabines, to visit his city with their wives and daughters, and when the visitors were off their guard, the young Romans seized the Sabine women and drove the men away with violence. After some time the Sabines returned in force to recover their women, and a bloody battle was fought in what was afterwards the Roman Forum. In the midst of the fight the Sabine women, whose affections had been won by their violent young captors, but who still were anxious for the safety of their relatives, rushed between the combatants and effected a reconciliation. The Sabines were now given a settlement on the Capitoline and Quirinal Hills, and the two races united in one state with a common meeting-place in the Forum, the valley between their respective settlements. Through the wise and strong rule of Romulus the new city grew rapidly, and successful wars were carried on against hostile neighbors. One day when the king was reviewing his army in the Campus Martius, or Field of Mars, outside the city walls, an eclipse of the sun, accompanied by a terrific storm, darkened the heavens and threw the assemblage into a panic. As the men dispersed, Mars descended in a fiery chariot and carried his son Romulus off to heaven. After this his people worshiped the deified Romulus under the name of Qui ri'nus, and side by side with the temples of their other gods, religiously preserved the little straw hut he had occupied as a shepherd. The stories of Romulus's six successors in the kingship, full of interest and adventure, belong rather to the legendary history of Rome than to mythology.

APPENDICES

APPENDICES

APPENDIX A

Notes on the Pronunciation of Greek and Latin Proper Names.

I. *Accent.*

(1) The last syllable (ultima) is never accented.

(2) The next to the last syllable (penult) is accented when it contains a long vowel or a diphthong or when its vowel is followed by two or more consonants or by *x or z*, e.g., A the'na, He phæs'tus, Min er'va.

(3) If the penult is not long, the accent falls on the third syllable from the end (antepenult), e.g., Ju'pi ter, Ni'o be.

II. *Consonants.*

(1) *Ch* is pronounced like *k*.

(2) *C* is soft before *e, i, y, æ, œ;* elsewhere it is hard.

III. *Vowels.*

(1) The vowel *e* is long in the terminations *c* and *es*.

(2) The vowel *e* is long before the terminations *a* and *us*.

(3) The diphthongs *æ* and *œ* are pronounced like *e*.

APPENDIX B

A Brief List of Poems and Dramas Based on the Myths.

Chapter I. The World of the Myths.

Keats, *Hyperion;* Æschylus, *Prometheus Bound* (translation in *Everyman's Library*); Mrs. E. B. Browning, *Prometheus Bound;* Shelley, *Prometheus Unbound;* Byron, *Prometheus;* Robert Bridges, *Prometheus;* J. R. Lowell, *Prometheus;* H. W. Longfellow, *Prometheus* and *Epimetheus;* D. G. Rossetti, *Pandora;* H. W. Longfellow's *Masque of Pandora;* Account of the Four Ages and the Flood in Ovid's *Metamorphoses* I. 89–415 (translation in *Bohn's Libraries*).

Chapter II. The Gods of Olympus: Zeus.

Dean Swift, *Baucis and Philemon, imitated from the Eighth Book of Ovid, Metamorphoses* (a burlesque), in the Scott-Saintsbury edition of Swift's Works; Ovid, *Metamorphoses* I. 583 ff., II. 410 ff., VIII. 620 ff. (translation in *Bohn's Libraries*).

Chapter III. Hera, Athena, Hephæstus.

Thomas Moore, *The Fall of Hebe;* J. R. Lowell, *Hebe;* John Ruskin, *The Queen of the Air* (lectures); Milton, *Paradise Lost* I. 740 ff.; Ovid, *Metamorphoses* VI. 1 ff. (translation in *Bohn's Libraries*).

Chapter IV. Apollo and Artemis.

Keats, *Hymn to Apollo;* Shelley, *Hymn of Apollo, Homer's Hymn to the Sun;* A. C. Swinburne, *The Last Oracle, Delphic Hymn to Apollo;* Stephen Phillips, *Marpessa;* W. S. Landor, *Niobe;* Chaucer, *Prolog of* the Legend of Good Women; W. Morris, *The Love of Alcestis*; R. Browning, *Apollo and the Fates, Balaustion's Adventure*; Euripides, *Alcestis* (translation in *Everyman's Library*); Ovid, *Metamorphoses* I. 452 ff., X. 162 ff., VI. 146 ff., I. 748 ff.; Shelley, *Homer's Hymn to the Moon, Arethusa*; A. H. Clough, *Actæon*; John Lyly, *Endymion*; Keats, *Endymion*; J. R. Lowell, *Endymion*; H. W. Longfellow, *Endymion, Occultation of Orion*; Ovid, *Metamorphoses* V. 577 ff., III. 138 ff.

Chapter V. Hermes and Hestia.

Shelley, *Homer's Hymn to Mercury*.

Chapter VI. Ares and Aphrodite.

Chaucer, *The Compleynt of Mars, Legend of Thisbe* (in *The Legend of Good Women*); Shakespeare, *Venus and Adonis, Midsummer Night's Dream*; Shelley, *Homer's Hymn to Venus*; Keats, *Sonnet On a Picture of Leander*; Byron, *Poem written after swimming from Sestos to Abydos*; Thomas Moore, *Hero and Leander*; Tom Hood, *Hero and Leander*; Tennyson, *Hero to Leander*; Sir Edwin Arnold, *Hero and Leander*; Leigh Hunt, *Hero and Leander*; D. G. Rossetti, *Sonnets, Venus Verticordia, Venus Victrix, Hero's Lamp* (in *The House of Life*); W. S. Landor, *Hippomenes and Atalanta*; W. Morris, *Pygmalion and the Image, Atalanta's Race* (in *The Earthly Paradise*); Andrew Lang, *The New Pygmalion*; Theocritus, *Idyl XV.*; Bion, *Idyl I.* (translations in *Bohn's Libraries* and in *The Loeb Classical Library*); Ovid, *Metamorphoses* X. 560 ff., IV. 55 ff.

Chapter VII. The Lesser Deities of Olympus.

Mrs. E. B. Browning, *Paraphrases on Apuleius*; Keats, *Ode to Psyche*; A. C. Swinburne, *Eros*; W.

Morris, *Cupid and Psyche* (in *The Earthly Paradise*);
Spenser, *The Tears of the Muses.*

Chapter VIII. The Gods of the Sea.

D. G. Rossetti, *A Sea-Spell;* J. R. Lowell, *The Sirens.*

Chapter IX. The Gods of the Earth.

Shelley, *Homer's Hymn to the Earth, Song of
Proserpine, Hymn of Pan; Pan, Echo, and the Satyr;*
Tennyson, *Demeter and Persephone;* A. C. Swinburne,
Hymn to Proserpine, At Eleusis, Pan and Thalassius;
D. G. Rossetti, *Proserpine;* Mrs. E. B. Browning,
Bacchus and Ariadne (paraphrase on Nonnus), *The
Dead Pan;* R. W. Emerson, *Bacchus;* W. S. Landor,
Cupid and Pan; R. Browning, *Pan and Luna;* Ovid,
Metamorphoses V. 341 ff.

Chapter X. The World of the Dead.

Dante, *The Divine Comedy;* Milton, *Paradise Lost;*
Sackville, *Induction to the Mirror for Magistrates;* L.
Morris, *The Epic of Hades;* A. C. Swinburne, *The
Garden of Proserpine, Eurydice;* A. Lang, *The For-
tunate Islands;* W. Morris, *The Earthly Paradise;*
Shelley, *Orpheus;* Wordsworth, *The Power of Music;*
R. Browning, *Eurydice to Orpheus, Ixion;* J. R. Lowell,
Eurydice.

Chapter XI. Stories of Argos.

Chaucer, *The Legend of Hypermnestra* (in *The
Legend of Good Women*); W. Morris, *The Doom of
King Acrisius* (in *The Earthly Paradise*); D. G.
Rossetti, *Aspecta Medusa;* Ovid, *Metamorphoses* IV.
610 ff.

Chapter XII. Heracles.

W. Morris, *The Golden Apples* (in *The Earthly Paradise*); Theocritus, *Idyl X.* (translation in *Bohn's Libraries* and in *The Loeb Classical Library*).

Chapter XIII. Stories of Crete, Sparta, Corinth, and Ætolia.

Shelley, *Homer's Hymn to Castor and Pollux;* Macaulay, *The Battle of Lake Regillus;* II. W. Longfellow, *Pegasus in Pound;* W. Morris, *Bellerophon in Argos and Lycia* (in *The Earthly Paradise*); G. Meredith, *Bellerophon;* A. C. Swinburne, *Atalanta in Calydon;* Moschus, *Idyl* II (translations in *Bohn's Libraries* and in *The Loeb Classical Library*); Ovid, *Metamorphoses* II. 833 ff., VIII. 183 ff., VIII. 260 ff.

Chapter XIV. Stories of Attica.

Chaucer, *The Legend of Philomela,* and *The Legend of Ariadne* (in *The Legend of Good Women*), *The Knight's Tale* (in *The Canterbury Tales*); A. C. Swinburne, *Erectheus, Itylus;* Thomas Moore, *Cephalus and Procris;* M. Arnold, *Philomela.*

Chapter XV. Stories of Thebes.

A. C. Swinburne, *Tiresias;* Tennyson, *Tiresias;* Shelley, *Swellfoot the Tyrant;* Sophocles, *Œdipus Tyrannus, Œdipus Coloneus, Antigone* (translations in *Everyman's Library*).

Chapter XVI. The Argonautic Expedition.

Chaucer, *The Legend of Hypsipyle and Medea* (in *The Legend of Good Women*); W. Morris, *The Life and Death of Jason;* Apollonius Rhodius, *Argonautica* (translation in *The Loeb Classical Library*); Theocritus, *Idyl* XIII. (translation in *Bohn's Libraries* and in *The Loeb Classical Library*); Euripides, *Medea* (translation in *Everyman's Library*).

Chapter XVII. The Trojan War.

Chaucer, *Troilus and Criseyde;* Shakespeare, *Troilus and Cressida;* Keats, *Sonnet on Chapman's Homer;* Tennyson, *Œnone, Dream of Fair Women;* W. S. Landor, *The Death of Paris and Œnone, Menelaüs and Helen, Iphigenia and Agamemnon, Shades of Iphigenia and Agamemnon;* A. Lang, *Helen of Troy, The Shade of Helen, Translation of Theocritus, Idyl XVIII.;* Mrs. E. B. Browning, *Hector and Andromache* (a paraphrase of Homer); W. Morris, *The Death of Paris* (in *The Earthly Paradise*); Wordsworth, *Laodamia;* M. Arnold, *Palladium;* D. G. Rossetti, *Cassandra;* Schiller, *Cassandra* (translation by Lord Lytton): Goethe, *Iphigenia in Tauris* (translation in *Bohn's Libraries*); Sophocles, *Ajax, Philoctetes;* Euripides, *Iphigenia at Aulis, Iphigenia Among the Taurians, Hecuba, Trojan Women, Andromache.*

Chapter XVIII. The Wanderings of Odysseus.

Tennyson, *Ulysses, The Lotus-Eaters;* W. S. Landor, *The Last of Ulysses, Penelope;* Stephen Phillips, *Ulysses;* M. Arnold, *The Strayed Reveller;* D. G. Rossetti, *The Wine of Circe;* J. R. Lowell, *The Sirens;* Shelley, *The Cyclops* (translation from Euripides); Milton, *Comus* (inspired by the story of Circe); Pope, *Argus;* Theocritus, *Idyl XI* (translation in *The Loeb Classical Library*). A. Lang. *Hesperothen, The Odyssey, The Sirens, In Ithaca.*

Chapter XIX. The Tragedy of Agamemnon.

Æschylus, *Agamemnon Choëphori, Eumenides;* Sophocles, *Electra;* Euripides, *Electra, Orestes; Iphigenia in Tauris* (translation in *Everyman's Library*).

Chapter XX. The Legendary Origin of Rome.

Chaucer, *The Legend of Dido* (in *The Legend of Good Women*); Christopher Marlowe, *The Tragedy of Dido*.

FOR GENERAL READING: *The Iliad* (translation by Lang, Leaf and Myers); *The Odyssey* (translation by Butcher and Lang); *The Homeric Hymns* (translation in *The Loeb Classical Library*); translations of the tragedies of Æschylus, Sophocles and Euripides in *Everyman's Library;* Ovid, *Metamorphoses* (translations in *Bohn's Libraries* and in *The Loeb Classical Library*).

FOR YOUNGER STUDENTS: A. C. Church, *Stories from Homer; Stories from the Greek Tragedians; Stories from Virgil.* These are excellent reading and retain remarkably well the spirit of the originals. Charles Kingsley, *The Heroes.*

INDEX

A çes'tes, 340

A cha'tes, 339

Ach e lo'us, 225

A'cher on, 187, 311, 343

A chil'les, 186, 280, 283, 288f.

A cris'i us, 200, 209

Ac tæ'on, 85f.

Ad me'tus, 77f.

A do'nis, 113f.

A dras'tus. 264

Æ'a cus, 189, 283

Æ e'tes, 267, 273

Æ.'geus, 248, 279

Æ gi'na, 283

Æ'gis, 44

Æ. gis'thus, 326f.

Æ gyp'tus, 199

Æ ne'as, 280, 331f.

Æ'o lus, 142, 309, 339

Æs cu la'pi us. See Asclepius

Æ'son, 267, 276

Æ'ther, 5

Æ'thra, 248

Ag a mem'non, 281, 287f.,
326f.

A ga've, daughter of Cad-
mus and mother of Pen-
theus.

A ge'nor, 256

Ages, the Four, 12

A glai'a, one of the Graces.

A'jax, 287, 294, 300

Alba Longa. 347

Al çes'tis, 77f.

Al çi'des, name of Heracles.

Al çin'o us, king of the
Phæacians.

Alc mæ'on, one of the Epigoni, son of Amphiaraus
and Eriphyle, who, fol-
lowing his father's injunction, killed his mother,
and who was, therefore,
pursued by the Furies.

Alc me'na, 210

A lec'to, one of the Furies

A læ'us, father of Otus and
Ephialtes.

Al phe'us, 84, 218

Al thæ'a, 241

Am al the'a, 7

Am'a zons, 219, 252, 300

Am bro'sia, 10

Am'mon, an Egyptian deity
identified with Zeus; he
had a famous shrine in
an oasis of the Libyan
desert.

Am phi a ra'us, 242, 264

Am phi'on, 26f.

Am phi tri'te, 144. 148, 247

Am phit'ry on, 210

A mul'i us, 348

An chi'ses, 331, 339, 345

An drom'a che, 298, 304. 335

An drom'eda. 207

An tæ'us, 222

An tig'o ne, 363. 364

An ti'a, Prœtus' wife, who

falsely accused Bellero-
phon.

An tin'o us, one of Penelope's suitors.

An ti'o pe, 26f., 252

Aph ro di'te, 106, 109f., 286

A pol'lo, 55f., 92, 144, 181,
224, 272, 291, 296

Apple of Discord, 108, 285

A rach'ne, 46f.

Ar'cas, 22

A re o'pa gus, 109, 329

A'res, 36, 105f., 256

Are thu'sa, 83f., 157

Ar'go, 269

Argonautic expedition, 269f.

Ar'gus (hundred-eyed), 25

Ar'gus (builder of the
Argo), 269

Ar'gus (Odysseus' dog), 323

A ri ad'ne, 171, 250

Ar is tæ'us, son of Apollo
and father of Actæon. It
was when he was pursu-
ing Eurydice that she
stepped upon the serpent
from whose sting she
died. In punishment, his
bees were destroyed by
the nymphs. On the ad-
vice of Proteus he offered
animals in sacrifice to the
shades of Orpheus and
Eurydice, whereupon bees
swarmed in the carcasses.
He taught men to keep
bees.

Ar'te mis, 69, 80f., 241, 288

As ca'ni us, 333, 347

As cle'pi us, 55, 74

A so'pus, 236

As sar'a cus, king of Troy,
son of Tros.

As ty'a nax, Hector's infant
son.

At a lan'ta in Caledon, 242

At a lan'ta's race, 115f.

Ath'a mas, 266

A the'na, 9, 40f., 111, 203,
238, 297

At'las, 206, 223

A'treus, 282

A tri'des, sons of Atreus,
Agamemnon and Mene-
laus

At'ro pus, 141

Au ge'as, 217

Au'lis, 288

Au'ra, 246

Au ro'ra, 71, 245

Au to'me don, charioteer of
Achilles

A ver'nus, 187, 341

Bac'cha na'li a, 171

Bac chan'tes, 167, 173, 192

Bac'chus, see Dionysus

Bau'çis, 28f.

Bear, the Great, 24

Bel ler'o phon, 237

Bel lo'na, 109

Be re cyn'thi a, Cybele, from
Mt. Berecynthus in Phry-
gia

Ber'o e, 165

Bona Dea, divinity wor-
shiped in secret by women
in Rome

Bo're as, 142, 245, 271

Bos'pho rus, 26

Bri a're us, a hundred-handed giant who aided Zeus
against the rebellious gods

Bri se'is, 291

Bronze Age, 13

Ca'cus, 221

Cad'mus, 256

Ca du'çe us, 97

Cal'chas, 291

Cal li'o pe, 139, 192

Cal lis'to, 22f.

Cal y do'ni an boar, 241f.

Ca lyp'so, 316

Ca mil'la, a princess of Italy who assisted Turnus against Æneas

Cas san'dra, 304, 327

Cas si o pe'a, 207

Cas'tor, 234, 241, 254, 269

Çe'crops, 46, 244

Ce læ'no, one of the Harpies

Çe'le us, king of Eleusis and father of Triptolemus

Çen'taurs, 253

Çeph'a lus, 245

Çe'pheus, 207

Çer'ber us, 188, 223, 254

Çe'res, 6, 165. See also Demeter.

Çer y ne'an doe, 217

Çestus, the girdle of Venus with power to enhance beauty

Çe'yx. See Halcyone

Cha'os, 5

Char'i tes, 139

Cha'ron, 187, 343

Char yb'dis, 151, 314, 315, 336

Chi mæ'ra, 238

Chi'ron, 267, 284

Chry se'is, 290

Çi co'ni ans, men with whom Odysseus fought early in his wanderings.

Çim me'ri ans, 311

Çir'çe, 310

Cli'o, 139

Clo'tho, 141

Clym'e ne, 70

Cly tem nes'tra, 234, 326f.

Cly'ti e, a water-nymph who loved Apollo and was changed into a sun-flower.

Co çy'tus, 188, 311

Col'chis, 273

Co lo'nus, 263

Con'sus, a Roman god of agriculture.

Co ro'nis, by Apollo, mother of Asclepius.

Cor y ban'tes, 154

Cre'on, 263

Cretan bull, 218

Cre u'sa, 333

Cro'nus, 6f., 12

Cu'mæ, 187

Cupid, 123. See also Eros.

Cu re'tes, 7

Çy'a ne, 157

Çy'be le, 117, 153

Çy clo'pes, 5, 7, 189, 306, 336

Çyc'nus, son of Poseidon, Apollo, or Ares, who was turned into a swan.

Çyn'thi a, name of Artemis derived from Mt. Cynthus in Delos, where she was born.

Çy pris, 114

Cyth er e'a, name of Aphrodite, derived from Cythera, an island near the Peloponnese.

Dæ'da lus, 233

Dan'a e, 200

Dan'a ids, 190, 199

Dan'a us, 199

Daph'ne, 62f.

Daph'nis, a son of Hermes who was made blind by

a jealous naiad. He was the ideal shepherd and musician.

Dar'da nus, 284, 334

Day, 5

De iph'o bus, son of Priam who married Helen at Paris' death.

De jan i'ra, 225

De'los, 60

Del'phi, 3, 56, 62, 98, 215, 224, 262

De me'ter, 6, 21, 154f.

Deu ca'li on, 14f.

Di an'a, 90. See also Artemis.

Dic'tys, 202, 208

Di'do, 339, 344

Di o me'des, 287, 301

Di o me'des, horses of, 219

Di o'ne, 109

Di on y'si a, 171

Di on y'sus, 165f.

Di os cu'ri, 234

Di'ræ, a name of the Furies.

Dir'çe, 26f.

Dis, name of *Pluto* or *Hades*

Do do'na, 34, 269

Dreams, gates of, 345

Dry'ads, 184

E'cho, 185

Ei lei thy'ia, the goddess who aided women in child-birth.

E lec'tra, 328

E lec'tra, one of the Pleiads

E lec'try on, 210

E leu'sis, 158

E leu sin'i an Mysteries, 158

E ly'sian Fields, 190, 345

En çel'a dus, one of the hundred-handed giants.

En dy'mi on, 87f.

E ny'o, goddess of war, companion of Ares.

E'os, the dawn goddess.

E pe'us, builder of the wooden horse.

Eph i al'tes, one of the giants who piled Pelion on Ossa in order to reach the gods.

Ep i dau'rus, 74

Ep ig'o ni, 265

Ep i me'theus, 12

Er'a to, 140

Er'e bus, 5

E rech'theus, 244

Er ich tho'ni us, 244

E rin'ys, the Furies

E ri'phy le, 264

E'ris, 111

E'ros, 5, 106, 112, 122f., 273

Er y man'thi an boar, 216

E te'o cles, 264

E thi o'pi ans, 4

Eu mæ'us, swineherd of Odysseus.

Eu men'i des, 189, 329

Eu phros'y ne, one of the Graces.

Eu ro'pa, 228f.

Eu ry'a le, one of the gorgons

Eu ry cle'a, 323

Eu ryd'i ce, 192

Eu ryl'o chus, a companion of Odysseus

Eu ryn'o me, mother of the Graces

Eu rys'theus, 213

Eu ter'pe, 140

E vad'ne, wife of Capaneus, who, when her husband was killed in the siege of Thebes, threw herself on his funeral pyre.

E van'der, 347

Fates, 140
Fau'nus, 180
Flood, 13
Furies, 344. See also *Eumenides*

Gæ a, 5, 7, 8, 153
Gal a te'a (the Nereid), 149
Gal a te'a (wife of Pygmalion), 118
Gan'y mede, 36, 220, 284
Garden of the Hes per'i des, 206
Gem'i ni, 235
Genius, the guardian spirit of each man, sometimes symbolized as a snake.
Ge'ry on, 220
Giants, 5, 8
Glau'cus, a prophetic sea deity
Golden Age, 12
Golden fleece, 266
Golden bough, 90
Gorgons, 203
Graces, 139
Græ'æ, 204

Ha'des, 6, 8, 154, 187f., 204, 311f.
Hæ'mon, son of Creon of Thebes. See p. 265.
Hal cy'o ne, daughter of Æolus who, when her husband perished in a shipwreck, drowned herself. The two were changed into birds.
Ham a dry'ads, 184
Har mo'ni a, 258, 264
Harpies, 150, 271, 335

He'be, 19, 36, 227
Hec'a te, 89, 274, 277
Hec'tor, 284, 292, 297, 332
Hec'u ba, 298
Helen, 112, 235, 254, 286
Hel'e nus, 335
Hel'i con, 139, 238
He'li os, 55
Hel'le, 266
Hel'len, son of Deucalion and mythical ancestor of all the Hellenes or Greeks.
Hel'les pont, 119, 267
Hem'er a, Day. See p. 5.
He phæs'tus, 36, 49f., 106, 295
He'ra, 6, 20, 36f., 111, 210
Her'a cles, 11, 78f., 144, 210f., 269
Her'cu les. See Heracles
Her'mes, 25, 91f., 187, 204
Her mi'o ne, daughter of Menelaus and Helen
He'ro, 118
He si'o ne, 144, 220
Hes'per us, the evening star, father of the Hesperides
Hes per'i des, 206, 222
Hes'ti a, 6, 98f.
Hip po cre'ne, 238
Hip po da mi'a, 147
Hip pol'y ta, 219
Hip pol'y tus, son of Theseus by Antiope
Hip pom'e nes, 115f.
Horn of plenty, 225
Hours, 16, 59
Hy a cin'thus, 64f.
Hy'a des, seven nymphs placed by Zeus in heaven as a constellation because of their care of the infant Dionysus.
Hy'dra. See *Lernæan*

Hy ge'a, daughter of Asclepius and goddess of health

Hy'las, 270

Hy'men, god of marriage, son of Apollo and a Muse

Hy per bo're ans, 4

Hy pe'ri on, a Titan, father of Helios and Selene

Hy perm nes'tra, 199

Hyp'nos, the god of sleep

I ac'cus (a name of Dionysus

I ap'e tus, a Titan, father of Prometheus, Epimetheus, and Atlas

Ic'a rus, 233

Ida, Mt., 111

I'das, 66

Il'i um (Troy), 284f.

I'lus, 284

In'a chus, 24, 199

I'o, 24f., 199

I o'ba tes, king of Lycia who sent Bellerophon after the Chimæra

I o la'us, 216

I'o le, 226

I o'ni an Sea, 26

Iph'i cles, son of Amphitryon and Alcmena

Iph i ge ni'a, 288, 329

I'ris, 39, 271, 294

Iron Age, 13

Islands of the Blest, 190

Is me'ne, 265

Ith'a ca, island home of Odysseus

It'y lus, 247

I'tys, same as Itylus

I u'lus. See Ascanius

Ix i'on, 190

Ja'nus, 347

Ja'son, 242, 267f.

Jo cas'ta, 259

Jove. See Jupiter

Ju'no, 40, 339. See also Hera

Ju'pi ter, 34. See also Zeus

Ko're, name of Persephone

Lab'da cus, father of Laius of Thebes

Lab'y rinth, 233, 250

Lach'e sis, 141

La er'tes, father of Odysseus

Læs try go'ni ans, 309

Lai'us, 259

La oc'o on, 303

La od a mi'a, 290

La om'e don, 144, 220, 225, 284

Lap'iths, 253

La'res, 101

La ti'nus, 346

Lat'mos, Mt., 87

La to'na. See Leto

La vin'i a, 346

Le an'der, 118

Le'da, 234

Ler næ an hydra, 216

Le'the, 345

Le'to, 60, 67f.

Leu coth'e a, Ino, wife of Athamas, became a sea nymph under this name.

Li'ber, Italian divinity, later identified with Bacchus

Li'ber a, Italian divinity, later identified with Proserpina

Li'chas, attendant of Heracles who brought him the poisoned garment.

Li'nus, a song of lamentation personified as a son of Apollo

Lotus-eaters, 305

Luna, the moon-goddess

Ly æ'us, a name of *Bacchus*

Ly cur'gus, king of Thrace who was killed for persecuting Bacchus

Ly'cus, 26

Lyn'ceus, 199

Ma cha'on, son of Asclepius, the physician in the Iliad

Mæ'nads, 173

Mag'na Ma'ter. See *Cybele*

Mai'a, 91

Ma'nes, souls of the dead, worshiped in Rome

Mar'a thon, battle of, 254

Marathonian bull, 250

Mar pes'sa, 66

Mars, 109. See also *Ares*

Mar'sy as, 181

Ma'ter Ma tu'ta, Italian goddess identified with Leucothea or Aurora.

Me de'a, 249, 273f.

Me du'sa, 203, 238

Mel e a'ger, 241, 269

Mel pom'e ne, 139

Mem'non, 300

Men e la'us, 281, 286, 294, 321

Men'tor, friend and adviser of Odysseus

Mer'cu ry, 97f. See also *Hermes*

Mer'o pe, wife of Sisyphus

Metis, "insight," Zeus's wife whom he swallowed before Athena's birth.

Mi'das, 170, 181

Mi lan'i on, sometimes this name is given to the suitor of Atalanta

Mi ner'va, 48. See also *Athena*

Mi'nos, 189, 219, 230, 250

Min'o taur, 233, 250

Mne mos'y ne, 22, 139

Mu sa'ge tes, Apollo as leader of the Muses

Muses, 22, 59, 139, 238

Myr'mi dons, 283, 293

Myr'ti lus, 147, 282

Mysteries, 158, 190

Nai'ads, 152, 184

Nar cis'sus, 185

Nau sic' a a, 317

Nectar, 19

Ne me'an lion, 216

Ne'me sis, 141

Ne'mi, Lake, 90

Ne op tol'e mus, 301, 325

Neph'e le, mother of Phrixus and Helle

Nep'tune, 148. See also *Poseidon*

Ne're ids, 148

Ne'reus, 144, 148, 222

Nes'sus, 225

Nes'tor, 287, 321

Night, 5

Ni'ke. See *Victory*

Ni'o be, 66f.

Nu'mi tor, 348

Nymphs, 151, 184f., 204

Nyx. See *Night*

Ocean, 4

O ce'a nus, 143

O dys'seus, 150, 287, 300, 301, 305f.

Œd'i pus, 259f.

Œ'neus, 241

Œ'n o ma'us, 147

Œ no'ne, a nymph, wife of Paris

Olympic games, 32f., 218

Olympic Council, 19, 122

Olympus, Mt., 7, 16f.

Om'pha le, 224

Oracle at Delphi. See *Delphi.*

Or'cus, the god of death and the place of the dead. See *Hades*

O're ads, 184

O res'tes, 328

O ri'on, 88f.

Or i thy'ia, 245

Or'pheus, 192, 269

Os'sa, Mt., in Thessaly. The giants tried to pile Pelion on Ossa in their attempt to overthrow the gods.

O'tus, one of the giants

Pæ an, 62

Pa læ'mon, son of Athamas and Ino, who was turned into a sea deity.

Pal a me'des, one of the Greek heroes who was driven to death by the enmity of Odysseus.

Pa'les, Roman god of flocks

Pal i nu'rus, 341, 343

Pal la'di um, 301

Pal'las. See *Athena*

Pan, 173f.

Pan di'on, father of Procne and Philomela

Pan do'ra, 11f.

Pan'dro sus, a daughter of Cecrops

Par'cæ, the Fates

Par'is, 111, 284, 286, 300, 301

Par nas'sus, Mt., 14, 56, 59, 139

Par'the non, 44

Par then o pæ'us, son of Meleager and Atalanta, one of the Seven against Thebes.

Pa siph'a e, wife of Minos and mother of the Minotaur

Pa tro'clus, 288, 293

Peg'a sus, 238

Pe'leus, 111, 269, 283

Pe'li as, 267, 276

Pe li'des, "son of Peleus," Achilles

Pe'li on, Mt. See *Ossa*

Pe'lops, 147, 282

Pe na'tes, 101, 334

Pe nel'o pe, 287, 320, 324

Pe ne'us, a river-god, father of Daphne

Pen thes i le'a, 300

Pen'theus, 168

Per i pha'tes, 248

Per seph'o ne, 21, 154f., 189, 254

Per'seus, 200f.

Phæ a'ci ans, 317

Phæ'dra, daughter of Minos and wife of Theseus

Pha'e thon, 70f.

Phi le'mon, 28f.

Phil oc te'tes, 227, 301

Phil o me'la, 246

Phi'neus, 208, 271

Phleg'e thon, 188, 311, 344

Phœ'be, name of *Artemis*

Phœ'bus. See *Apollo*

Pho'lus, a centaur whom Heracles accidentally killed.

Phor'cys, a sea deity, father of Gorgons and Grææ

Phrix'us, 266
Pi er'i a, 139
Pi re'ne, 236
Pi rith'o us, 242, 253
Ple'ia des, 89
Plu'to. See *Hades*
Plu'tus, god of wealth
Pol'lux. See *Polydeuces*
Pol'y bus, king of Corinth who adopted Œdipus
Pol y dec'tes, 202, 208
Pol y deu'ces, 234, 241, 254, 269
Pol y do'rus, 334
Po lym'ni a, 140
Pol y ni'ces, 264
Pol y phe'mus, 149, 306, 336
Pol yx'e na, daughter of Priam, sacrificed on Achilles' tomb
Po sei'don, 6, 8, 45, 143f., 233
Pri'am, 225, 284, 298f., 304
Pri a'pus, god of fruitfulness
Proc'ne, 246
Pro'cris, 245
Pro crus'tes, 249
Prœ'tus, 237
Pro me'theus, 9f., 223, 273
Pro ser'pi na. See *Persephone*
Pro tes i la'us, 290
Pro'teus, 149, 321
Psy'che, 123f.
Psy'cho pom'pus, "leader of souls," title of Hermes
Pyg ma'li on, 118
Pyg'mies, 4, 222
Py'la des, 328
Pyr'a mus, 119f.
Pyr'rha, 14
Pyr'rhus. See *Neoptolemus*

Pyth'i a, priestess of Apollo at Delphi
Py'thon, 62

Qui ri'nus, 351

Re gil'lus, battle of Lake, 235
Re'mus, 347
Rhad a man'thus, 189, 230
Rhe'a, 6f., 153
Rhe'a Sil'vi a, 348
River-gods, 151
Rom'u lus, 104, 345, 347
Rut'u li, the people of Turnus

Sabines, 350
Sal mo'neus, a son of Æolus who was punished in the lower world for trying to equal Zeus.
Sa'mos, 36
Sar pe'don, an ally of the Trojans
Sat'urn, 12
Sat ur na'li a, feast of Saturn, occurring about the time of our Christmas.
Sat'yrs, 173, 179f.
Sca man'der, one of the rivers by Troy
Sci'ron, 248
Scyl'la, 151, 314
Se le'ne, 80
Sem'e le, 165, 259
Sib'yl, 80, 165, 341
Si le'nus, 166, 173, 181f.
Sil va'nus, a Roman divinity of woods and fields.
Silver Age, 13
Si'nis, 248
Si'non, 303

Si'rens, 150, 313
Sir'i us, 89
Sis'y phus, 190, 236
Sphinx, 261
Stroph'a des, 335
Stym pha'li an birds, 217
Styx, 188, 283
Sun, cattle of the, 315
Sy chæ'us, husband of Dido
Sym pleg'a des, 271
Syr'inx, 178

Ta'lus, a bronze giant
Tan'ta lus, 190, 281
Tar'ta rus, 7, 190, 344
Tau'ri ans, 329
Tel'a mon, 269
Te lem'a chus, 287, 320
Te'reus, 246
Terp sich'o re, 139
Te'thys, one of the Titans
Teu'cer (1) First king of Troy, (2) one of the Greek heroes in the Trojan War.
Tha li'a, one of the Graces
Tha li'a, 139
The'mis, goddess of order and justice; by Zeus she was the mother of the Hours and Fates.
Ther si'tes, a deformed and impudent Greek at the siege of Troy.
The'seus, 242, 247f.
The'tis, 111, 148, 283, 292
This'be, 119f.
Thy es'tes, 282
Thyr'sus, 168
Ti'ber, 347
Ti re'si as, 311
Ti si'pho ne, one of the Furies

Ti'tans, 5, 7
Ti tho'nus, brother of Priam, beloved by the Dawn, through whom he gained perpetual life but not perpetual youth.
Ti'ty us, a giant who was cast into Tartarus for offering violence to a goddess.
Trip tol'e mus, 161
Tri to gen i'a, a name of Athena; origin unknown.
Tri'tons, 144
Troi'lus, son of Priam
Trojan War, 280f.
Tros, 284
Tur'nus, 346
Tyn da'reus, 234
Ty'phon, 8

U lys'ses. See Odysseus
Underworld. See Hades
U ra'ni a, 140
U'ra nus, 5, 8

Ve'nus, 115, 124. See also Aphrodite
Ves'ta, 100. See also Hestia
Vestal Virgins, 100
Victory, 20, 45
Vul'can, 52. See also Hephæstus

Winds. See Æolus
Wooden horse, 301

X an'thus, 296

Zeph'yr, 125, 142
Ze'thus, 26f.
Zeus, 7f., 19f., 200, 210, 229

2003178R00214

Printed in Great Britain
by Amazon.co.uk, Ltd.,
Marston Gate.